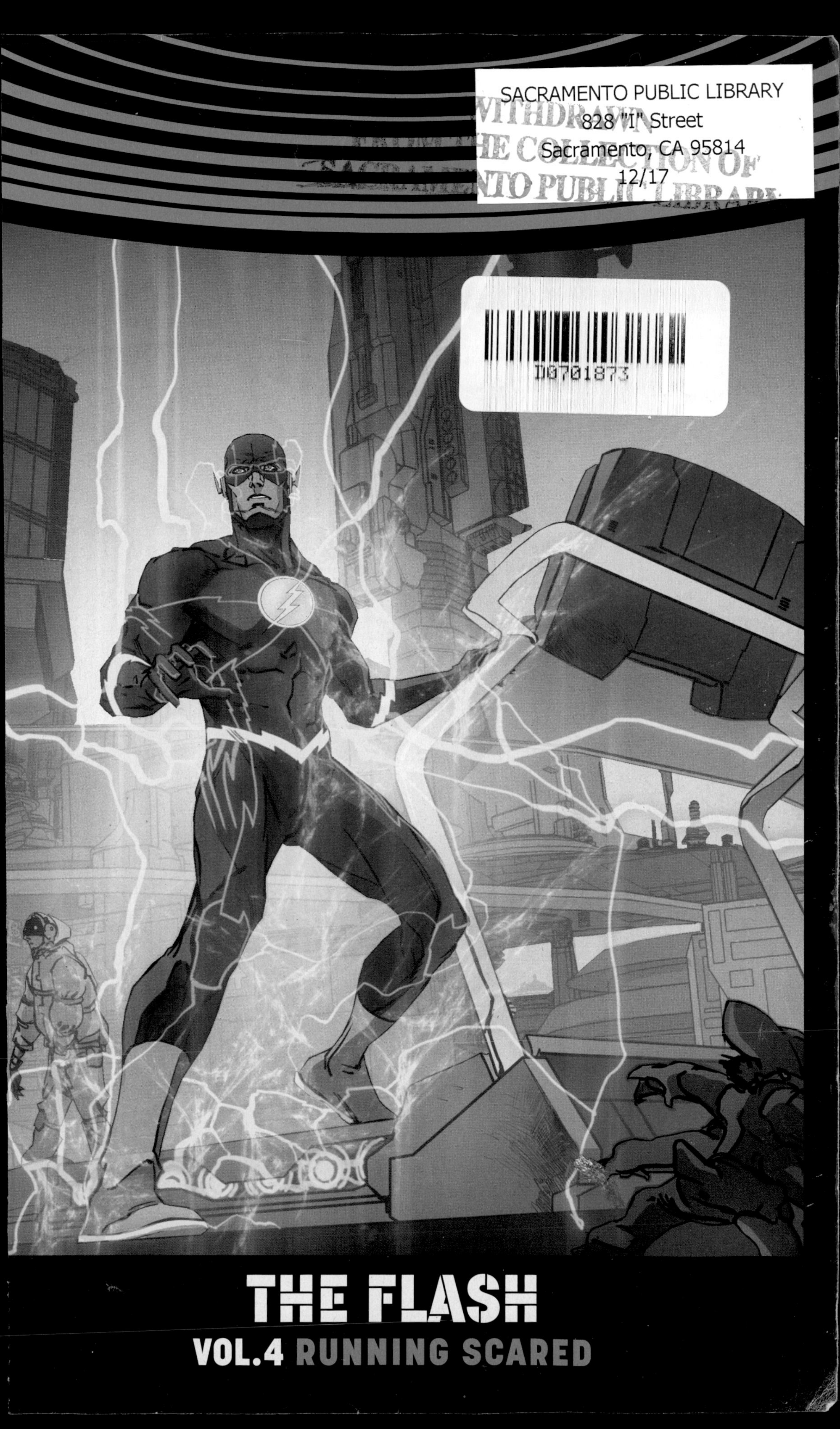

THE FLASH

VOL.4 RUNNING SCARED

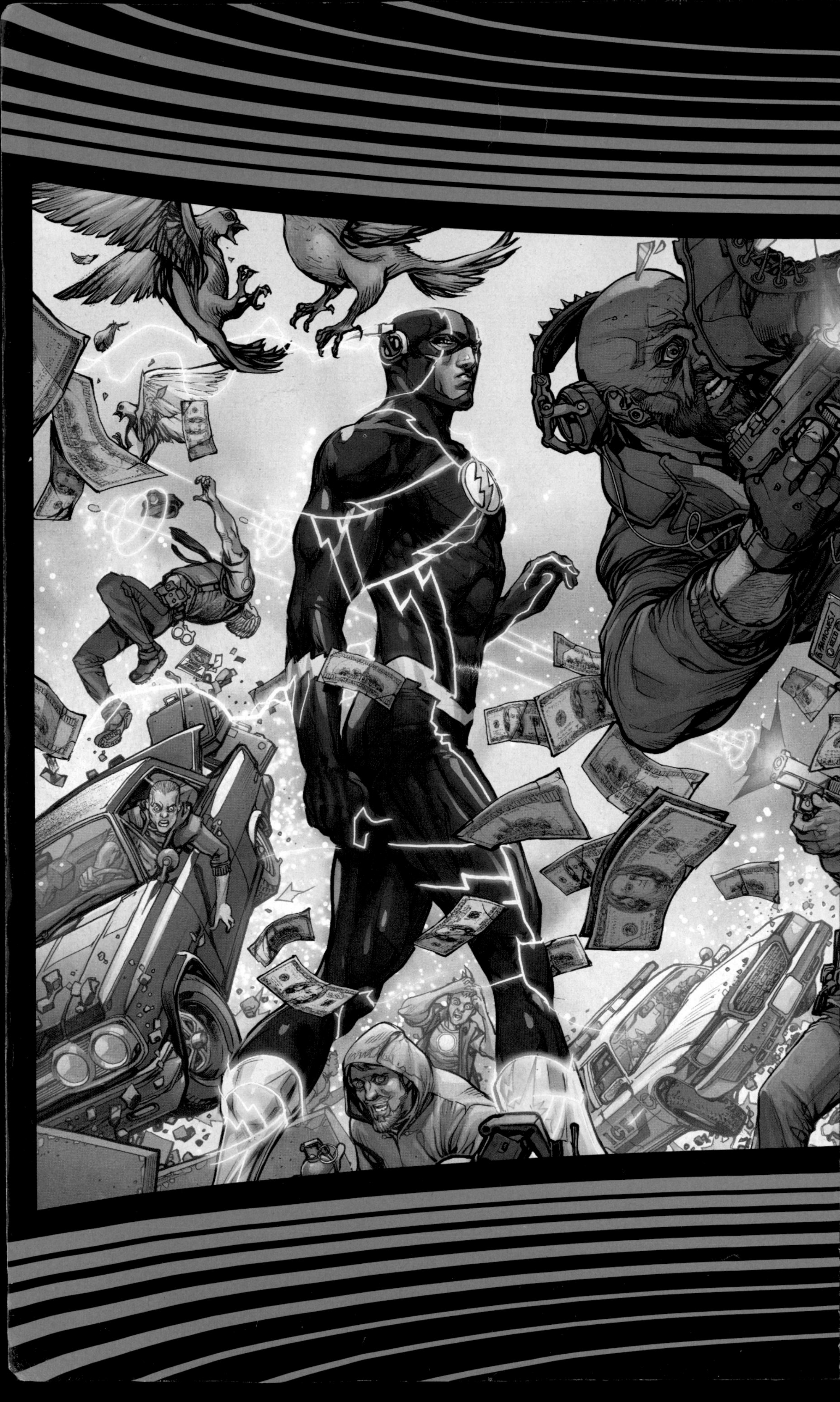

HOWARD PORTER * CARMINE DI GIANDOMENICO
POP MHAN * NEIL GOOGE * RYAN SOOK
PAUL PELLETIER * ANDREW HENNESSY
artists

IVAN PLASCENCIA * HI-FI
DAVE McCAIG
colorists

STEVE WANDS
TOM NAPOLITANO
letterers

CARMINE DI GIANDOMENICO
series and collection cover artist

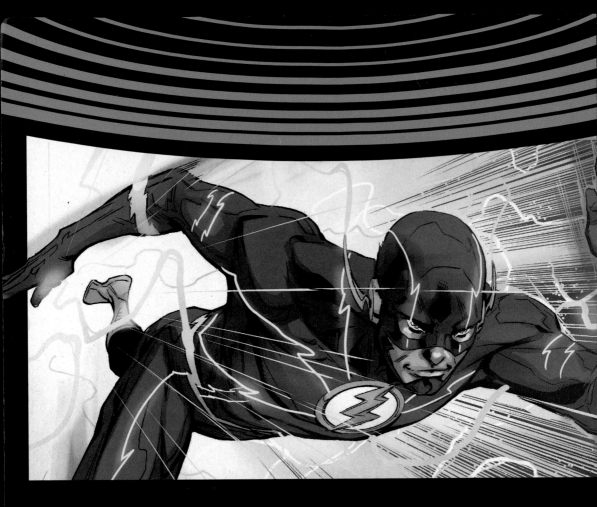

BRIAN CUNNINGHAM Editor - Original Series ＊ **AMEDEO TURTURRO** Associate Editor - Original Series
JEB WOODARD Group Editor - Collected Editions ＊ **ERIKA ROTHBERG** Editor - Collected Edition
STEVE COOK Design Director - Books ＊ **MONIQUE NARBONETA** Publication Design

BOB HARRAS Senior VP - Editor-in-Chief, DC Comics
PAT McCALLUM Executive Editor, DC Comics

DIANE NELSON President ＊ **DAN DiDIO** Publisher ＊ **JIM LEE** Publisher ＊ **GEOFF JOHNS** President & Chief Creative Officer
AMIT DESAI Executive VP - Business & Marketing Strategy, Direct to Consumer & Global Franchise Management
SAM ADES Senior VP & General Manager, Digital Services ＊ **BOBBIE CHASE** VP & Executive Editor, Young Reader & Talent Development
MARK CHIARELLO Senior VP - Art, Design & Collected Editions ＊ **JOHN CUNNINGHAM** Senior VP - Sales & Trade Marketing
ANNE DePIES Senior VP - Business Strategy, Finance & Administration ＊ **DON FALLETTI** VP - Manufacturing Operations
LAWRENCE GANEM VP - Editorial Administration & Talent Relations ＊ **ALISON GILL** Senior VP - Manufacturing & Operations
HANK KANALZ Senior VP - Editorial Strategy & Administration ＊ **JAY KOGAN** VP - Legal Affairs ＊ **JACK MAHAN** VP - Business Affairs
NICK J. NAPOLITANO VP - Manufacturing Administration ＊ **EDDIE SCANNELL** VP - Consumer Marketing
COURTNEY SIMMONS Senior VP - Publicity & Communications ＊ **JIM (SKI) SOKOLOWSKI** VP - Comic Book Specialty Sales & Trade Marketing
NANCY SPEARS VP - Mass, Book, Digital Sales & Trade Marketing ＊ **MICHELE R. WELLS** VP - Content Strategy

THE FLASH VOL. 4: RUNNING SCARED

Published by DC Comics. Compilation and all new material Copyright © 2017 DC Comics. All Rights Reserved.
Originally published in single magazine form in THE FLASH 23-27. Copyright © 2017 DC Comics. All Rights Reserved.
All characters, their distinctive likenesses and related elements featured in this publication are trademarks of DC Comics.
The stories, characters and incidents featured in this publication are entirely fictional.
DC Comics does not read or accept unsolicited submissions of ideas, stories or artwork.

DC Comics, 2900 West Alameda Ave., Burbank, CA 91505.
Printed by Solisco Printers, Scott, QC, Canada. 10/13/17. First Printing.
ISBN: 978-1-4012-7462-7

Library of Congress Cataloging-in-Publication Data is available.

PEFC Certified

This product is from
sustainably managed
forests, recycled and
controlled sources

PEFC/26-31-02   www.pefc.org

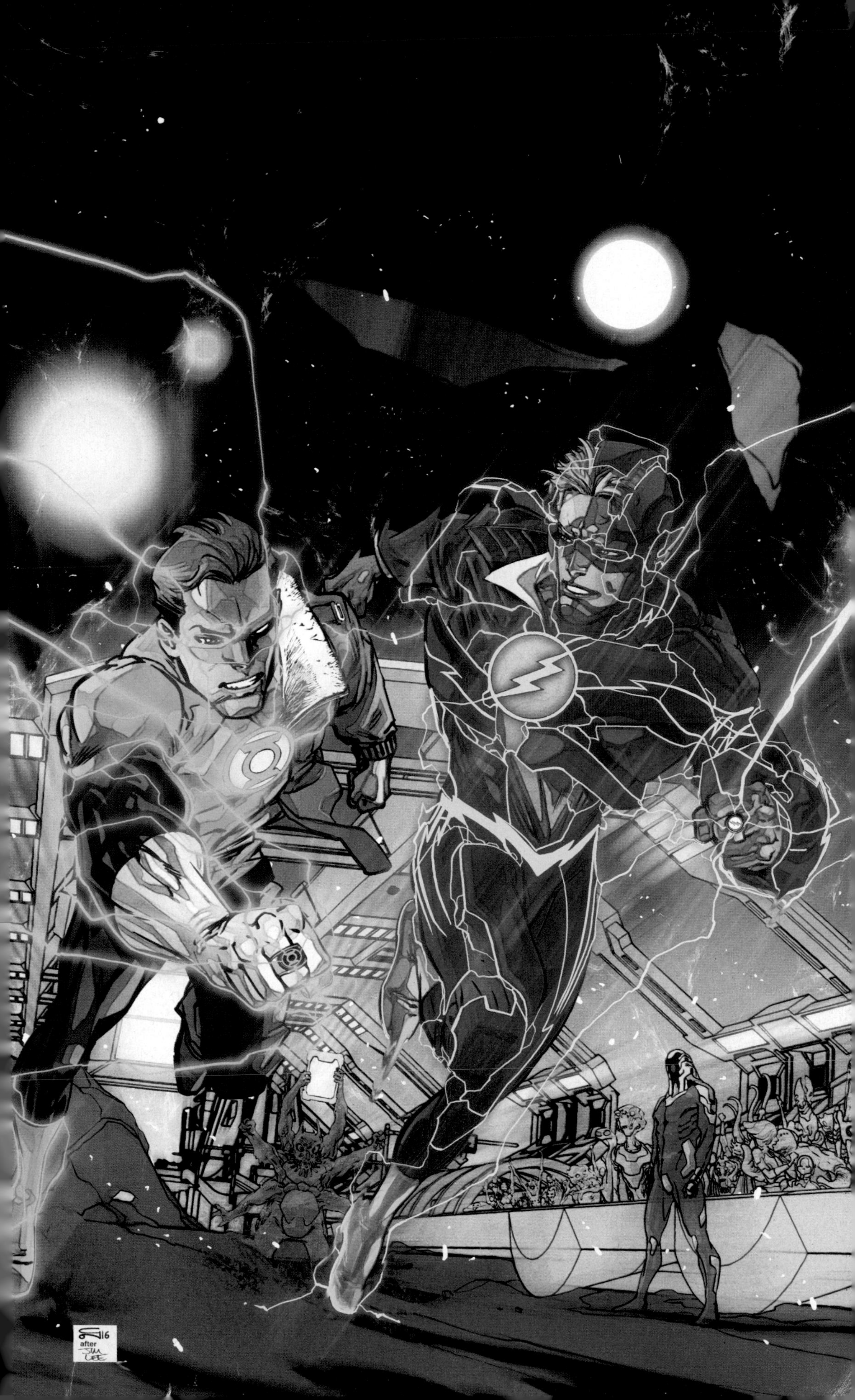
16
after
JIM LEE

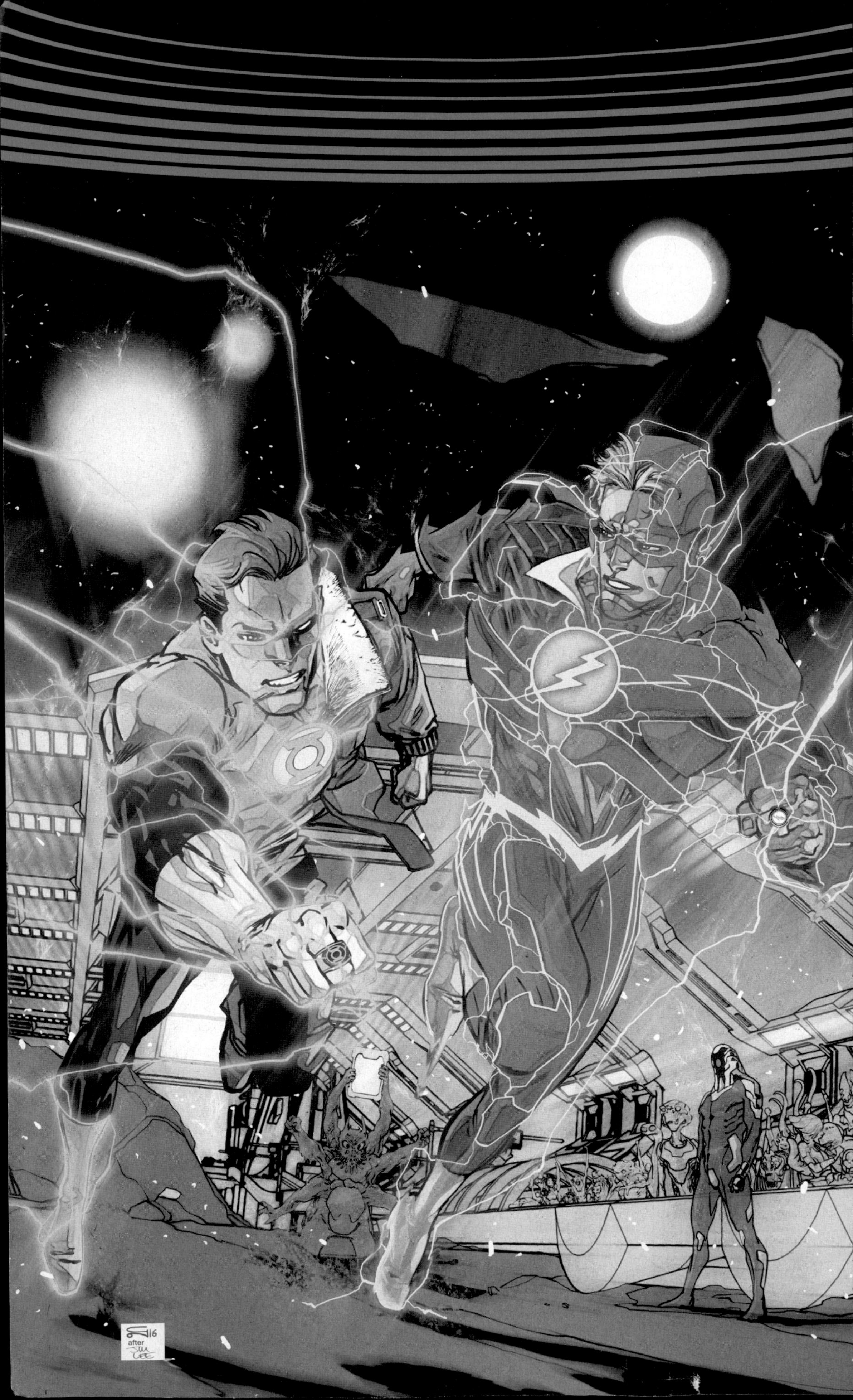

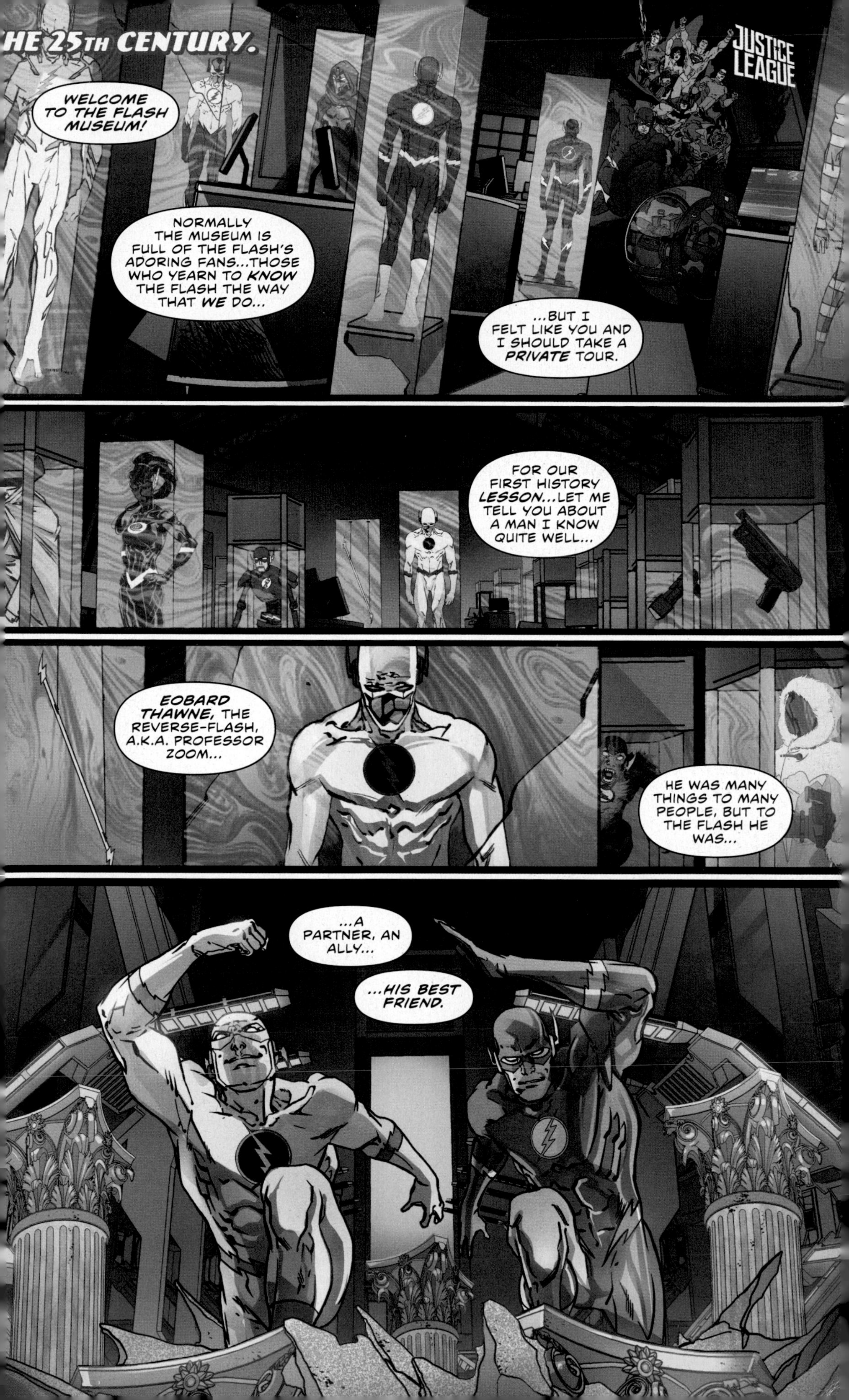
HE 25TH CENTURY.
JUSTICE LEAGUE
WELCOME TO THE FLASH MUSEUM!
NORMALLY THE MUSEUM IS FULL OF THE FLASH'S ADORING FANS...THOSE WHO YEARN TO KNOW THE FLASH THE WAY THAT WE DO...
...BUT I FELT LIKE YOU AND I SHOULD TAKE A PRIVATE TOUR.
FOR OUR FIRST HISTORY LESSON...LET ME TELL YOU ABOUT A MAN I KNOW QUITE WELL...
EOBARD THAWNE, THE REVERSE-FLASH, A.K.A. PROFESSOR ZOOM...
HE WAS MANY THINGS TO MANY PEOPLE, BUT TO THE FLASH HE WAS...
...A PARTNER, AN ALLY...
...HIS BEST FRIEND.

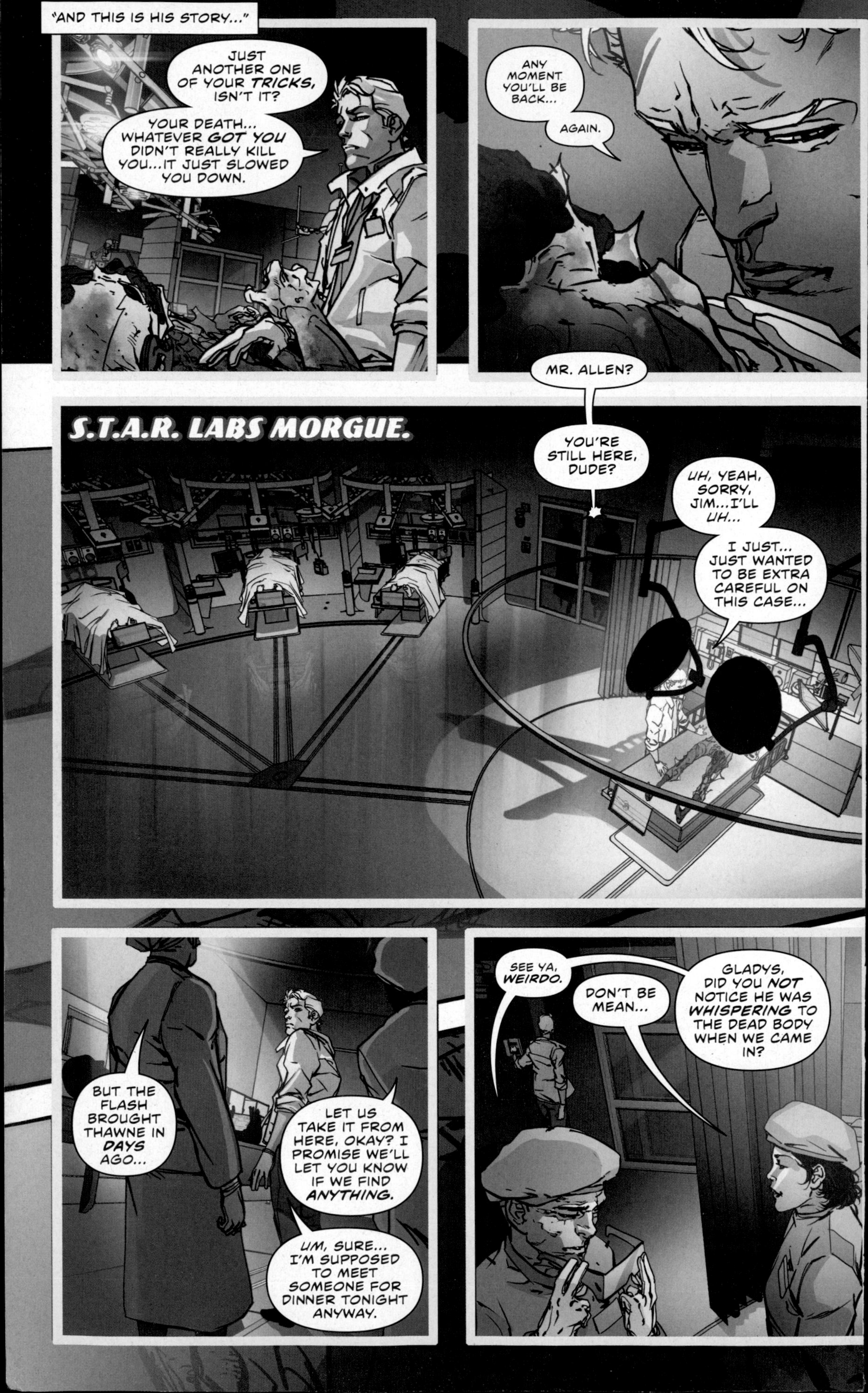
"AND THIS IS HIS STORY..."
JUST ANOTHER ONE OF YOUR TRICKS, ISN'T IT?
YOUR DEATH... WHATEVER GOT YOU DIDN'T REALLY KILL YOU...IT JUST SLOWED YOU DOWN.
ANY MOMENT YOU'LL BE BACK...
AGAIN.
MR. ALLEN?
S.T.A.R. LABS MORGUE.
YOU'RE STILL HERE, DUDE?
UH, YEAH, SORRY, JIM...I'LL UH...
I JUST... JUST WANTED TO BE EXTRA CAREFUL ON THIS CASE...
BUT THE FLASH BROUGHT THAWNE IN DAYS AGO...
LET US TAKE IT FROM HERE, OKAY? I PROMISE WE'LL LET YOU KNOW IF WE FIND ANYTHING.
UM, SURE... I'M SUPPOSED TO MEET SOMEONE FOR DINNER TONIGHT ANYWAY.
SEE YA, WEIRDO.
DON'T BE MEAN...
GLADYS, DID YOU NOT NOTICE HE WAS WHISPERING TO THE DEAD BODY WHEN WE CAME IN?

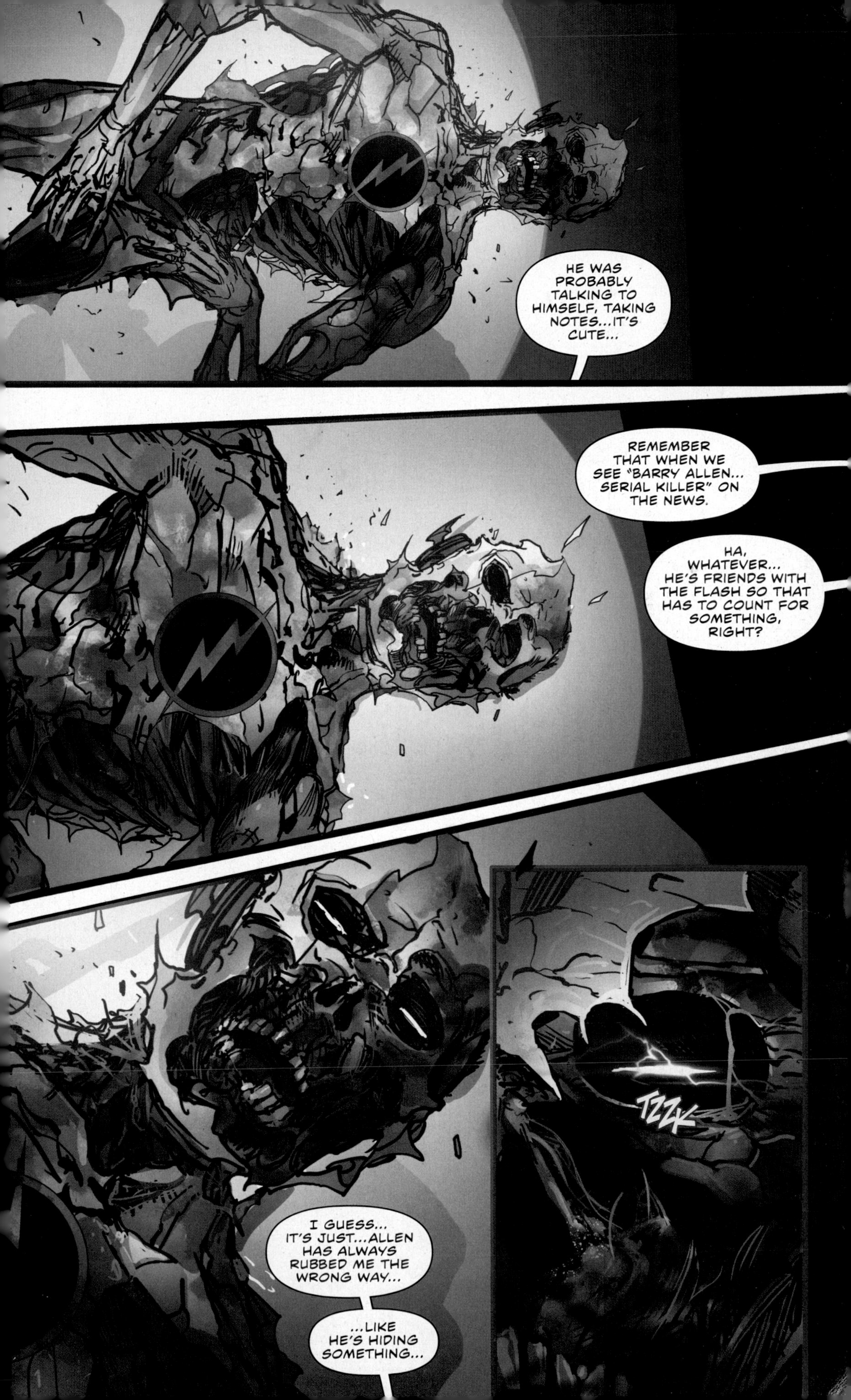
HE WAS PROBABLY TALKING TO HIMSELF, TAKING NOTES...IT'S CUTE...
REMEMBER THAT WHEN WE SEE "BARRY ALLEN... SERIAL KILLER" ON THE NEWS.
HA, WHATEVER... HE'S FRIENDS WITH THE FLASH SO THAT HAS TO COUNT FOR SOMETHING, RIGHT?
I GUESS... IT'S JUST...ALLEN HAS ALWAYS RUBBED ME THE WRONG WAY...
...LIKE HE'S HIDING SOMETHING...
TZZK

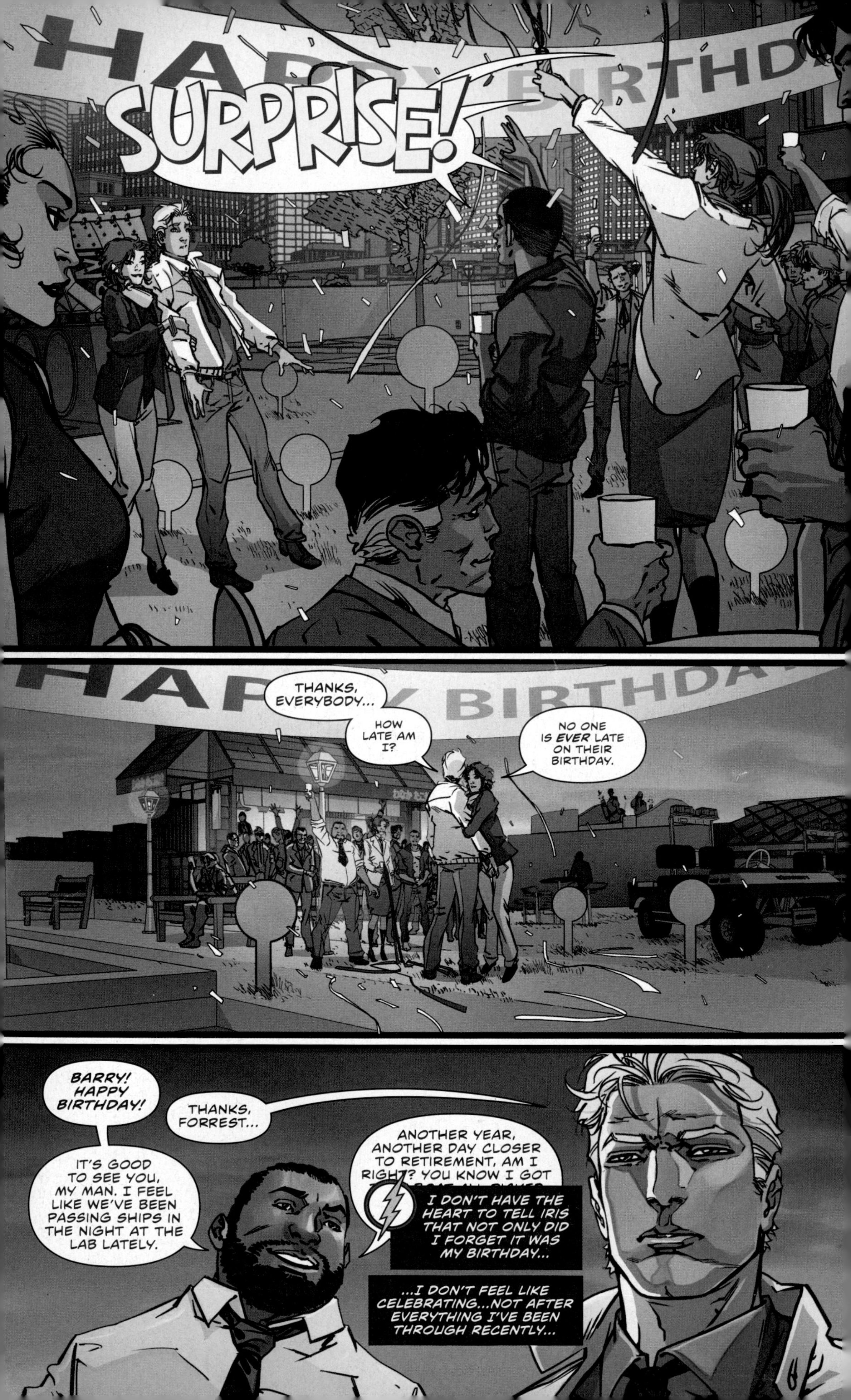
SURPRISE!
THANKS, EVERYBODY...
HOW LATE AM I?
NO ONE IS *EVER* LATE ON THEIR BIRTHDAY.
BARRY! HAPPY BIRTHDAY!
THANKS, FORREST...
IT'S GOOD TO SEE YOU, MY MAN. I FEEL LIKE WE'VE BEEN PASSING SHIPS IN THE NIGHT AT THE LAB LATELY.
ANOTHER YEAR, ANOTHER DAY CLOSER TO RETIREMENT, AM I RIGHT? YOU KNOW I GOT
I DON'T HAVE THE HEART TO TELL IRIS THAT NOT ONLY DID I FORGET IT WAS MY BIRTHDAY...
...I DON'T FEEL LIKE CELEBRATING...NOT AFTER EVERYTHING I'VE BEEN THROUGH RECENTLY...

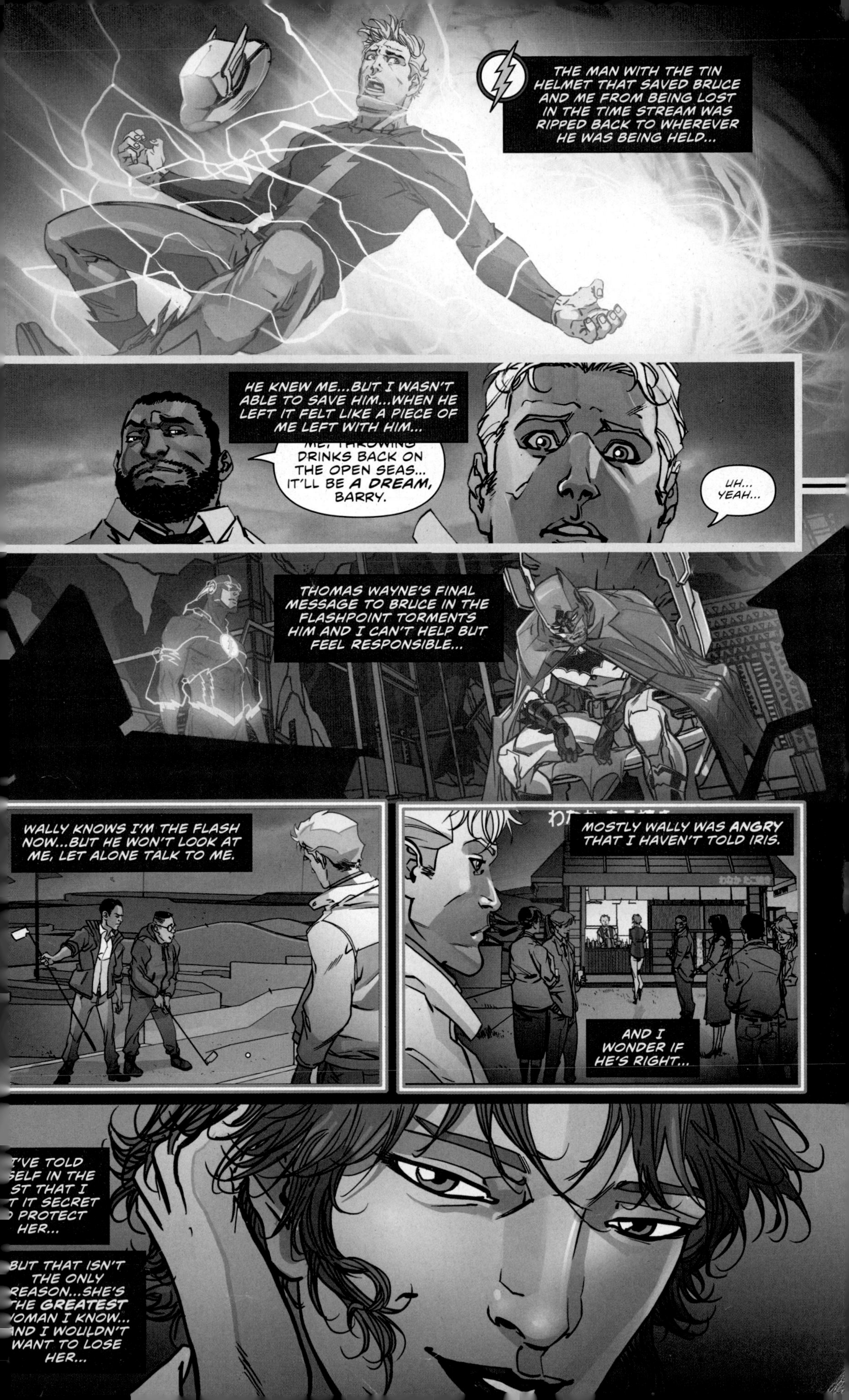

THE MAN WITH THE TIN HELMET THAT SAVED BRUCE AND ME FROM BEING LOST IN THE TIME STREAM WAS RIPPED BACK TO WHEREVER HE WAS BEING HELD...
HE KNEW ME...BUT I WASN'T ABLE TO SAVE HIM...WHEN HE LEFT IT FELT LIKE A PIECE OF ME LEFT WITH HIM...
DRINKS BACK ON THE OPEN SEAS... IT'LL BE A DREAM, BARRY.
UH... YEAH...
THOMAS WAYNE'S FINAL MESSAGE TO BRUCE IN THE FLASHPOINT TORMENTS HIM AND I CAN'T HELP BUT FEEL RESPONSIBLE...
WALLY KNOWS I'M THE FLASH NOW...BUT HE WON'T LOOK AT ME, LET ALONE TALK TO ME.
MOSTLY WALLY WAS ANGRY THAT I HAVEN'T TOLD IRIS.
AND I WONDER IF HE'S RIGHT...
'VE TOLD SELF IN THE ST THAT I T IT SECRET PROTECT HER...
BUT THAT ISN'T THE ONLY REASON...SHE'S THE GREATEST WOMAN I KNOW... AND I WOULDN'T WANT TO LOSE HER...

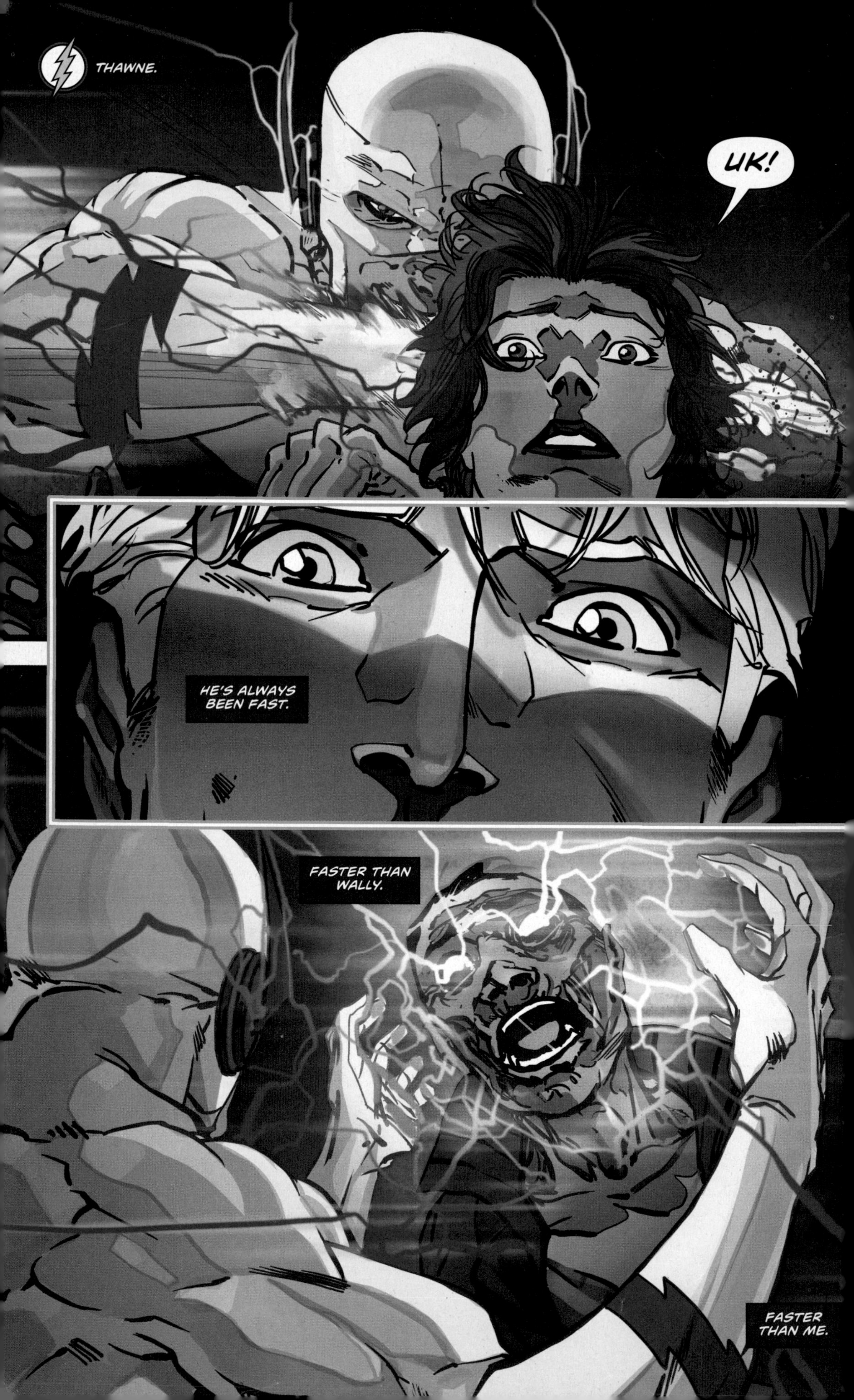
THAWNE.
UK!
HE'S ALWAYS BEEN FAST.
FASTER THAN WALLY.
FASTER THAN ME.

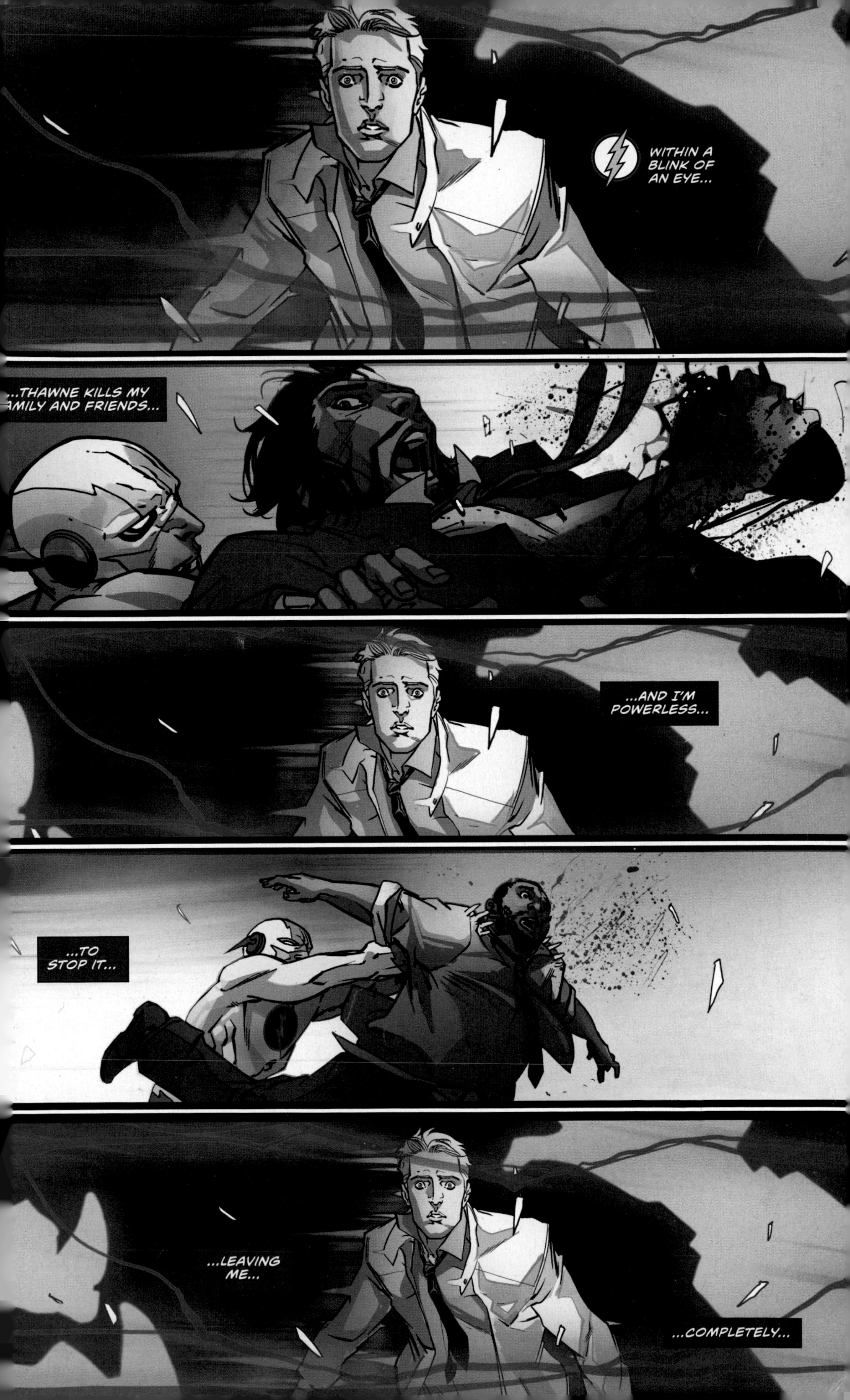
WITHIN A BLINK OF AN EYE...
...THAWNE KILLS MY
AMILY AND FRIENDS...
...AND I'M POWERLESS...
...TO STOP IT...
...LEAVING ME...
...COMPLETELY...

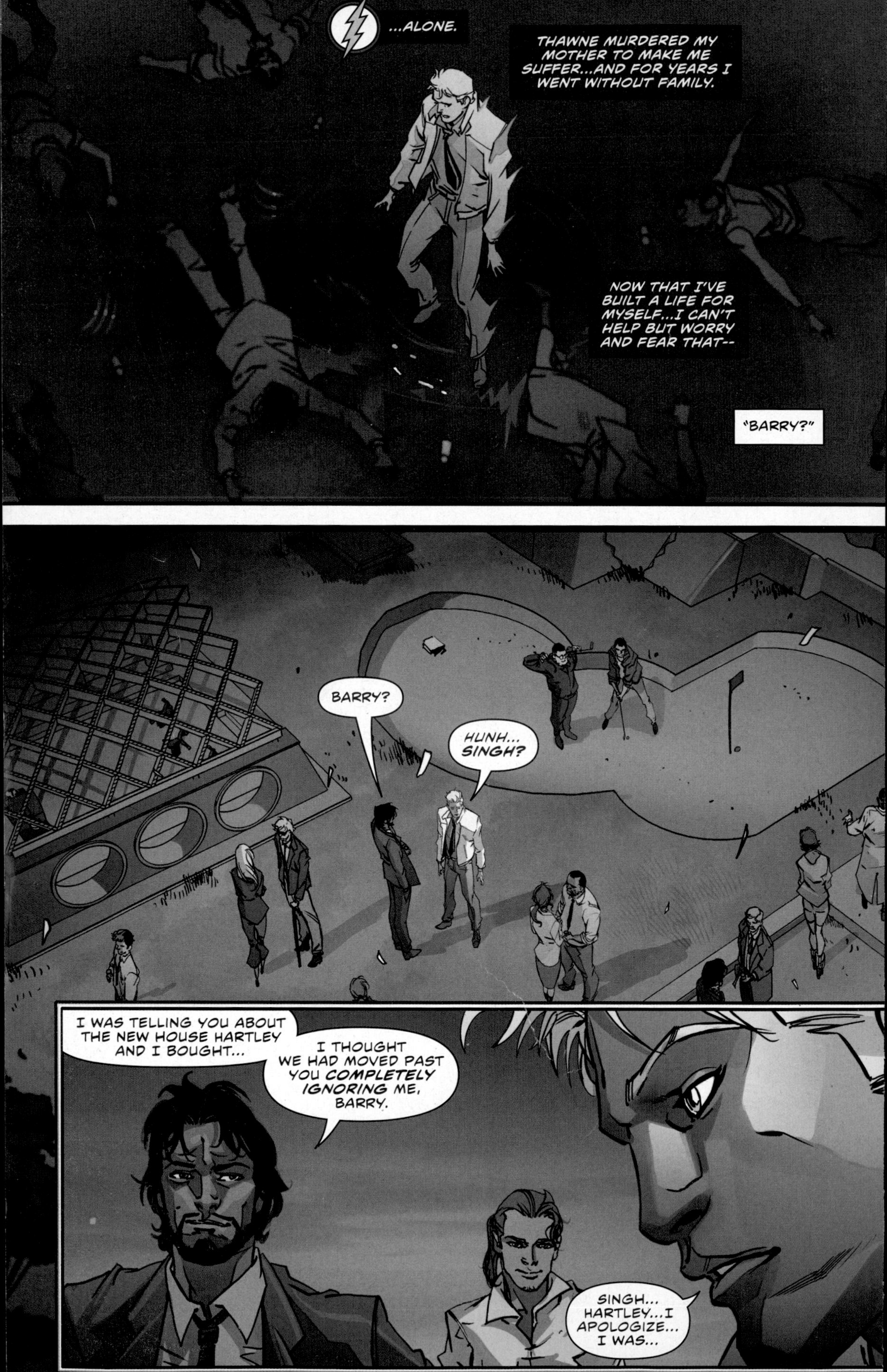
...ALONE.
THAWNE MURDERED MY MOTHER TO MAKE ME SUFFER...AND FOR YEARS I WENT WITHOUT FAMILY.
NOW THAT I'VE BUILT A LIFE FOR MYSELF...I CAN'T HELP BUT WORRY AND FEAR THAT--
"BARRY?"
BARRY?
HUNH... SINGH?
I WAS TELLING YOU ABOUT THE NEW HOUSE HARTLEY AND I BOUGHT...
I THOUGHT WE HAD MOVED PAST YOU COMPLETELY IGNORING ME, BARRY.
SINGH... HARTLEY...I APOLOGIZE... I WAS...

...I WAS JUST THINKING ABOUT A--

DON'T SAY YOU'RE DISTRACTED BY A *CASE*.

WE ALL HAVE CASES.

THE CRIME LAB CAME OUT FOR *YOUR* BIRTHDAY. THEY PUT ASIDE THEIR LIVES *FOR YOU*.

I EVEN DRAGGED *KRISTEN* AWAY FROM HER DESK.

SO... ENLIGHTEN ME, BARRY.

WHAT'S *REALLY* ON YOUR MIND?

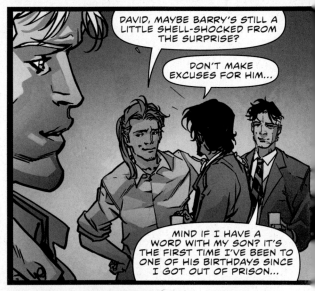

DAVID, MAYBE BARRY'S STILL A LITTLE SHELL-SHOCKED FROM THE SURPRISE?

DON'T MAKE EXCUSES FOR HIM...

MIND IF I HAVE A WORD WITH MY SON? IT'S THE FIRST TIME I'VE BEEN TO ONE OF HIS BIRTHDAYS SINCE I GOT OUT OF PRISON...

GO RIGHT AHEAD, HENRY...MAYBE YOU'LL HAVE BETTER LUCK GETTING BARRY TO OPEN UP...

RRY... OKAY, ON?

SORRY, I'M REALLY GLAD TO SEE EVERYONE... JUST...

JUST... GIMME A MINUTE...

BARRY?

TELL ME YOU'RE NOT ABOUT TO PULL ONE OF YOUR INFAMOUS DISAPPEARING ACTS.

NO...NO... OF COURSE NOT...

HEY, BUDDY...

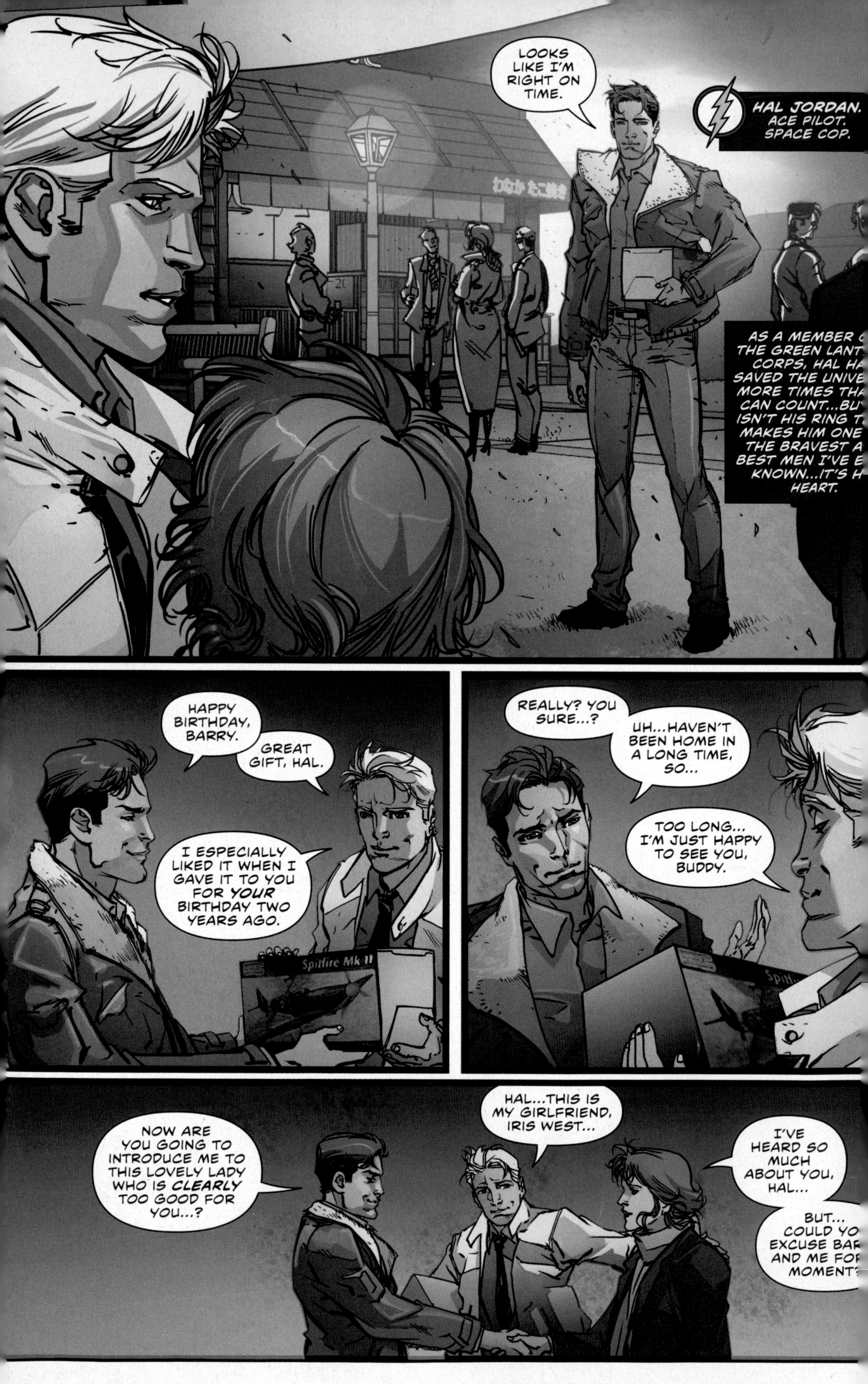

LOOKS LIKE I'M RIGHT ON TIME.
HAL JORDAN. ACE PILOT. SPACE COP.
わなか たこ焼き
AS A MEMBER O THE GREEN LANT CORPS, HAL HA SAVED THE UNIVE MORE TIMES THA CAN COUNT...BU ISN'T HIS RING T MAKES HIM ONE THE BRAVEST A BEST MEN I'VE E KNOWN...IT'S H HEART.
HAPPY BIRTHDAY, BARRY.
GREAT GIFT, HAL.
I ESPECIALLY LIKED IT WHEN I GAVE IT TO YOU FOR *YOUR* BIRTHDAY TWO YEARS AGO.
Spitfire Mk II
REALLY? YOU SURE...?
UH...HAVEN'T BEEN HOME IN A LONG TIME, SO...
TOO LONG... I'M JUST HAPPY TO SEE YOU, BUDDY.
NOW ARE YOU GOING TO INTRODUCE ME TO THIS LOVELY LADY WHO IS *CLEARLY* TOO GOOD FOR YOU...?
HAL...THIS IS MY GIRLFRIEND, IRIS WEST...
I'VE HEARD SO MUCH ABOUT YOU, HAL...
BUT... COULD YO EXCUSE BAR AND ME FOR MOMENT?

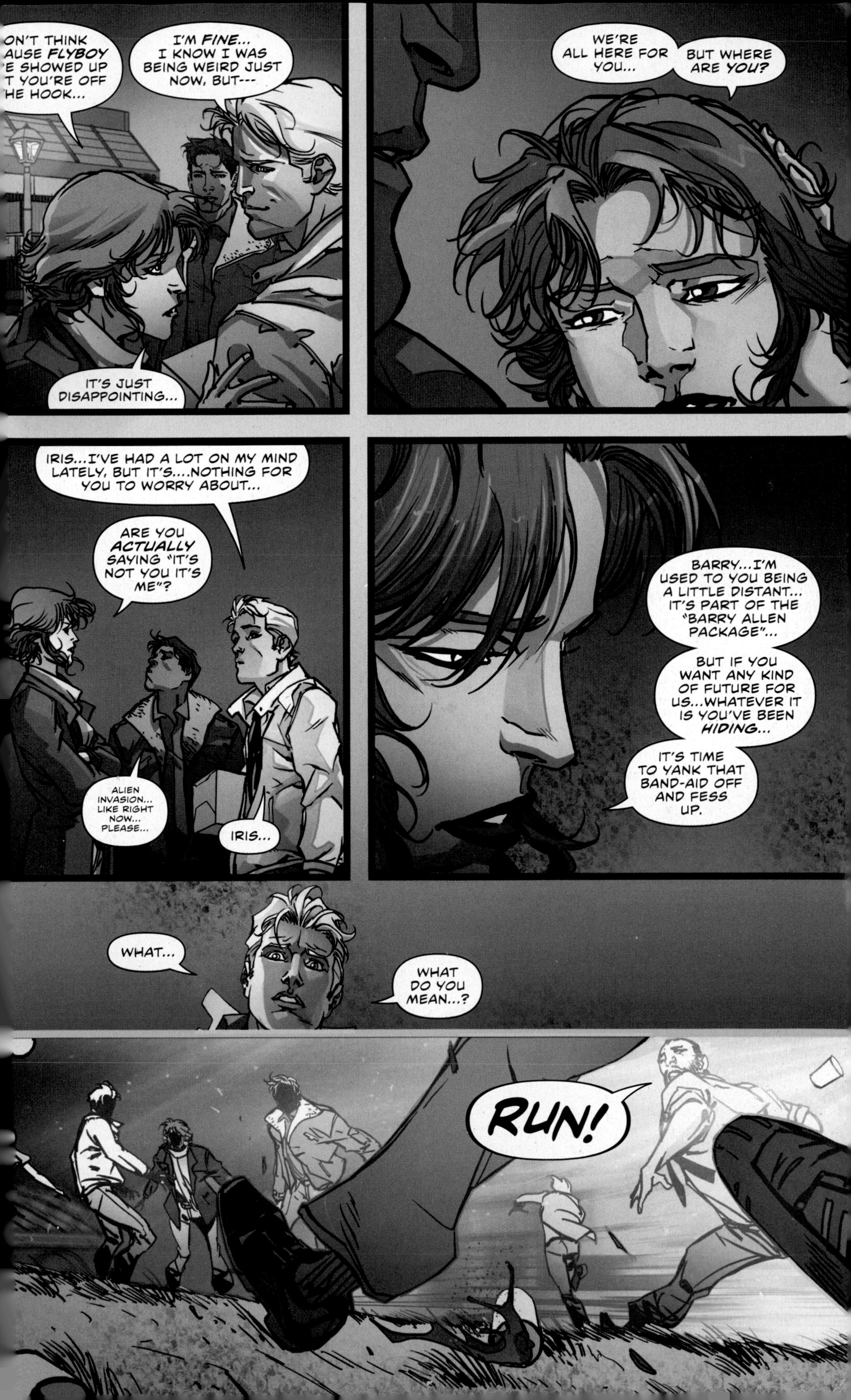
ON'T THINK
AUSE FLYBOY
'E SHOWED UP
T YOU'RE OFF
HE HOOK...
I'M FINE...
I KNOW I WAS
BEING WEIRD JUST
NOW, BUT---
IT'S JUST
DISAPPOINTING...
WE'RE
ALL HERE FOR
YOU...
BUT WHERE
ARE YOU?
IRIS...I'VE HAD A LOT ON MY MIND
LATELY, BUT IT'S....NOTHING FOR
YOU TO WORRY ABOUT...
ARE YOU
ACTUALLY
SAYING "IT'S
NOT YOU IT'S
ME"?
ALIEN
INVASION...
LIKE RIGHT
NOW...
PLEASE...
IRIS...
BARRY...I'M
USED TO YOU BEING
A LITTLE DISTANT...
IT'S PART OF THE
"BARRY ALLEN
PACKAGE"...
BUT IF YOU
WANT ANY KIND
OF FUTURE FOR
US...WHATEVER IT
IS YOU'VE BEEN
HIDING...
IT'S TIME
TO YANK THAT
BAND-AID OFF
AND FESS
UP.
WHAT...
WHAT
DO YOU
MEAN...?
RUN!

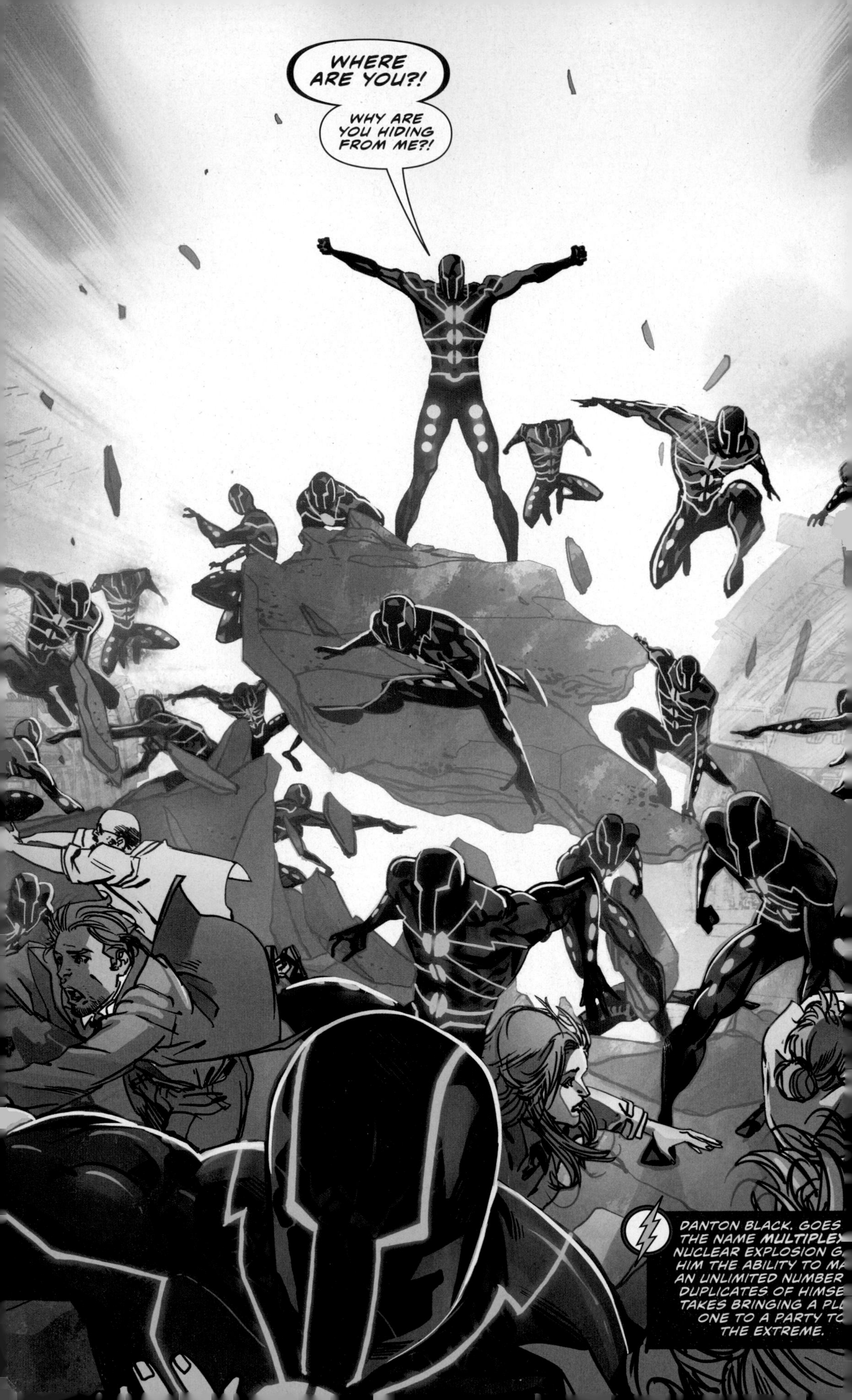
WHERE ARE YOU?!
WHY ARE YOU HIDING FROM ME?!
DANTON BLACK. GOES THE NAME MULTIPLEX NUCLEAR EXPLOSION G HIM THE ABILITY TO M AN UNLIMITED NUMBER DUPLICATES OF HIMSE TAKES BRINGING A PL ONE TO A PARTY TO THE EXTREME.

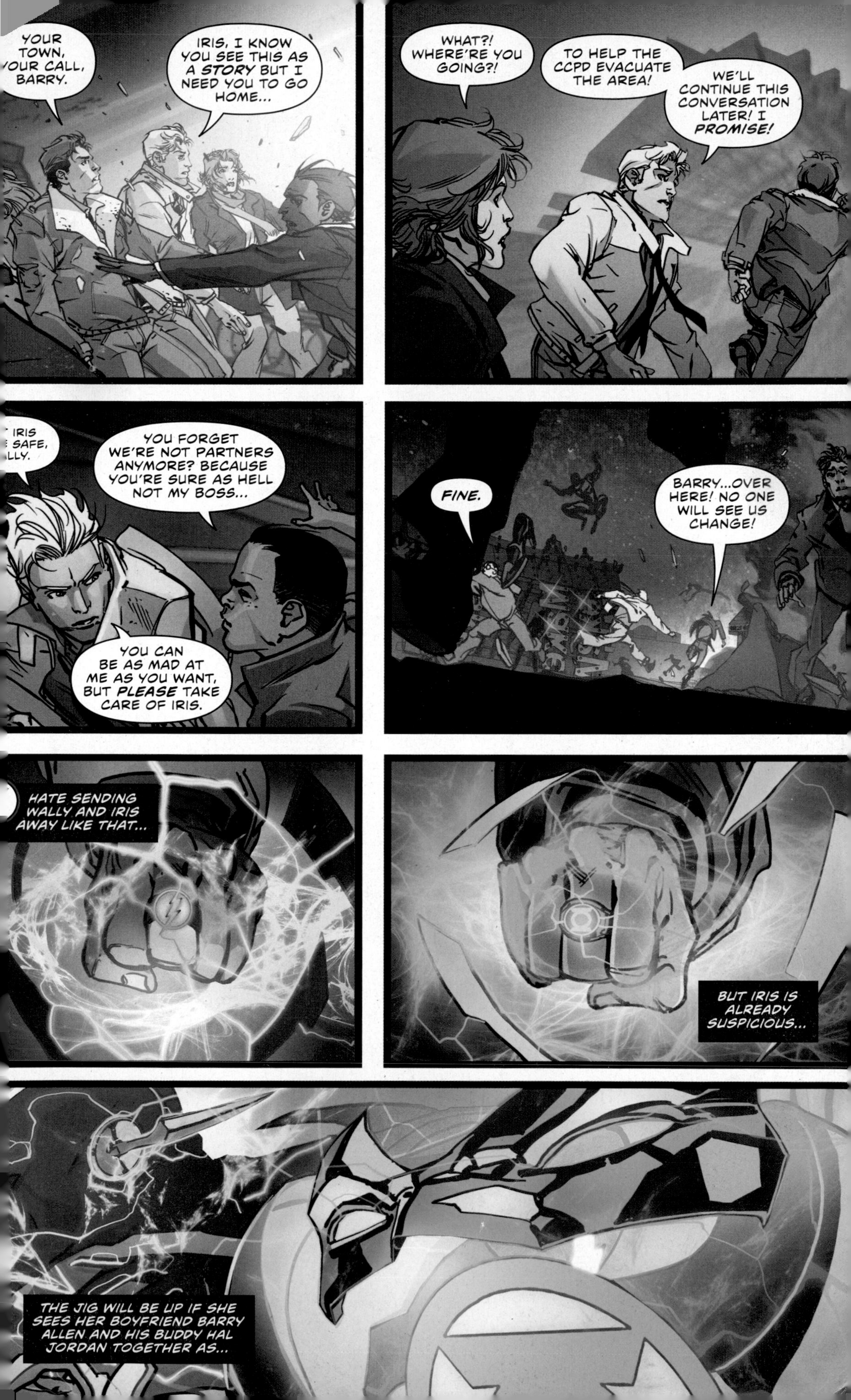
YOUR TOWN, YOUR CALL, BARRY.
IRIS, I KNOW YOU SEE THIS AS A STORY BUT I NEED YOU TO GO HOME...
WHAT?! WHERE'RE YOU GOING?!
TO HELP THE CCPD EVACUATE THE AREA!
WE'LL CONTINUE THIS CONVERSATION LATER! I PROMISE!
IRIS SAFE, LLY.
YOU FORGET WE'RE NOT PARTNERS ANYMORE? BECAUSE YOU'RE SURE AS HELL NOT MY BOSS...
YOU CAN BE AS MAD AT ME AS YOU WANT, BUT PLEASE TAKE CARE OF IRIS.
FINE.
BARRY...OVER HERE! NO ONE WILL SEE US CHANGE!
HATE SENDING WALLY AND IRIS AWAY LIKE THAT...
BUT IRIS IS ALREADY SUSPICIOUS...
THE JIG WILL BE UP IF SHE SEES HER BOYFRIEND BARRY ALLEN AND HIS BUDDY HAL JORDAN TOGETHER AS...

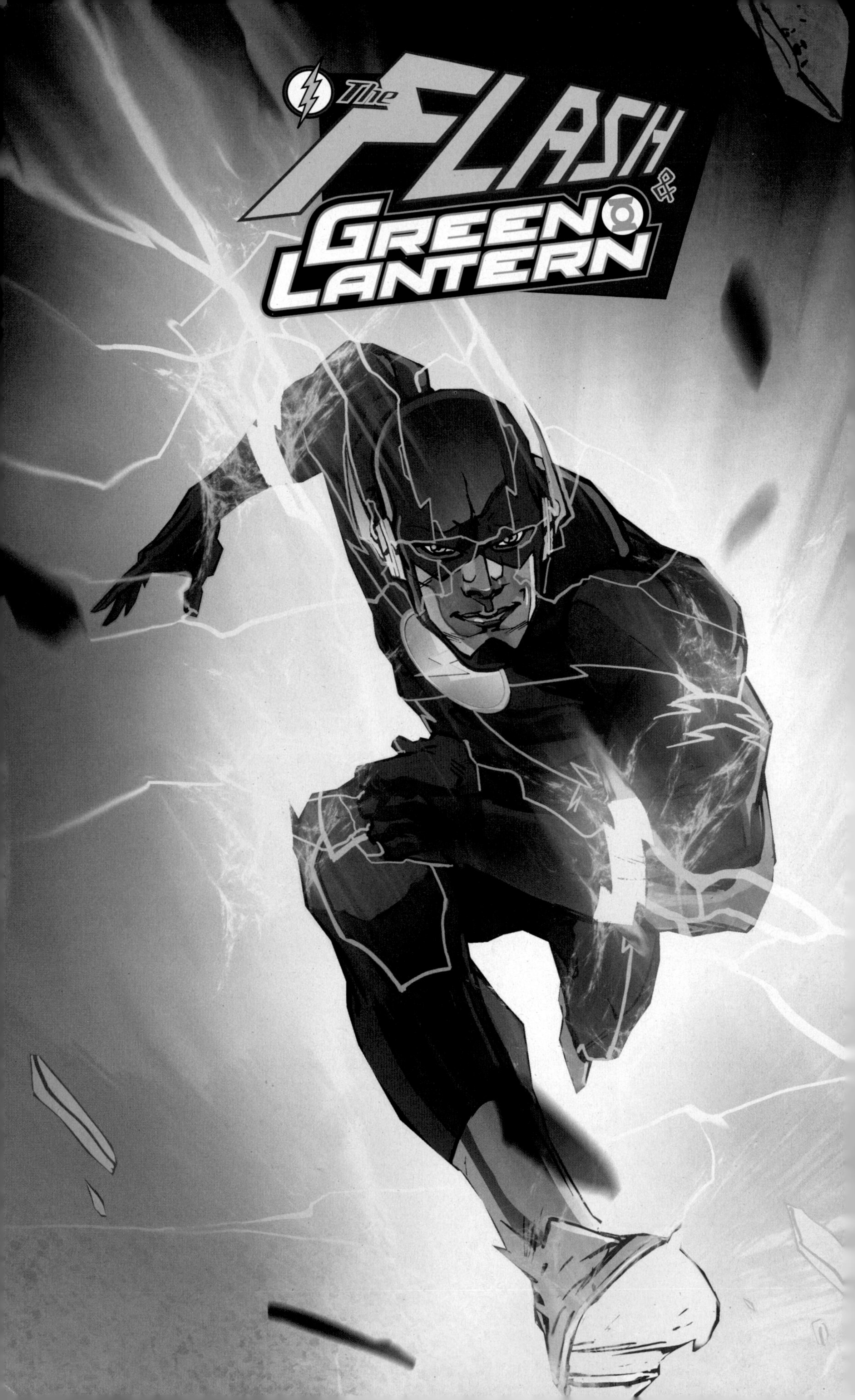
The FLASH
&
GREEN LANTERN

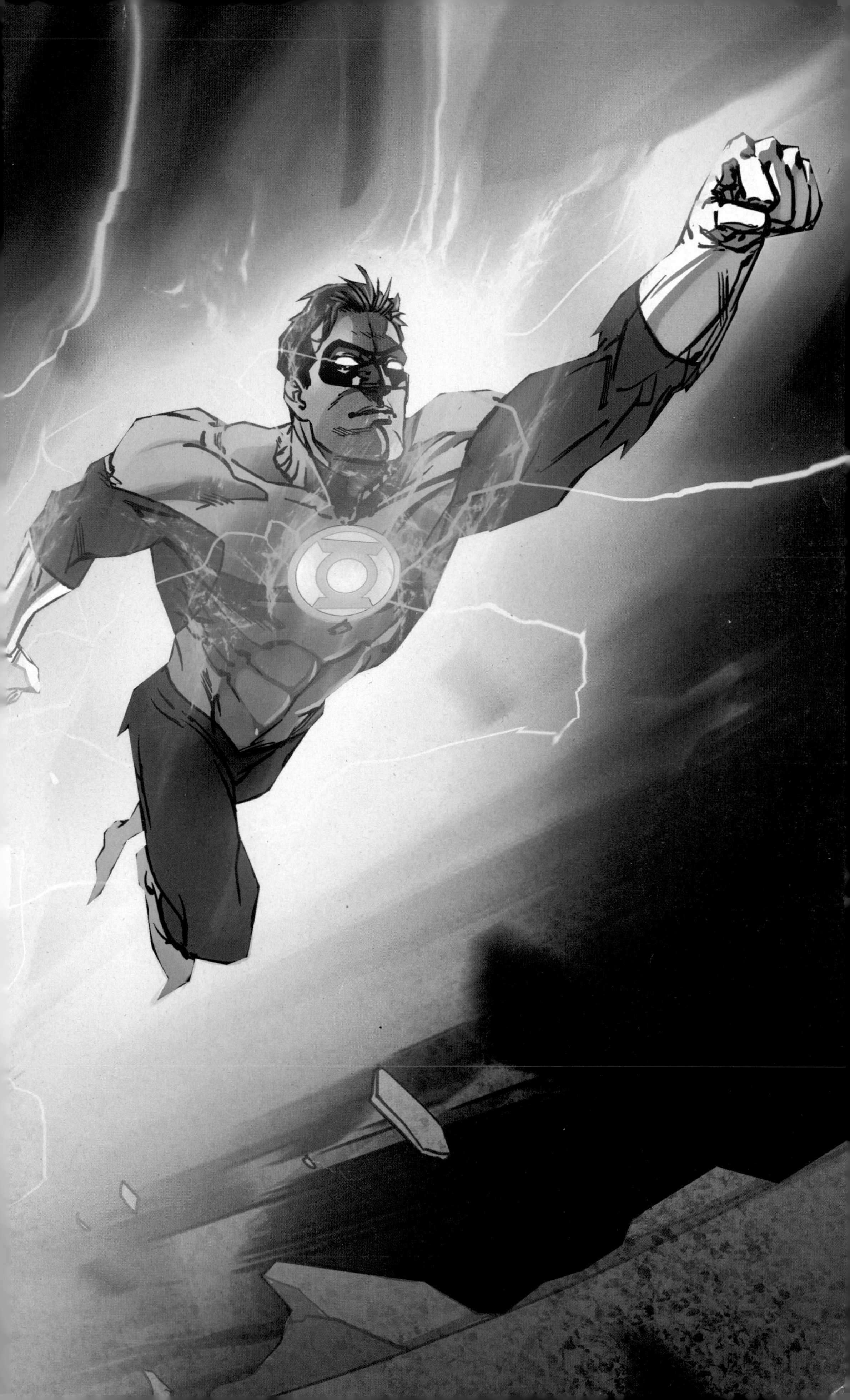

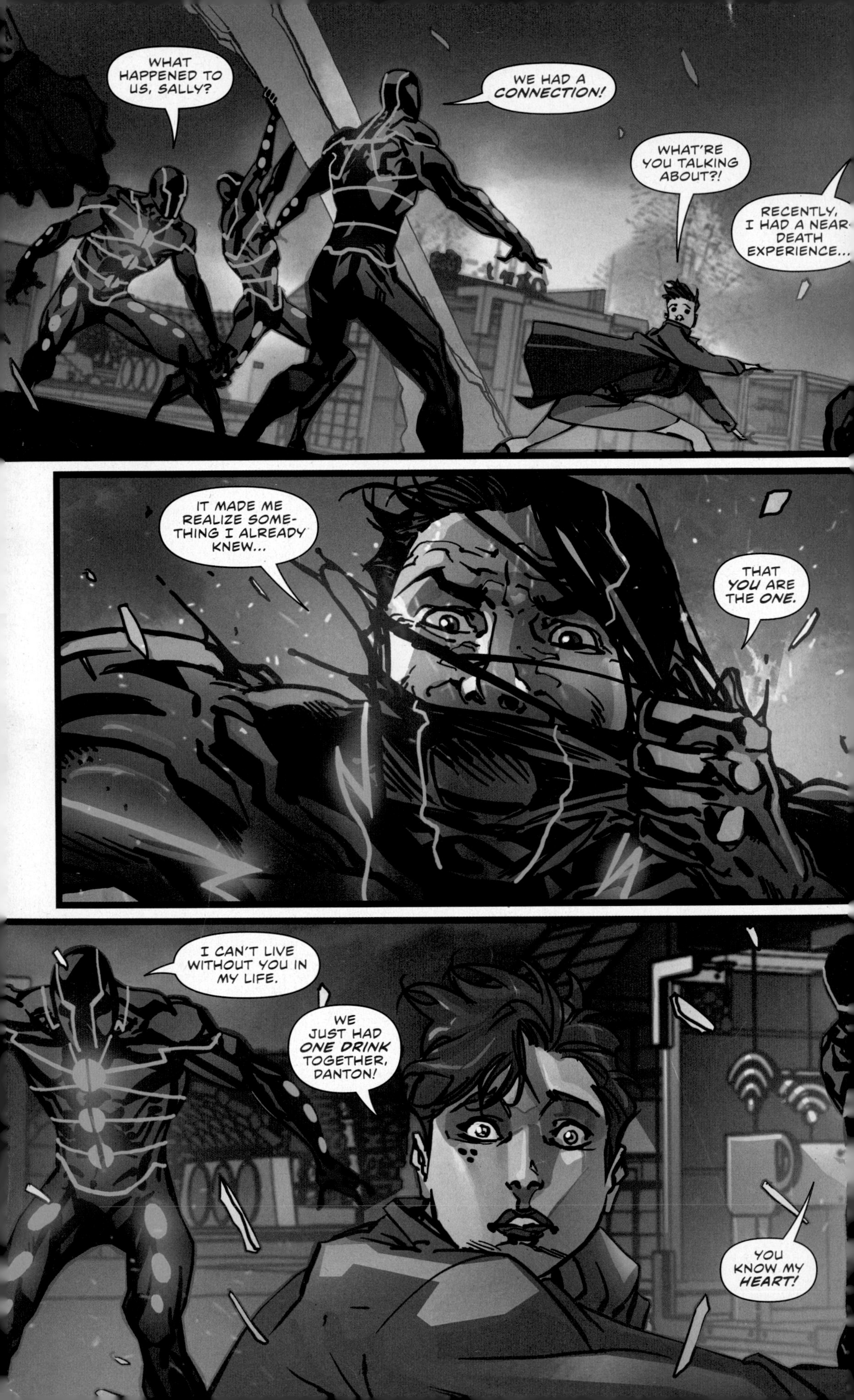
WHAT HAPPENED TO US, SALLY?
WE HAD A CONNECTION!
WHAT'RE YOU TALKING ABOUT?!
RECENTLY, I HAD A NEAR DEATH EXPERIENCE...
IT MADE ME REALIZE SOMETHING I ALREADY KNEW...
THAT YOU ARE THE ONE.
I CAN'T LIVE WITHOUT YOU IN MY LIFE.
WE JUST HAD ONE DRINK TOGETHER, DANTON!
YOU KNOW MY HEART!

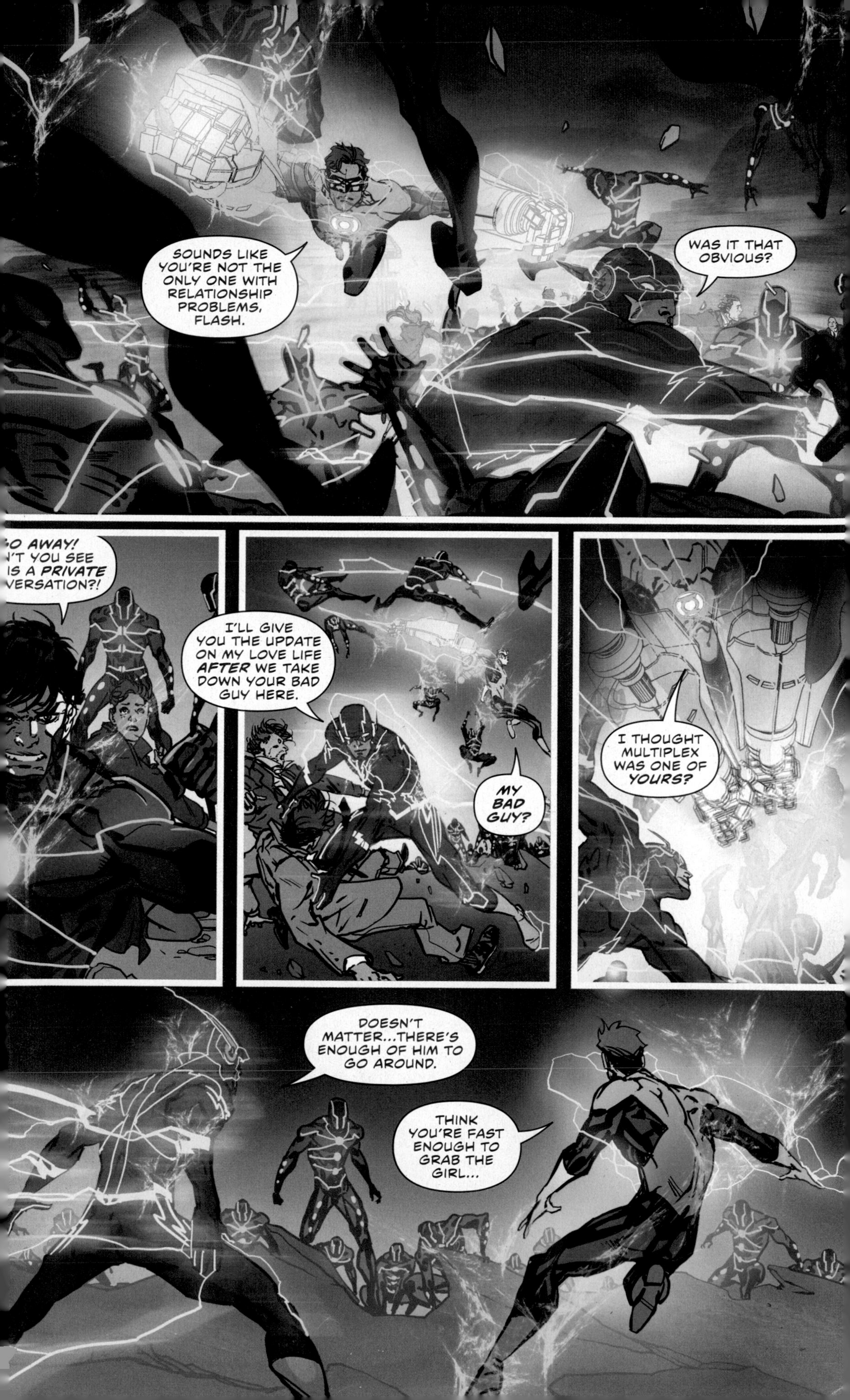
SOUNDS LIKE YOU'RE NOT THE ONLY ONE WITH RELATIONSHIP PROBLEMS, FLASH.
WAS IT THAT OBVIOUS?
GO AWAY! N'T YOU SEE IS A PRIVATE VERSATION?!
I'LL GIVE YOU THE UPDATE ON MY LOVE LIFE AFTER WE TAKE DOWN YOUR BAD GUY HERE.
MY BAD GUY?
I THOUGHT MULTIPLEX WAS ONE OF YOURS?
DOESN'T MATTER...THERE'S ENOUGH OF HIM TO GO AROUND.
THINK YOU'RE FAST ENOUGH TO GRAB THE GIRL...

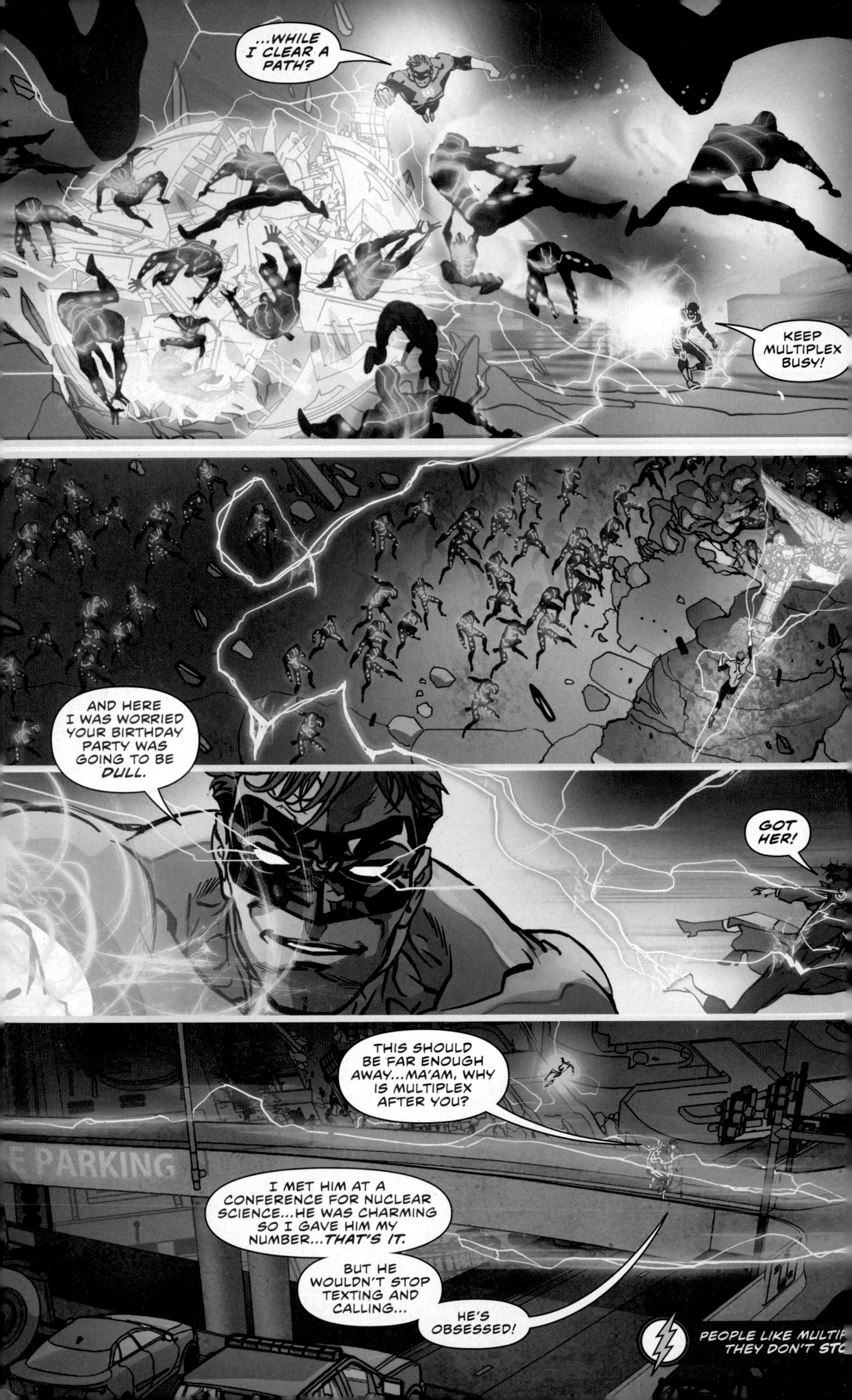
...WHILE I CLEAR A PATH?
KEEP MULTIPLEX BUSY!
AND HERE I WAS WORRIED YOUR BIRTHDAY PARTY WAS GOING TO BE *DULL.*
GOT HER!
THIS SHOULD BE FAR ENOUGH AWAY...MA'AM, WHY IS MULTIPLEX AFTER YOU?
PARKING
I MET HIM AT A CONFERENCE FOR NUCLEAR SCIENCE...HE WAS CHARMING SO I GAVE HIM MY NUMBER...*THAT'S IT.*
BUT HE WOULDN'T STOP TEXTING AND CALLING...
HE'S OBSESSED!
PEOPLE LIKE MULTIP
THEY DON'T STO

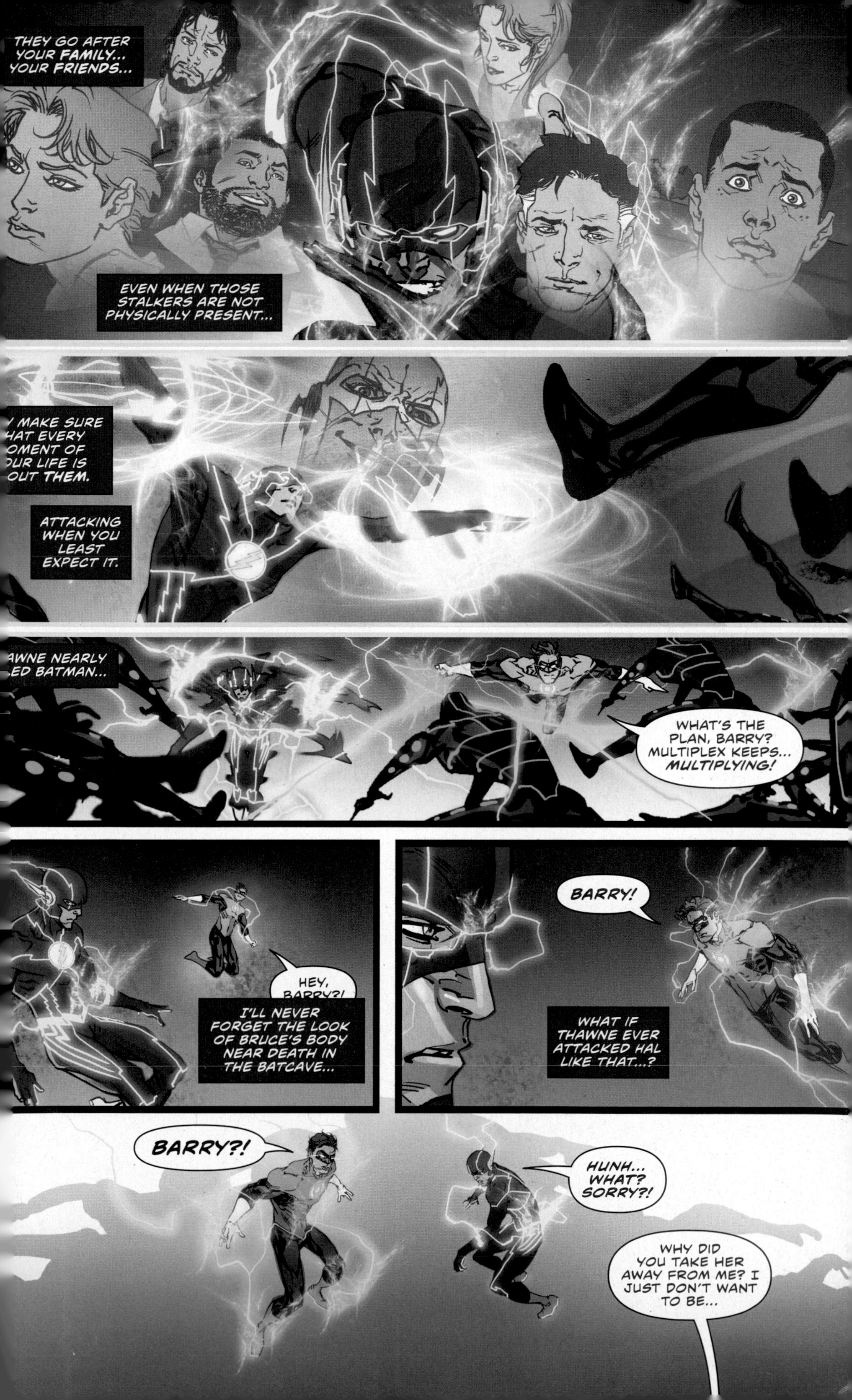
THEY GO AFTER YOUR FAMILY... YOUR FRIENDS...
EVEN WHEN THOSE STALKERS ARE NOT PHYSICALLY PRESENT...
Y MAKE SURE HAT EVERY OMENT OF OUR LIFE IS OUT THEM.
ATTACKING WHEN YOU LEAST EXPECT IT.
AWNE NEARLY ED BATMAN...
WHAT'S THE PLAN, BARRY? MULTIPLEX KEEPS... MULTIPLYING!
HEY, BARRY?!
I'LL NEVER FORGET THE LOOK OF BRUCE'S BODY NEAR DEATH IN THE BATCAVE...
BARRY!
WHAT IF THAWNE EVER ATTACKED HAL LIKE THAT...?
BARRY?!
HUNH... WHAT? SORRY?!
WHY DID YOU TAKE HER AWAY FROM ME? I JUST DON'T WANT TO BE...

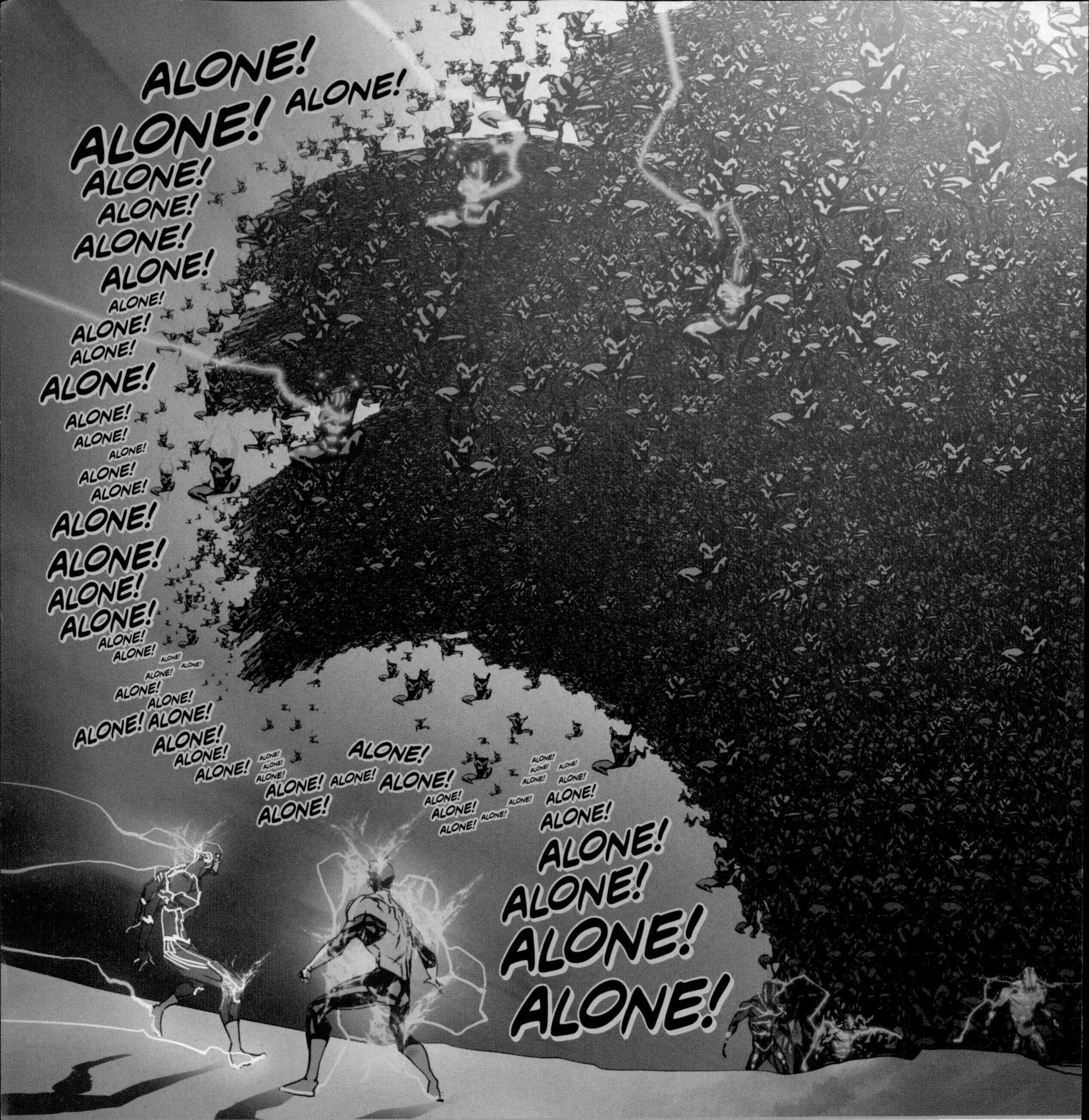
ALONE!
ALONE! ALONE!
ALONE!
ALONE!
ALONE!
ALONE!
ALONE!
ALONE!
ALONE!
ALONE!
ALONE!
ALONE!
ALONE!
ALONE!
ALONE!
ALONE!
ALONE!
ALONE!
ALONE!
ALONE! ALONE!
ALONE!
ALONE!
ALONE!
ALONE!
ALONE! ALONE! ALONE!
ALONE!
ALONE!
ALONE!
ALONE!
ALONE!
ALONE!
ALONE!

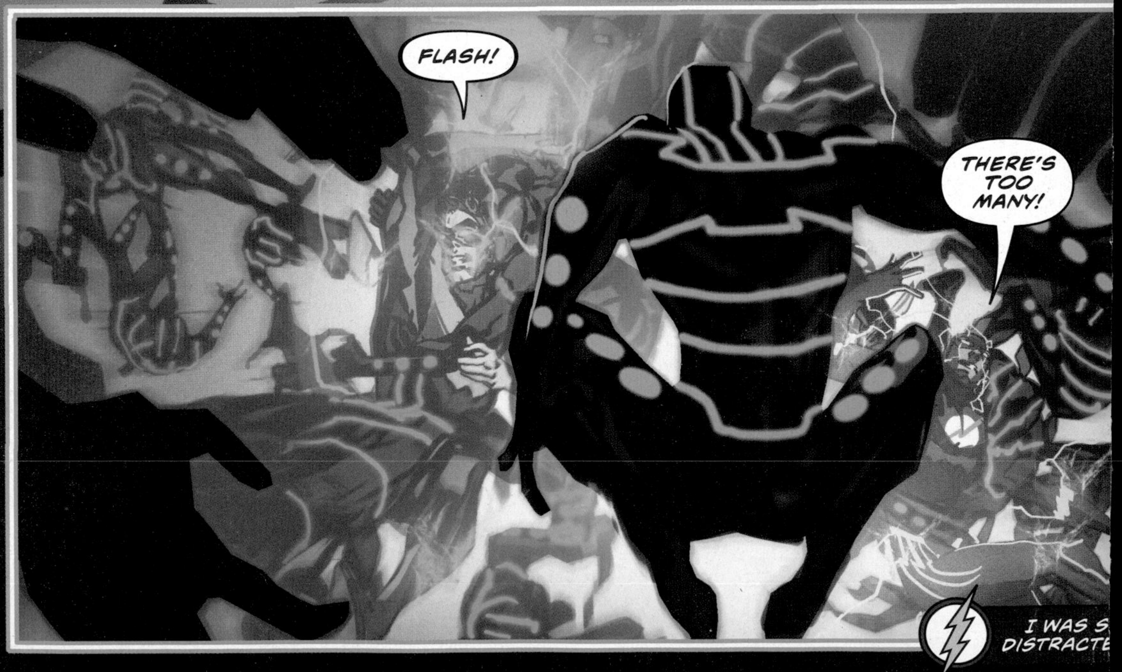
FLASH!
THERE'S TOO MANY!
I WAS S
DISTRACTE

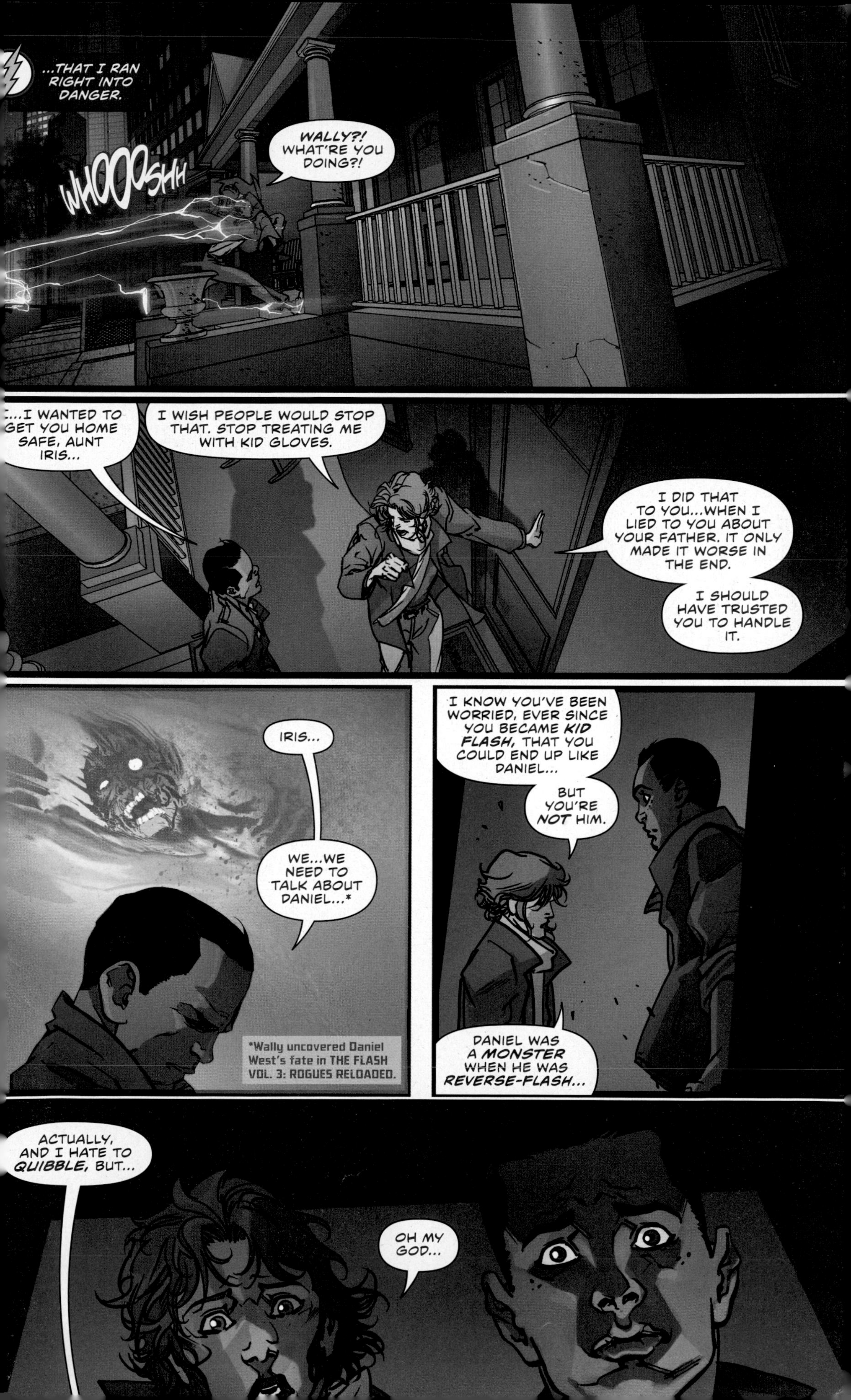
...THAT I RAN RIGHT INTO DANGER.
WALLY?! WHAT'RE YOU DOING?!
WHOOOSHH
...I WANTED TO GET YOU HOME SAFE, AUNT IRIS...
I WISH PEOPLE WOULD STOP THAT. STOP TREATING ME WITH KID GLOVES.
I DID THAT TO YOU...WHEN I LIED TO YOU ABOUT YOUR FATHER. IT ONLY MADE IT WORSE IN THE END.
I SHOULD HAVE TRUSTED YOU TO HANDLE IT.
IRIS...
WE...WE NEED TO TALK ABOUT DANIEL...*
*Wally uncovered Daniel West's fate in THE FLASH VOL. 3: ROGUES RELOADED.
I KNOW YOU'VE BEEN WORRIED, EVER SINCE YOU BECAME KID FLASH, THAT YOU COULD END UP LIKE DANIEL...
BUT YOU'RE NOT HIM.
DANIEL WAS A MONSTER WHEN HE WAS REVERSE-FLASH...
ACTUALLY, AND I HATE TO QUIBBLE, BUT...
OH MY GOD...

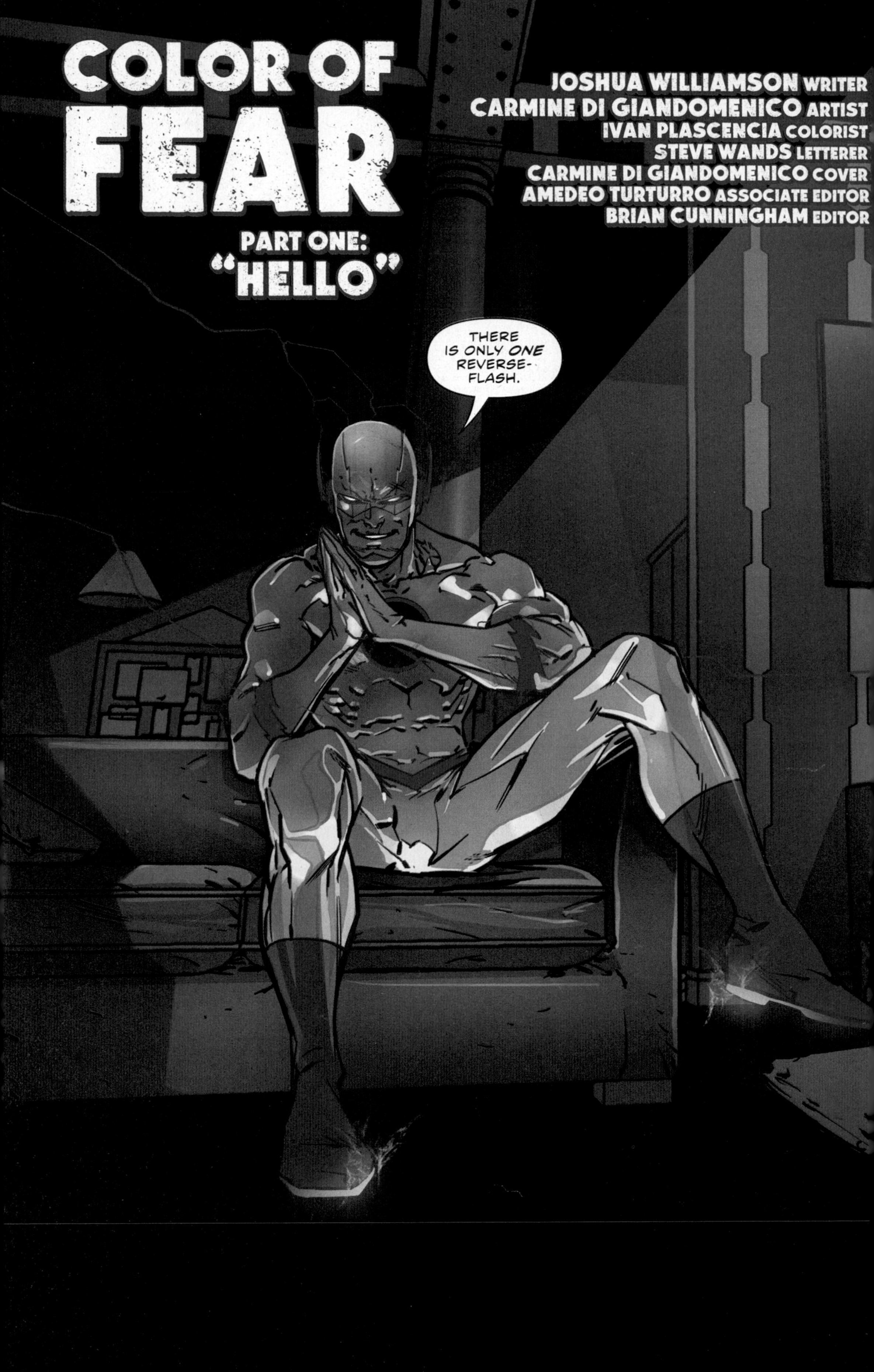
COLOR OF FEAR
PART ONE: "HELLO"
JOSHUA WILLIAMSON WRITER
CARMINE DI GIANDOMENICO ARTIST
IVAN PLASCENCIA COLORIST
STEVE WANDS LETTERER
CARMINE DI GIANDOMENICO COVER
AMEDEO TURTURRO ASSOCIATE EDITOR
BRIAN CUNNINGHAM EDITOR
THERE IS ONLY ONE REVERSE-FLASH.

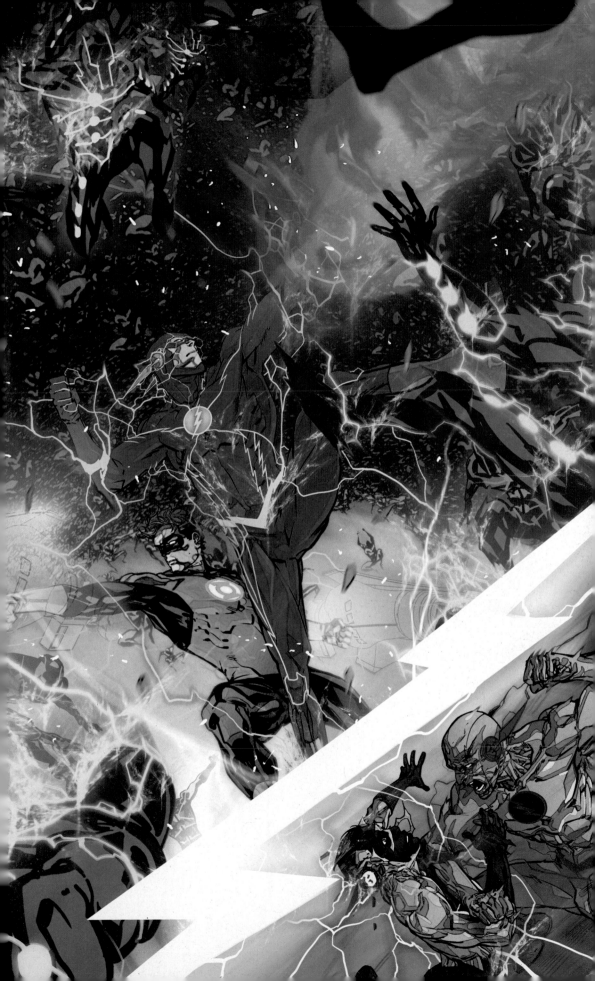

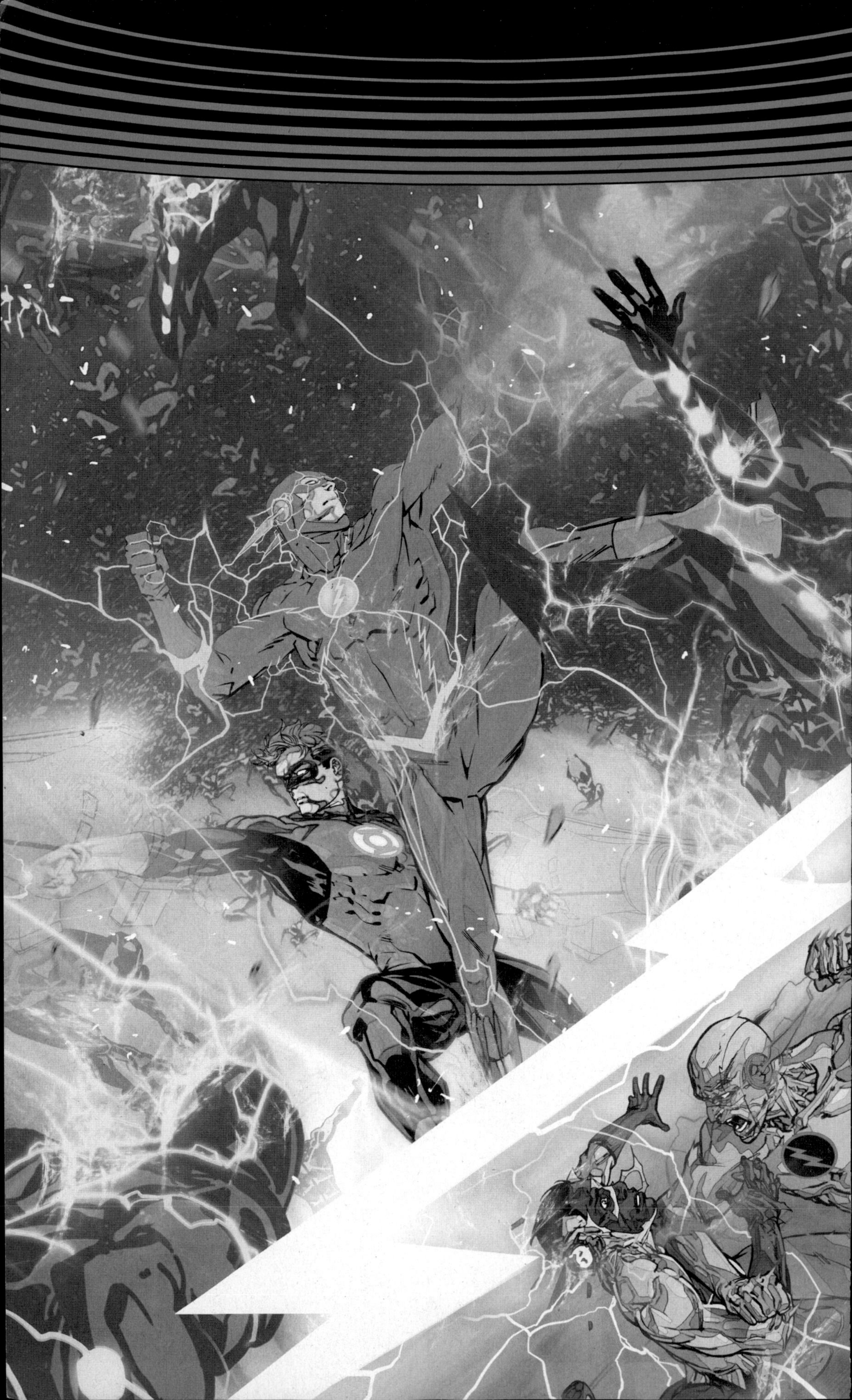

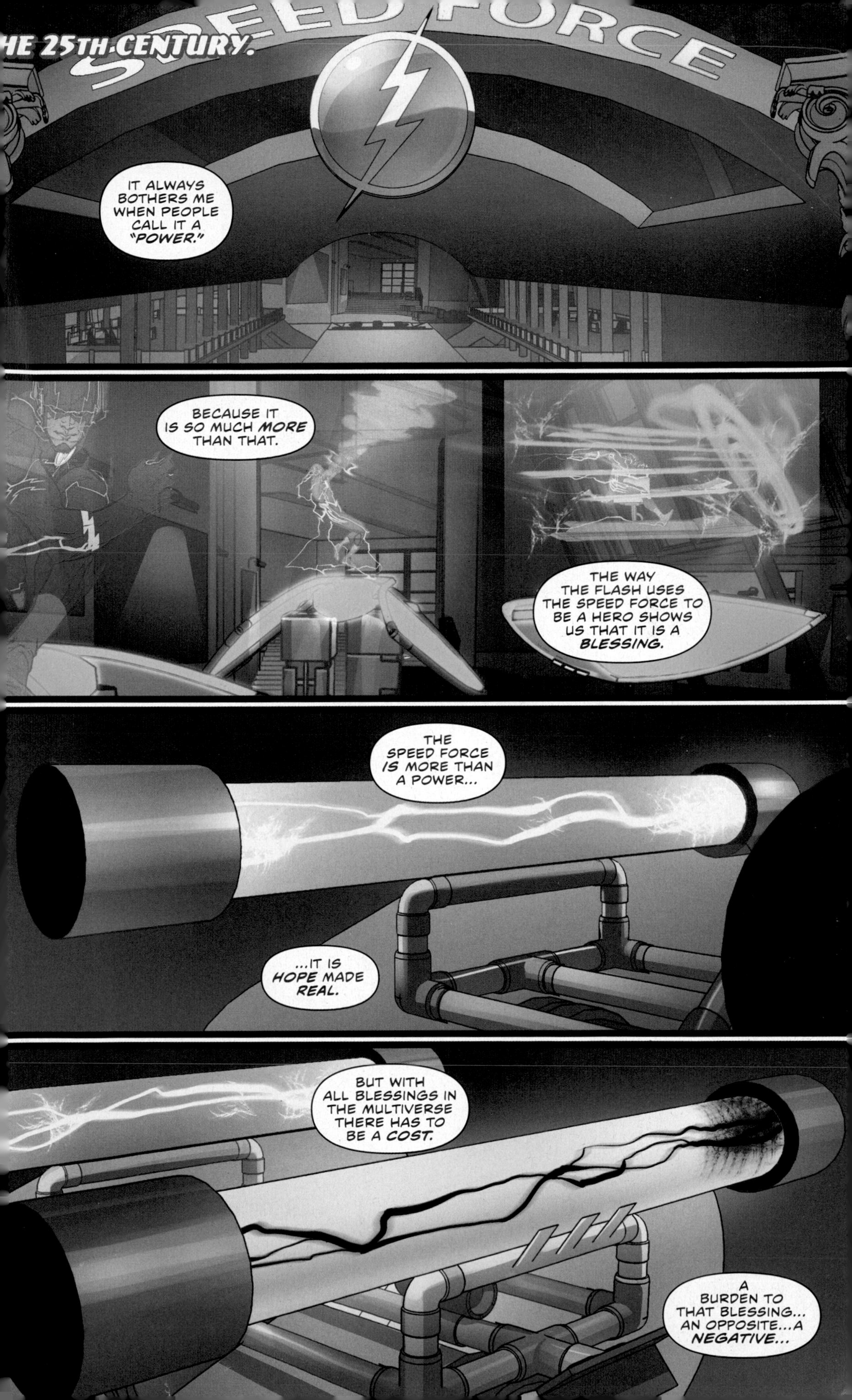
THE 25TH CENTURY.
SPEED FORCE
IT ALWAYS BOTHERS ME WHEN PEOPLE CALL IT A "POWER."
BECAUSE IT IS SO MUCH MORE THAN THAT.
THE WAY THE FLASH USES THE SPEED FORCE TO BE A HERO SHOWS US THAT IT IS A BLESSING.
THE SPEED FORCE IS MORE THAN A POWER...
...IT IS HOPE MADE REAL.
BUT WITH ALL BLESSINGS IN THE MULTIVERSE THERE HAS TO BE A COST.
A BURDEN TO THAT BLESSING... AN OPPOSITE...A NEGATIVE...

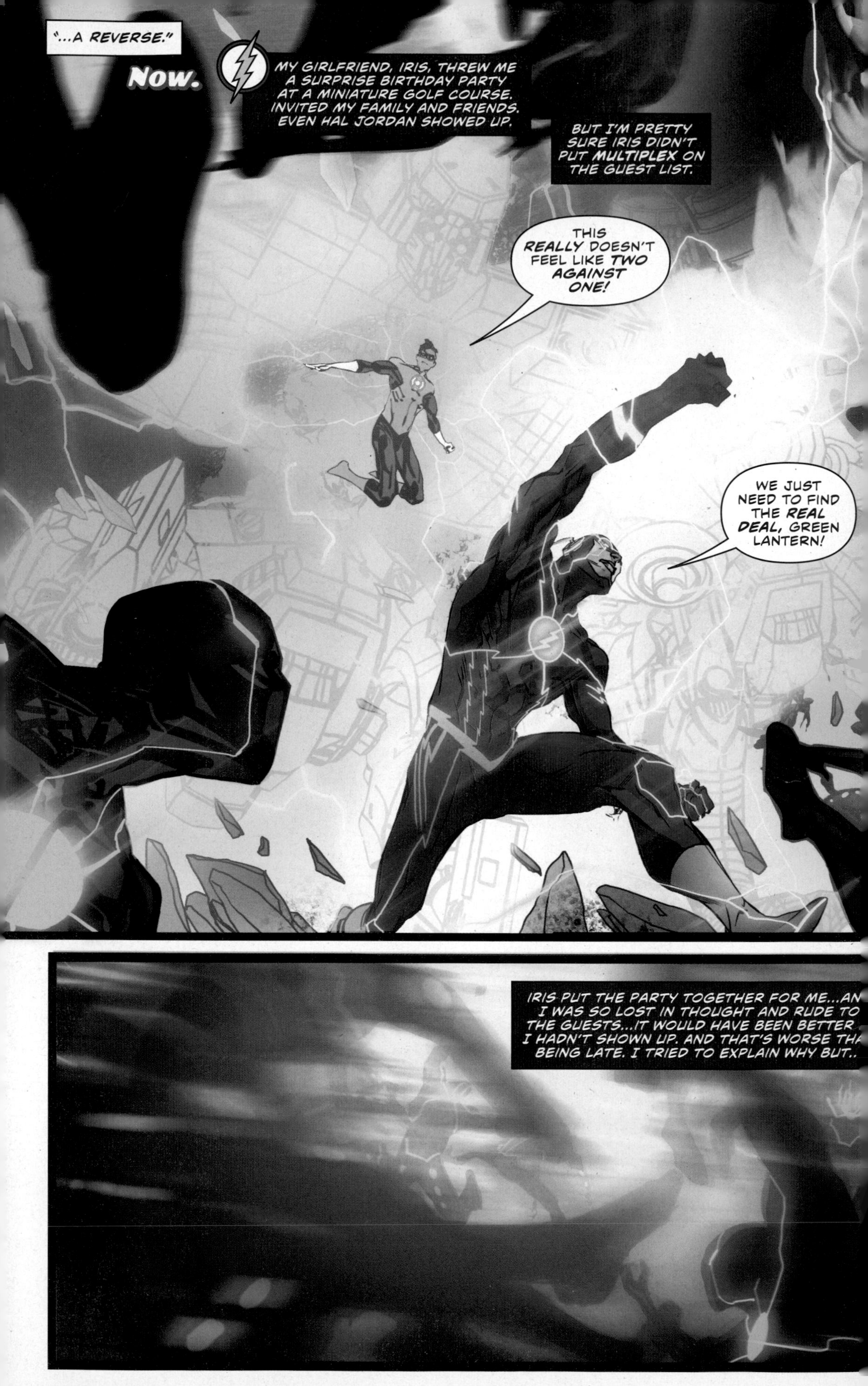
"...A REVERSE."
Now.
MY GIRLFRIEND, IRIS, THREW ME A SURPRISE BIRTHDAY PARTY AT A MINIATURE GOLF COURSE. INVITED MY FAMILY AND FRIENDS. EVEN HAL JORDAN SHOWED UP.
BUT I'M PRETTY SURE IRIS DIDN'T PUT MULTIPLEX ON THE GUEST LIST.
THIS REALLY DOESN'T FEEL LIKE TWO AGAINST ONE!
WE JUST NEED TO FIND THE REAL DEAL, GREEN LANTERN!
IRIS PUT THE PARTY TOGETHER FOR ME...AN I WAS SO LOST IN THOUGHT AND RUDE TO THE GUESTS...IT WOULD HAVE BEEN BETTER I HADN'T SHOWN UP. AND THAT'S WORSE THA BEING LATE. I TRIED TO EXPLAIN WHY BUT..

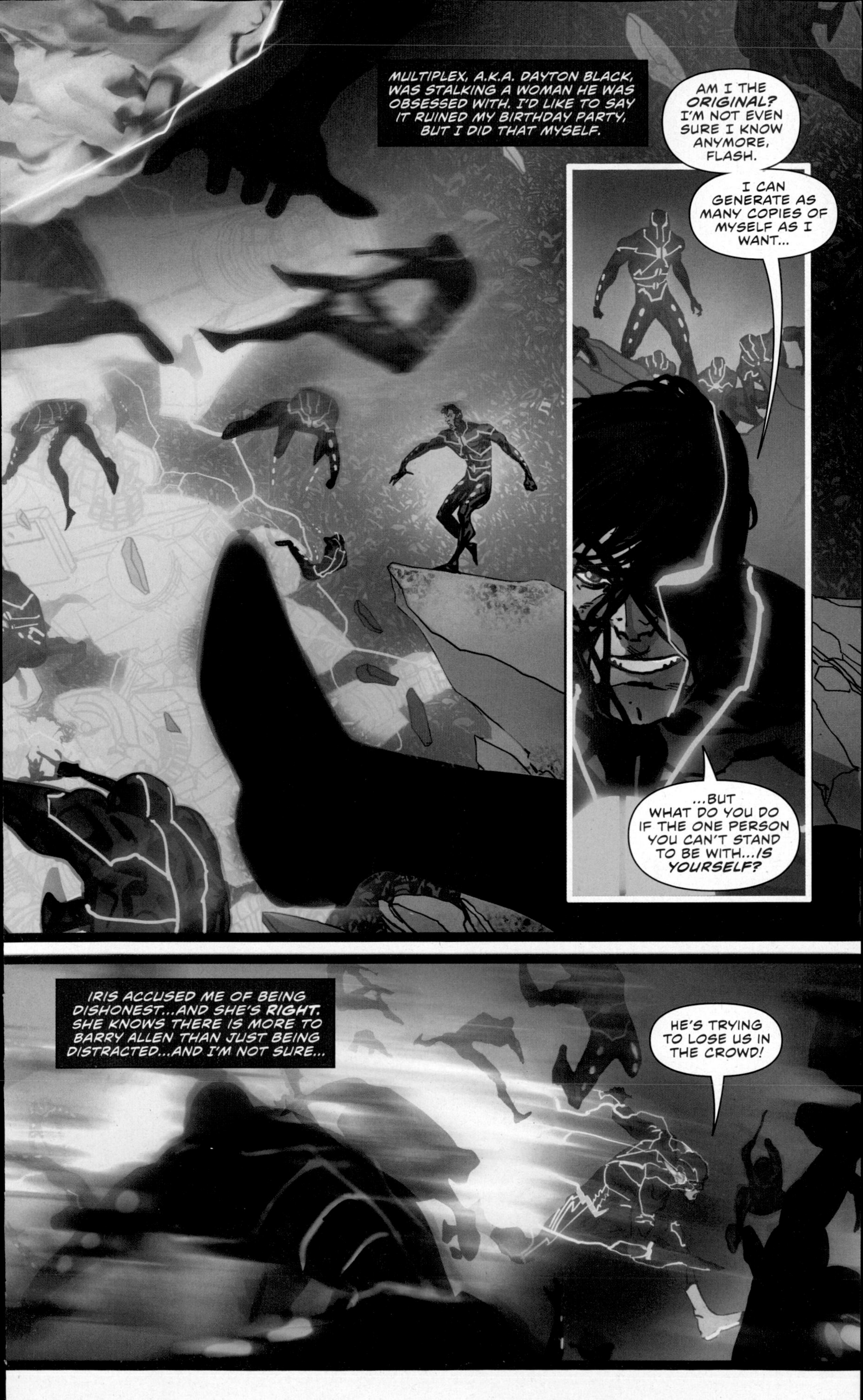
MULTIPLEX, A.K.A. DAYTON BLACK, WAS STALKING A WOMAN HE WAS OBSESSED WITH. I'D LIKE TO SAY IT RUINED MY BIRTHDAY PARTY, BUT I DID THAT MYSELF.
AM I THE ORIGINAL? I'M NOT EVEN SURE I KNOW ANYMORE, FLASH.
I CAN GENERATE AS MANY COPIES OF MYSELF AS I WANT...
...BUT WHAT DO YOU DO IF THE ONE PERSON YOU CAN'T STAND TO BE WITH...IS YOURSELF?
IRIS ACCUSED ME OF BEING DISHONEST...AND SHE'S RIGHT. SHE KNOWS THERE IS MORE TO BARRY ALLEN THAN JUST BEING DISTRACTED...AND I'M NOT SURE...
HE'S TRYING TO LOSE US IN THE CROWD!

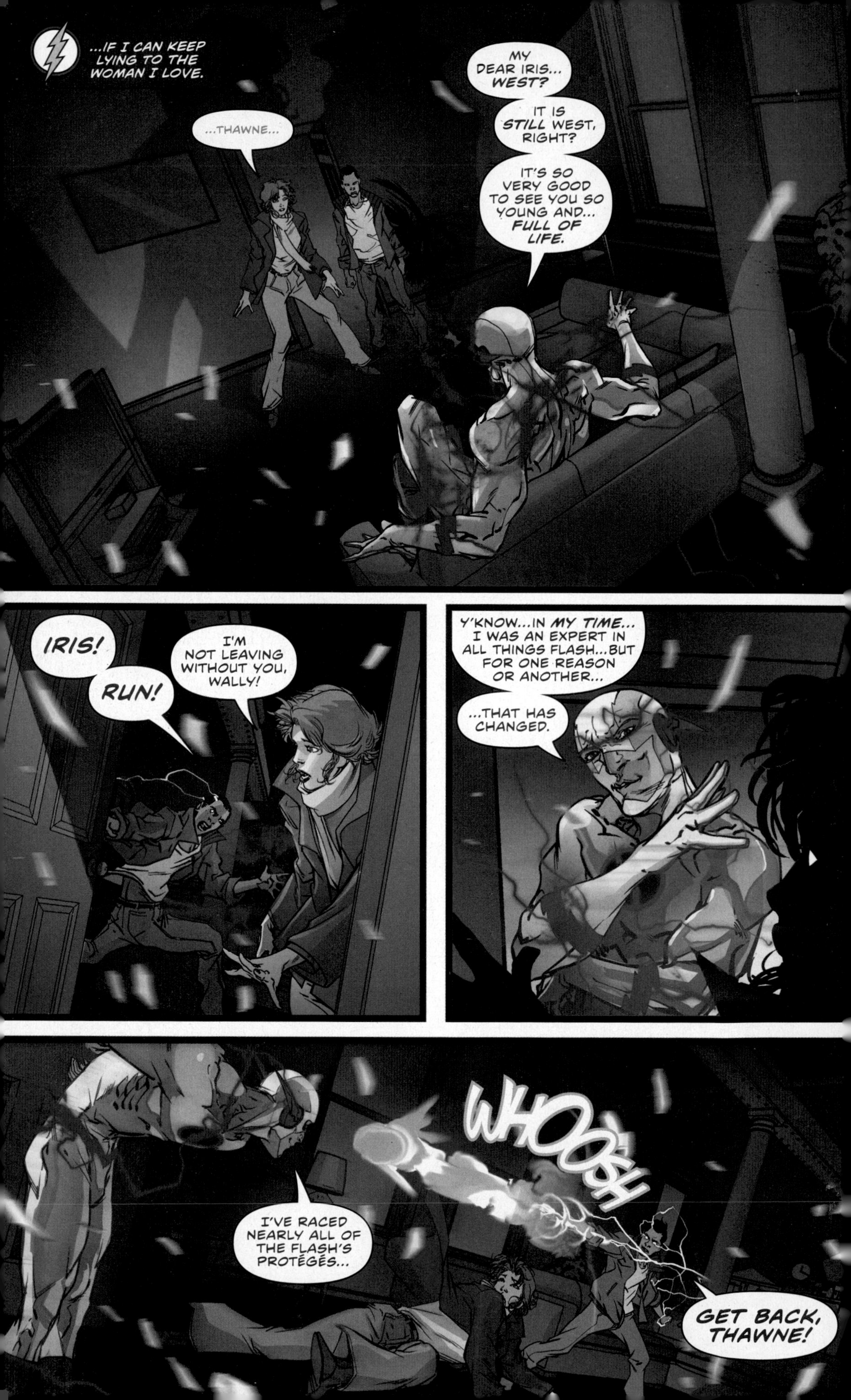
...IF I CAN KEEP LYING TO THE WOMAN I LOVE.
...THAWNE...
MY DEAR IRIS... WEST?
IT IS STILL WEST, RIGHT?
IT'S SO VERY GOOD TO SEE YOU SO YOUNG AND... FULL OF LIFE.
IRIS!
RUN!
I'M NOT LEAVING WITHOUT YOU, WALLY!
Y'KNOW...IN MY TIME... I WAS AN EXPERT IN ALL THINGS FLASH...BUT FOR ONE REASON OR ANOTHER...
...THAT HAS CHANGED.
WHOOOSH
I'VE RACED NEARLY ALL OF THE FLASH'S PROTÉGÉS...
GET BACK, THAWNE!

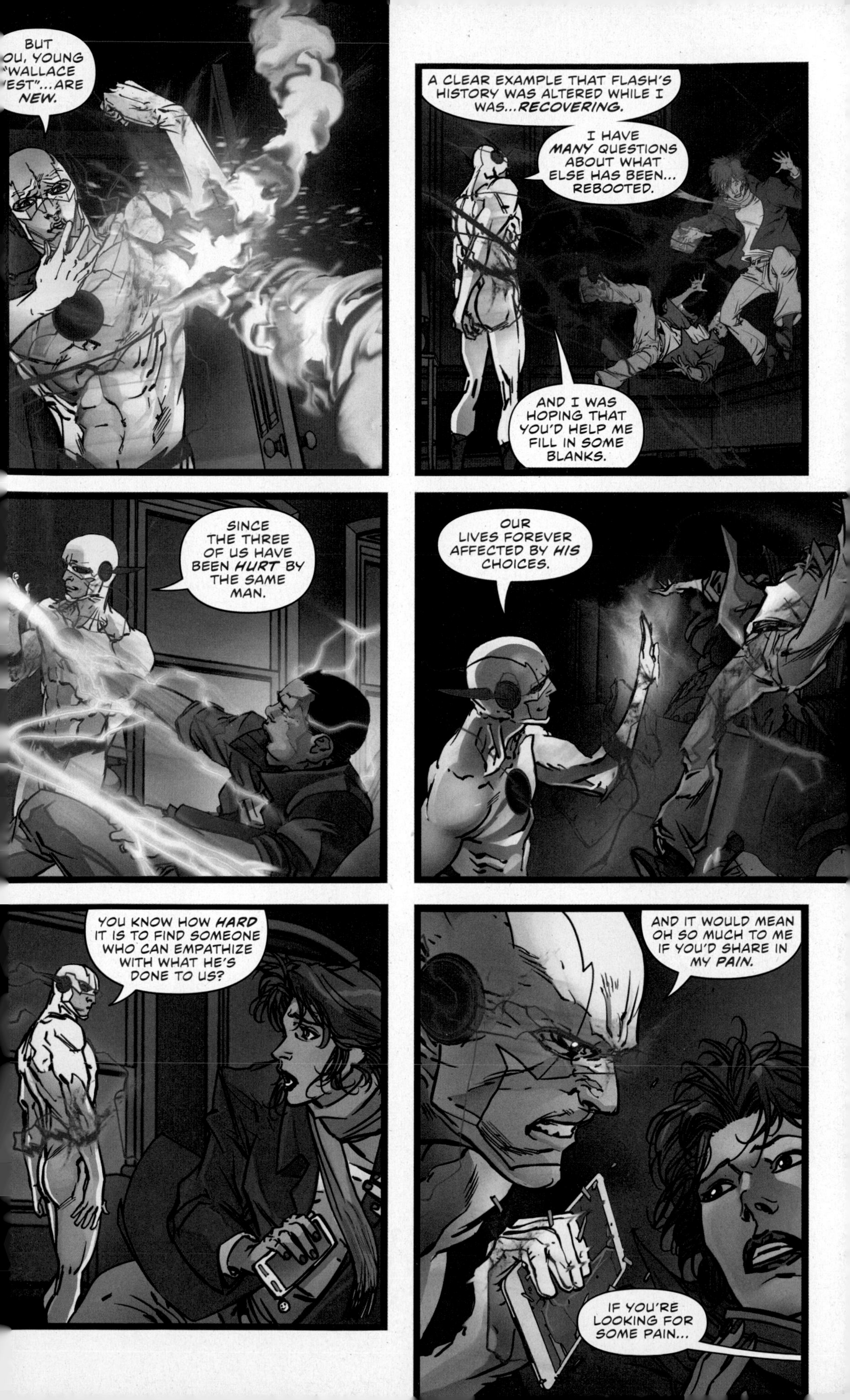
BUT
OU, YOUNG
"WALLACE
EST"...ARE
NEW.
A CLEAR EXAMPLE THAT FLASH'S HISTORY WAS ALTERED WHILE I WAS...RECOVERING.
I HAVE MANY QUESTIONS ABOUT WHAT ELSE HAS BEEN... REBOOTED.
AND I WAS HOPING THAT YOU'D HELP ME FILL IN SOME BLANKS.
SINCE THE THREE OF US HAVE BEEN HURT BY THE SAME MAN.
OUR LIVES FOREVER AFFECTED BY HIS CHOICES.
YOU KNOW HOW HARD IT IS TO FIND SOMEONE WHO CAN EMPATHIZE WITH WHAT HE'S DONE TO US?
AND IT WOULD MEAN OH SO MUCH TO ME IF YOU'D SHARE IN MY PAIN.
IF YOU'RE LOOKING FOR SOME PAIN...

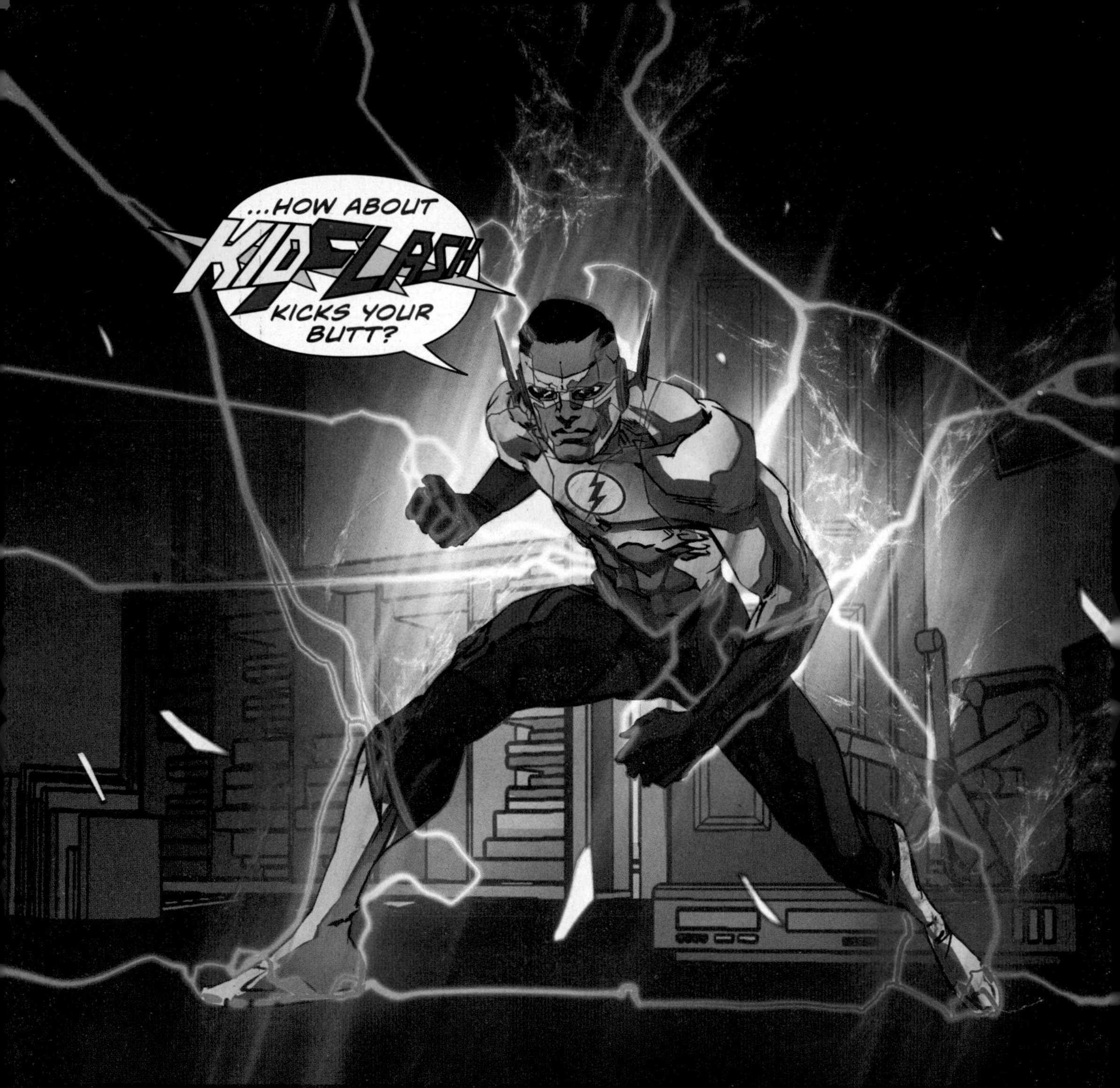
...HOW ABOUT KID FLASH KICKS YOUR BUTT?

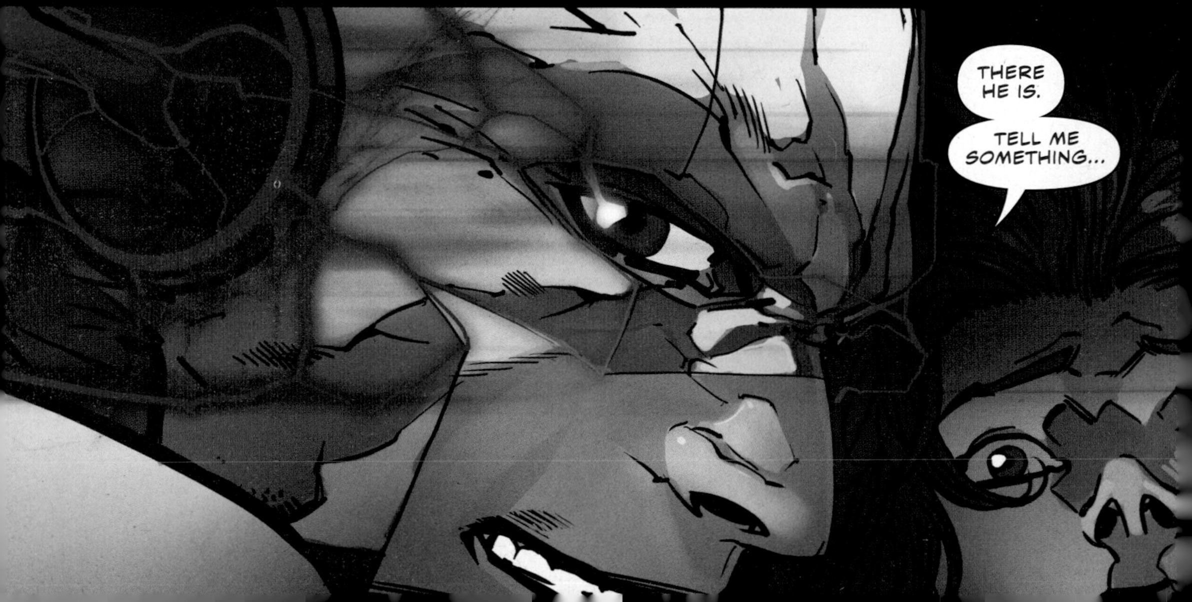
THERE HE IS.
TELL ME SOMETHING...

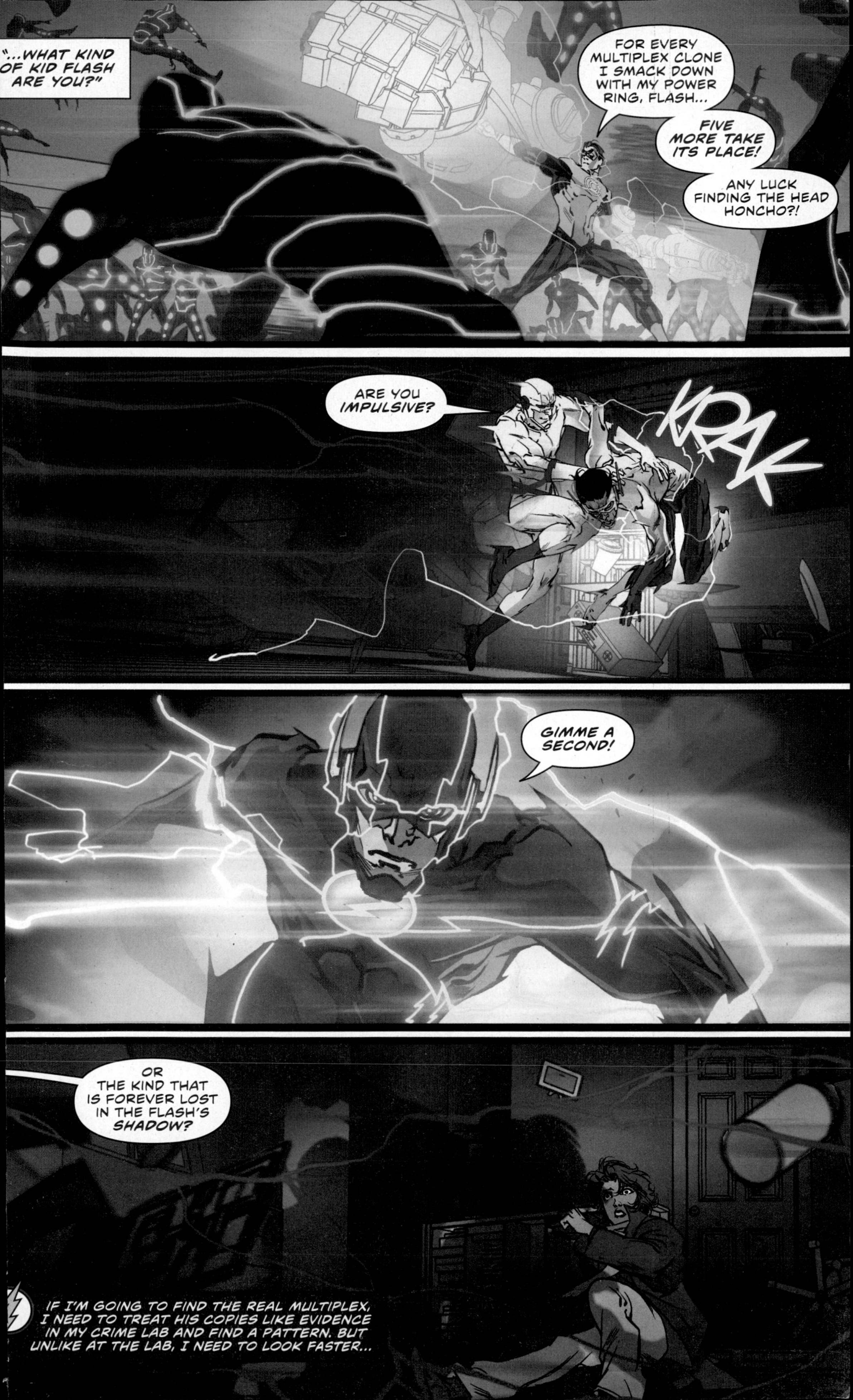

"...WHAT KIND OF KID FLASH ARE YOU?"
FOR EVERY MULTIPLEX CLONE I SMACK DOWN WITH MY POWER RING, FLASH...
FIVE MORE TAKE ITS PLACE!
ANY LUCK FINDING THE HEAD HONCHO?!
ARE YOU IMPULSIVE?
KRAK
GIMME A SECOND!
OR THE KIND THAT IS FOREVER LOST IN THE FLASH'S SHADOW?
IF I'M GOING TO FIND THE REAL MULTIPLEX, I NEED TO TREAT HIS COPIES LIKE EVIDENCE IN MY CRIME LAB AND FIND A PATTERN. BUT UNLIKE AT THE LAB, I NEED TO LOOK FASTER...

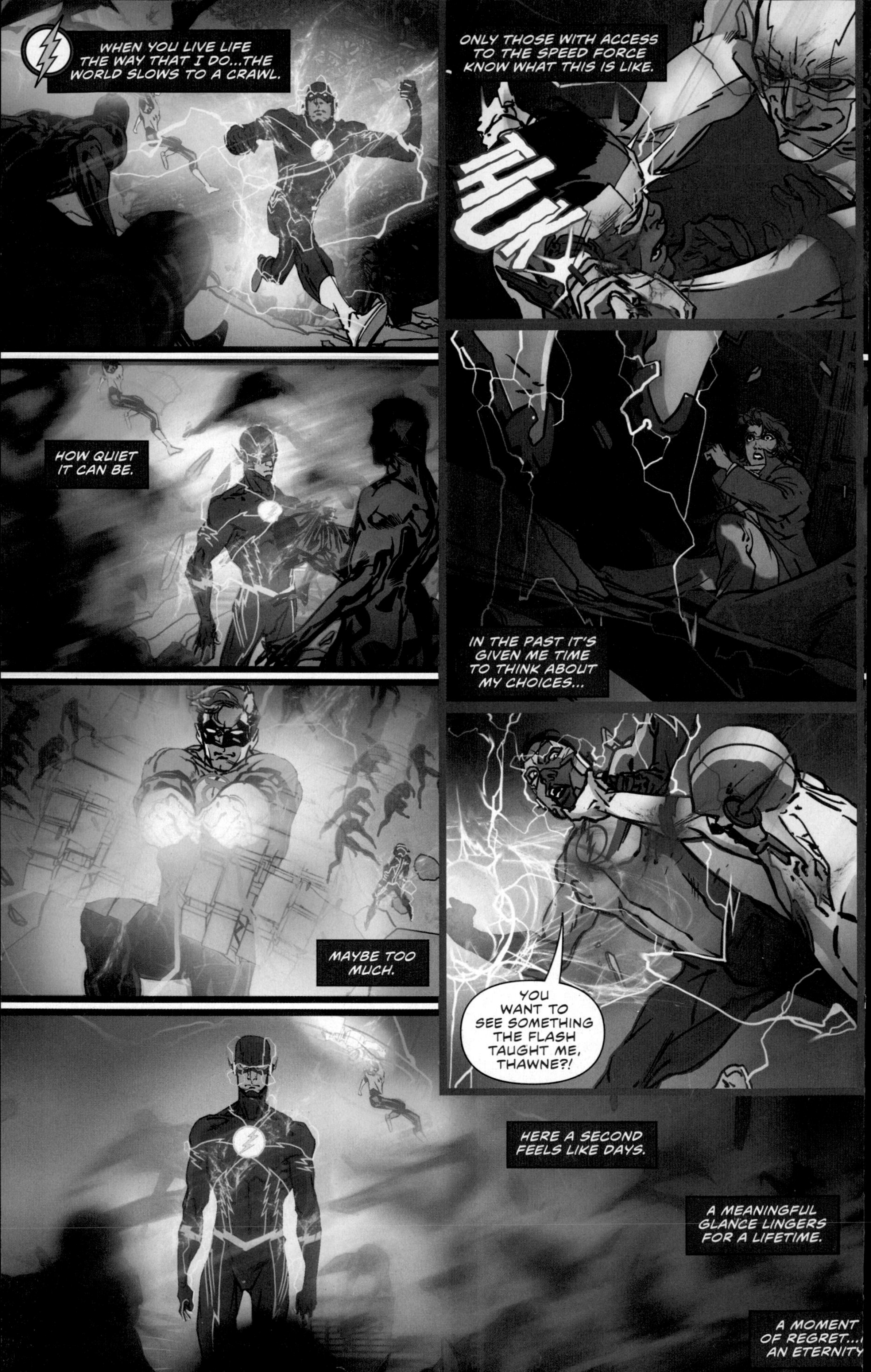

WHEN YOU LIVE LIFE THE WAY THAT I DO...THE WORLD SLOWS TO A CRAWL.
ONLY THOSE WITH ACCESS TO THE SPEED FORCE KNOW WHAT THIS IS LIKE.
THUK
HOW QUIET IT CAN BE.
IN THE PAST IT'S GIVEN ME TIME TO THINK ABOUT MY CHOICES...
MAYBE TOO MUCH.
YOU WANT TO SEE SOMETHING THE FLASH TAUGHT ME, THAWNE?!
HERE A SECOND FEELS LIKE DAYS.
A MEANINGFUL GLANCE LINGERS FOR A LIFETIME.
A MOMENT OF REGRET... AN ETERNITY

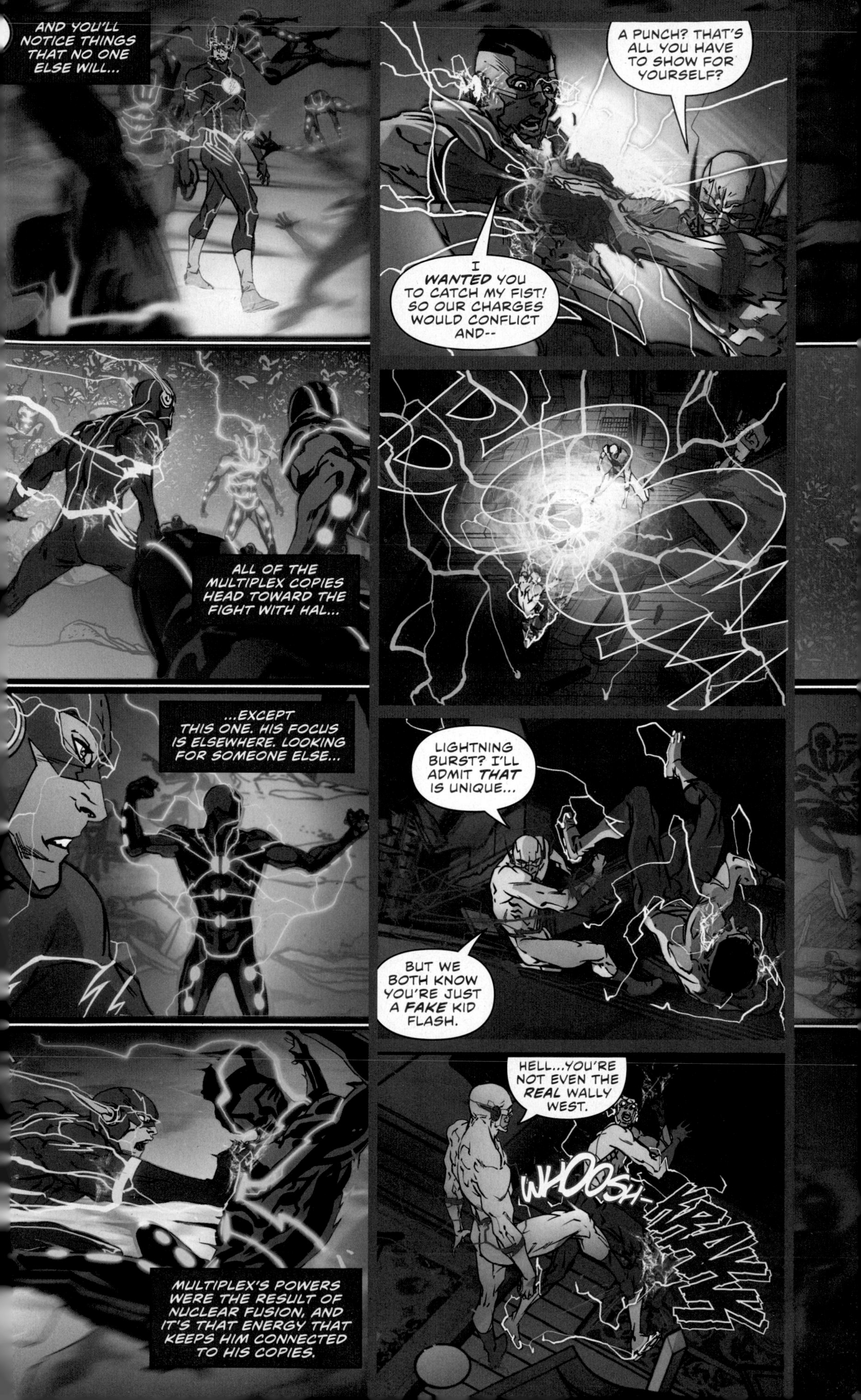
AND YOU'LL NOTICE THINGS THAT NO ONE ELSE WILL...
A PUNCH? THAT'S ALL YOU HAVE TO SHOW FOR YOURSELF?
I WANTED YOU TO CATCH MY FIST! SO OUR CHARGES WOULD CONFLICT AND--
ALL OF THE MULTIPLEX COPIES HEAD TOWARD THE FIGHT WITH HAL...
...EXCEPT THIS ONE. HIS FOCUS IS ELSEWHERE. LOOKING FOR SOMEONE ELSE...
LIGHTNING BURST? I'LL ADMIT THAT IS UNIQUE...
BUT WE BOTH KNOW YOU'RE JUST A FAKE KID FLASH.
MULTIPLEX'S POWERS WERE THE RESULT OF NUCLEAR FUSION, AND IT'S THAT ENERGY THAT KEEPS HIM CONNECTED TO HIS COPIES.
HELL...YOU'RE NOT EVEN THE REAL WALLY WEST.
WHOOSH-

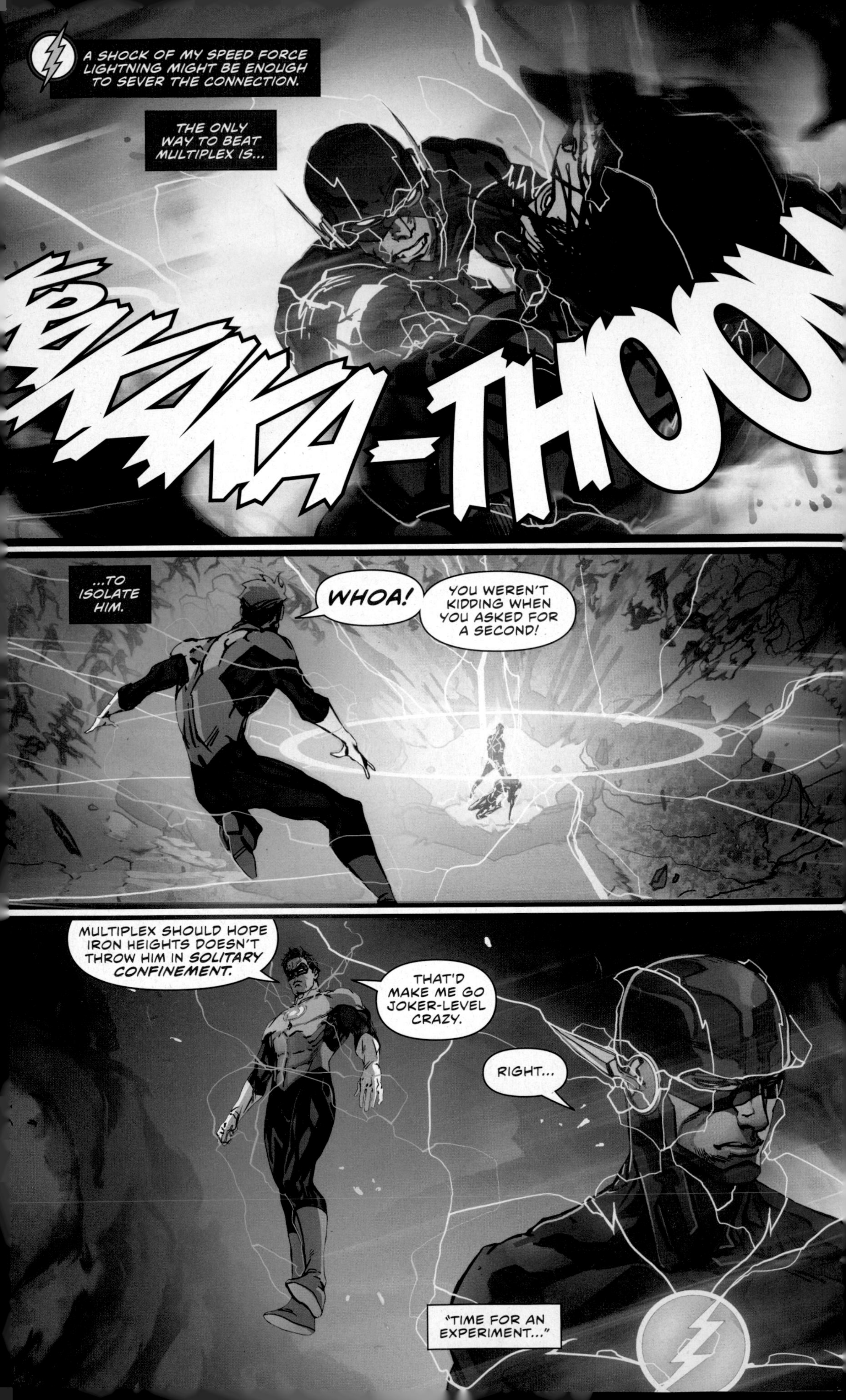
A SHOCK OF MY SPEED FORCE LIGHTNING MIGHT BE ENOUGH TO SEVER THE CONNECTION.
THE ONLY WAY TO BEAT MULTIPLEX IS...
KAKAKA-THOO
...TO ISOLATE HIM.
WHOA!
YOU WEREN'T KIDDING WHEN YOU ASKED FOR A SECOND!
MULTIPLEX SHOULD HOPE IRON HEIGHTS DOESN'T THROW HIM IN SOLITARY CONFINEMENT.
THAT'D MAKE ME GO JOKER-LEVEL CRAZY.
RIGHT...
"TIME FOR AN EXPERIMENT..."

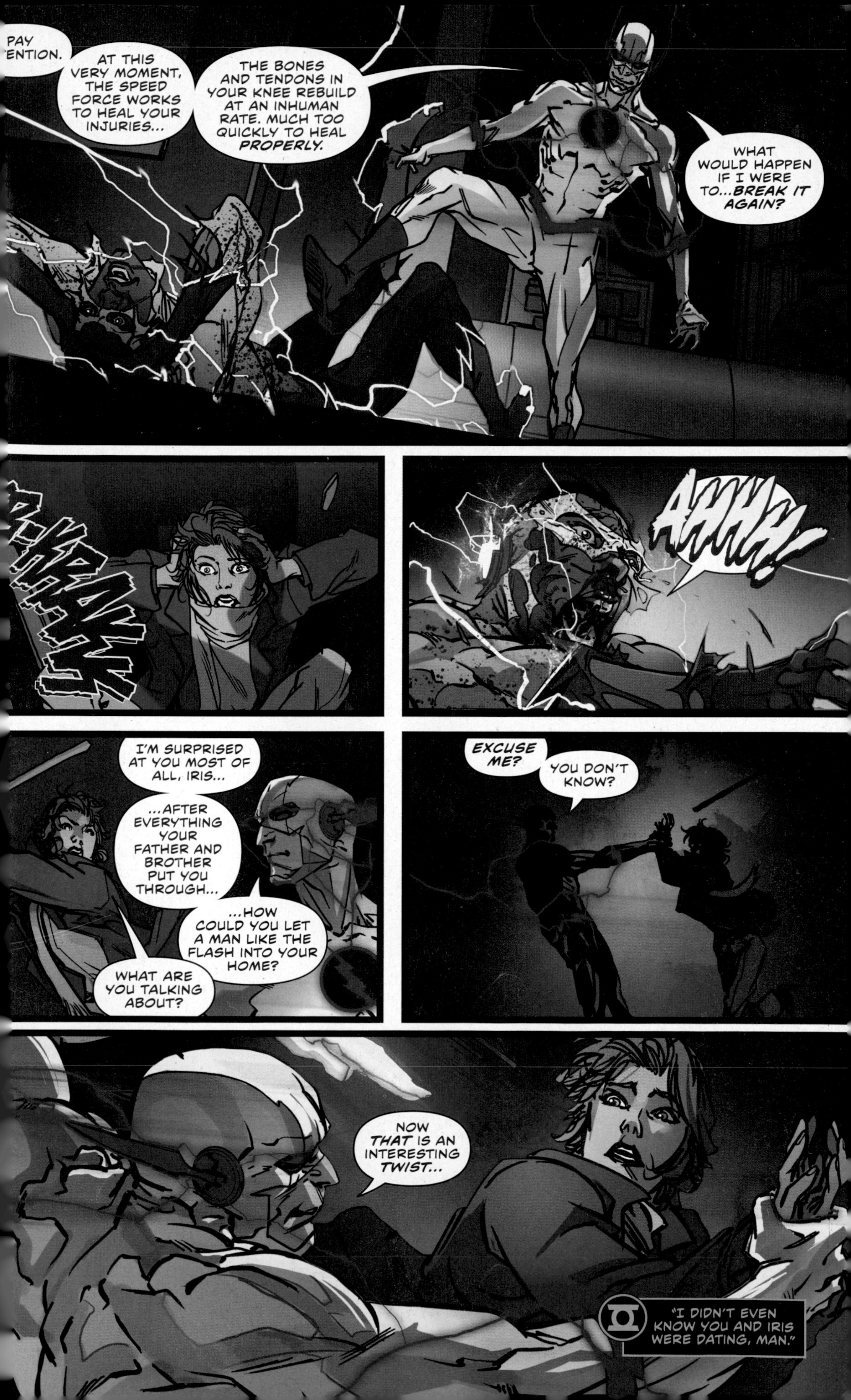

PAY
TENTION.
AT THIS VERY MOMENT, THE SPEED FORCE WORKS TO HEAL YOUR INJURIES...
THE BONES AND TENDONS IN YOUR KNEE REBUILD AT AN INHUMAN RATE. MUCH TOO QUICKLY TO HEAL PROPERLY.
WHAT WOULD HAPPEN IF I WERE TO...BREAK IT AGAIN?
AHHH!
I'M SURPRISED AT YOU MOST OF ALL, IRIS...
...AFTER EVERYTHING YOUR FATHER AND BROTHER PUT YOU THROUGH...
...HOW COULD YOU LET A MAN LIKE THE FLASH INTO YOUR HOME?
WHAT ARE YOU TALKING ABOUT?
EXCUSE ME?
YOU DON'T KNOW?
NOW THAT IS AN INTERESTING TWIST...
"I DIDN'T EVEN KNOW YOU AND IRIS WERE DATING, MAN."

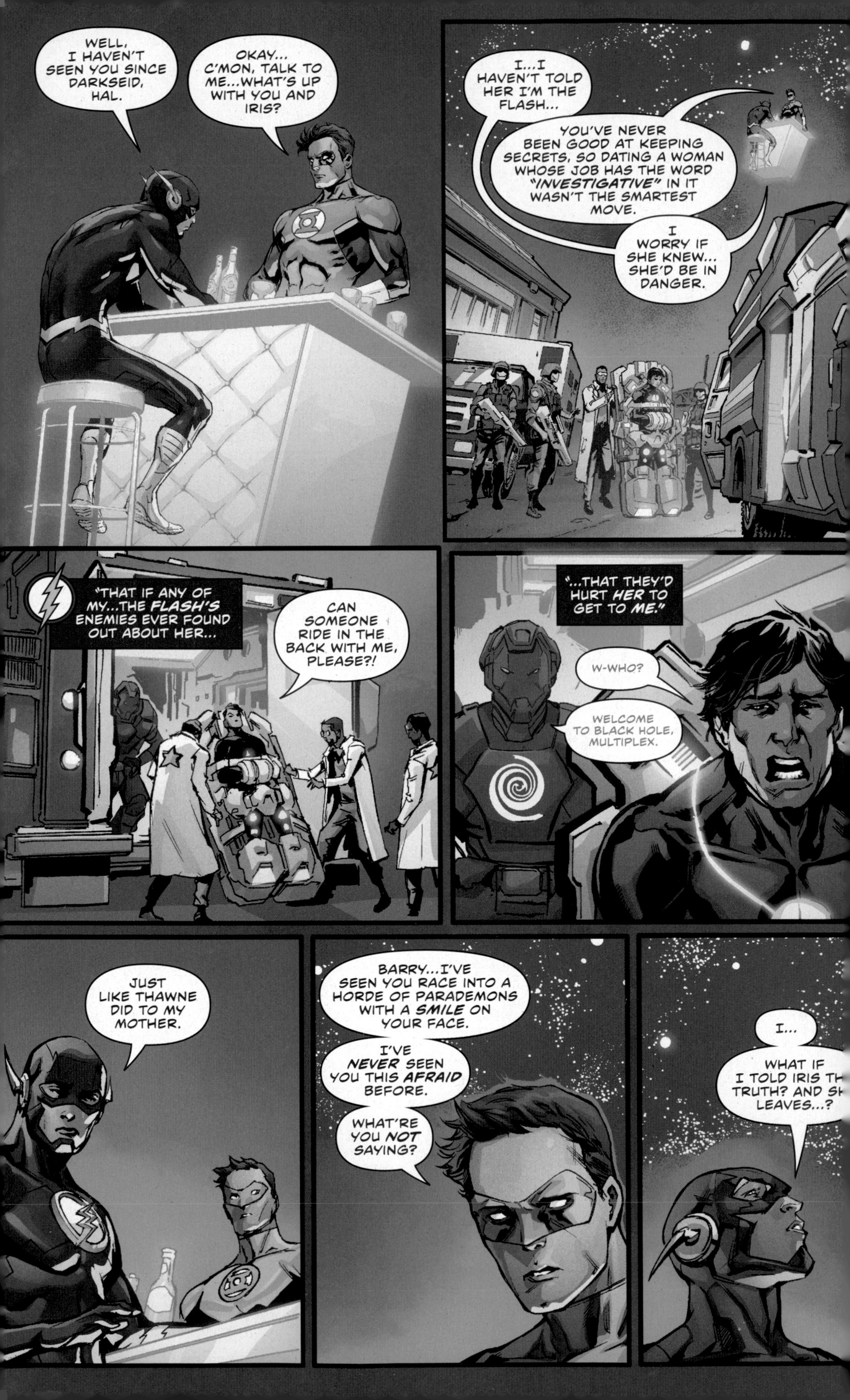

WELL, I HAVEN'T SEEN YOU SINCE DARKSEID, HAL.
OKAY... C'MON, TALK TO ME...WHAT'S UP WITH YOU AND IRIS?
I...I HAVEN'T TOLD HER I'M THE FLASH...
YOU'VE NEVER BEEN GOOD AT KEEPING SECRETS, SO DATING A WOMAN WHOSE JOB HAS THE WORD *"INVESTIGATIVE"* IN IT WASN'T THE SMARTEST MOVE.
I WORRY IF SHE KNEW... SHE'D BE IN DANGER.
"THAT IF ANY OF MY...THE *FLASH'S* ENEMIES EVER FOUND OUT ABOUT HER...
CAN SOMEONE RIDE IN THE BACK WITH ME, PLEASE?!
"...THAT THEY'D HURT *HER* TO GET TO *ME.*"
W-WHO?
WELCOME TO BLACK HOLE, MULTIPLEX.
JUST LIKE THAWNE DID TO MY MOTHER.
BARRY...I'VE SEEN YOU RACE INTO A HORDE OF PARADEMONS WITH A *SMILE* ON YOUR FACE.
I'VE *NEVER* SEEN YOU THIS *AFRAID* BEFORE.
WHAT'RE YOU *NOT* SAYING?
I...

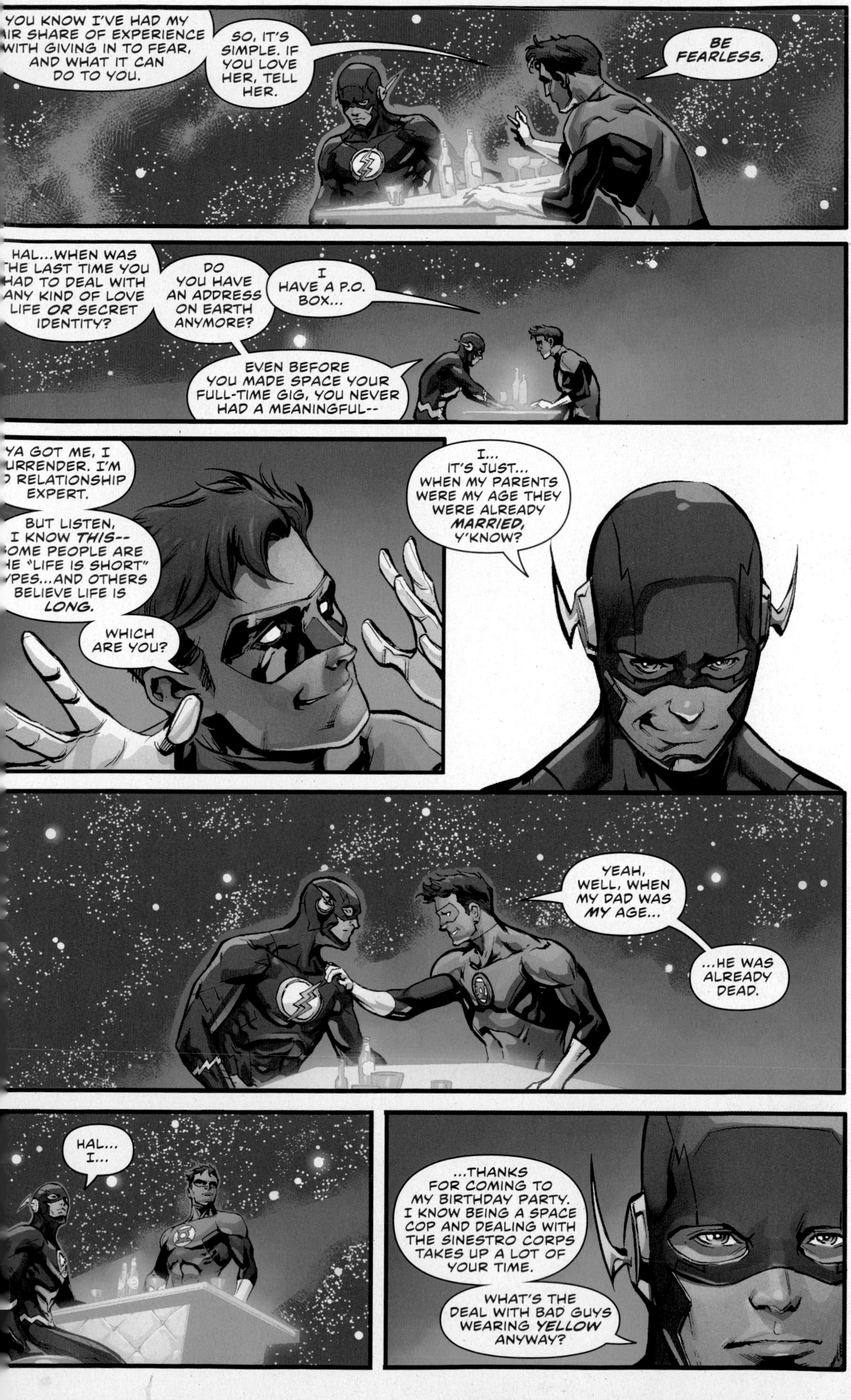
YOU KNOW I'VE HAD MY IR SHARE OF EXPERIENCE WITH GIVING IN TO FEAR, AND WHAT IT CAN DO TO YOU.
SO, IT'S SIMPLE. IF YOU LOVE HER, TELL HER.
BE FEARLESS.
HAL...WHEN WAS HE LAST TIME YOU HAD TO DEAL WITH ANY KIND OF LOVE LIFE *OR* SECRET IDENTITY?
DO YOU HAVE AN ADDRESS ON EARTH ANYMORE?
I HAVE A P.O. BOX...
EVEN BEFORE YOU MADE SPACE YOUR FULL-TIME GIG, YOU NEVER HAD A MEANINGFUL--
YA GOT ME, I URRENDER. I'M O RELATIONSHIP EXPERT.
BUT LISTEN, I KNOW *THIS*-- OME PEOPLE ARE HE "LIFE IS SHORT" YPES...AND OTHERS BELIEVE LIFE IS *LONG.*
WHICH ARE YOU?
I... IT'S JUST... WHEN MY PARENTS WERE MY AGE THEY WERE ALREADY *MARRIED,* Y'KNOW?
YEAH, WELL, WHEN MY DAD WAS *MY* AGE...
...HE WAS ALREADY DEAD.
HAL... I...
...THANKS FOR COMING TO MY BIRTHDAY PARTY. I KNOW BEING A SPACE COP AND DEALING WITH THE SINESTRO CORPS TAKES UP A LOT OF YOUR TIME.
WHAT'S THE DEAL WITH BAD GUYS WEARING *YELLOW* ANYWAY?

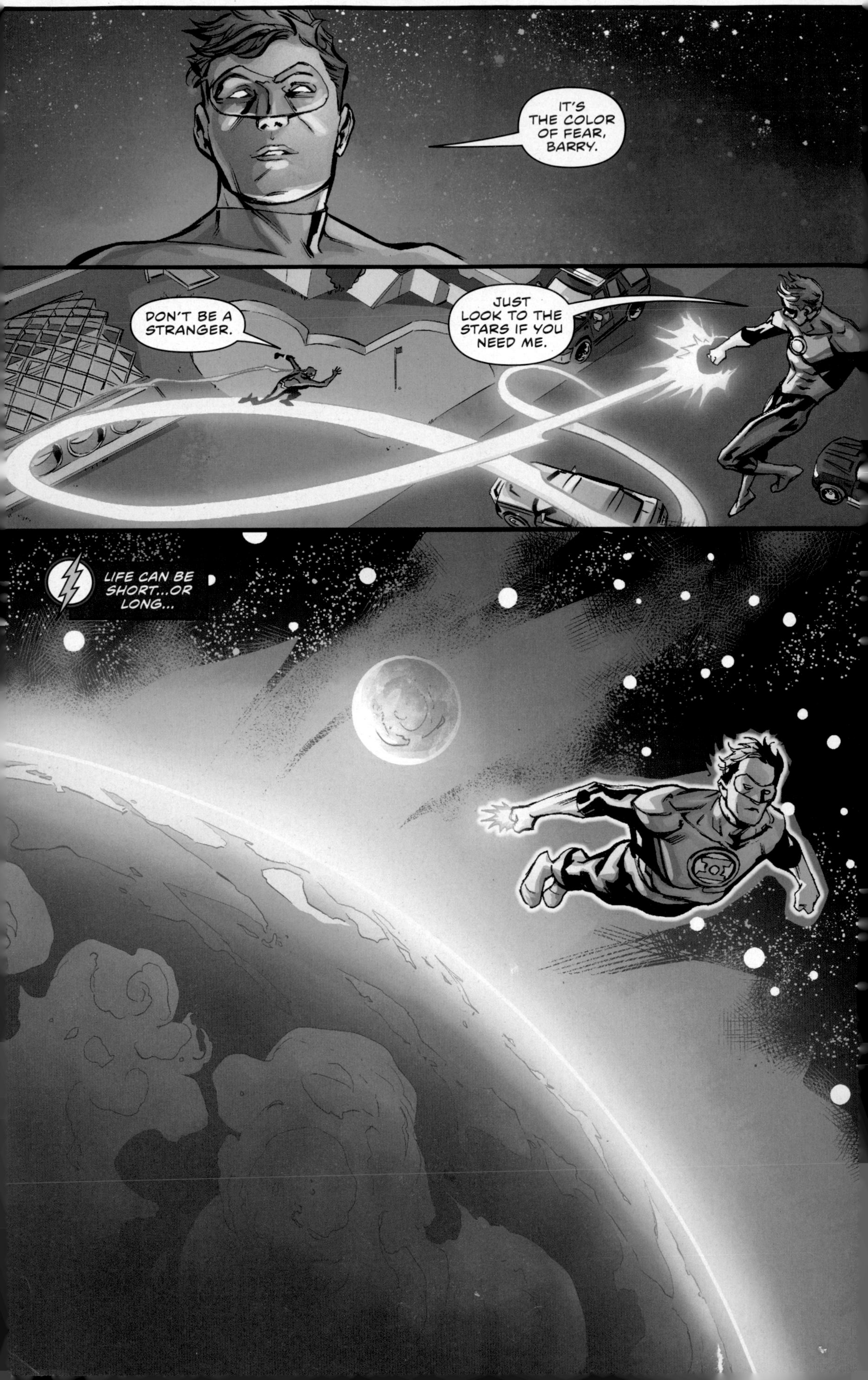
IT'S THE COLOR OF FEAR, BARRY.
DON'T BE A STRANGER.
JUST LOOK TO THE STARS IF YOU NEED ME.
LIFE CAN BE SHORT...OR LONG...

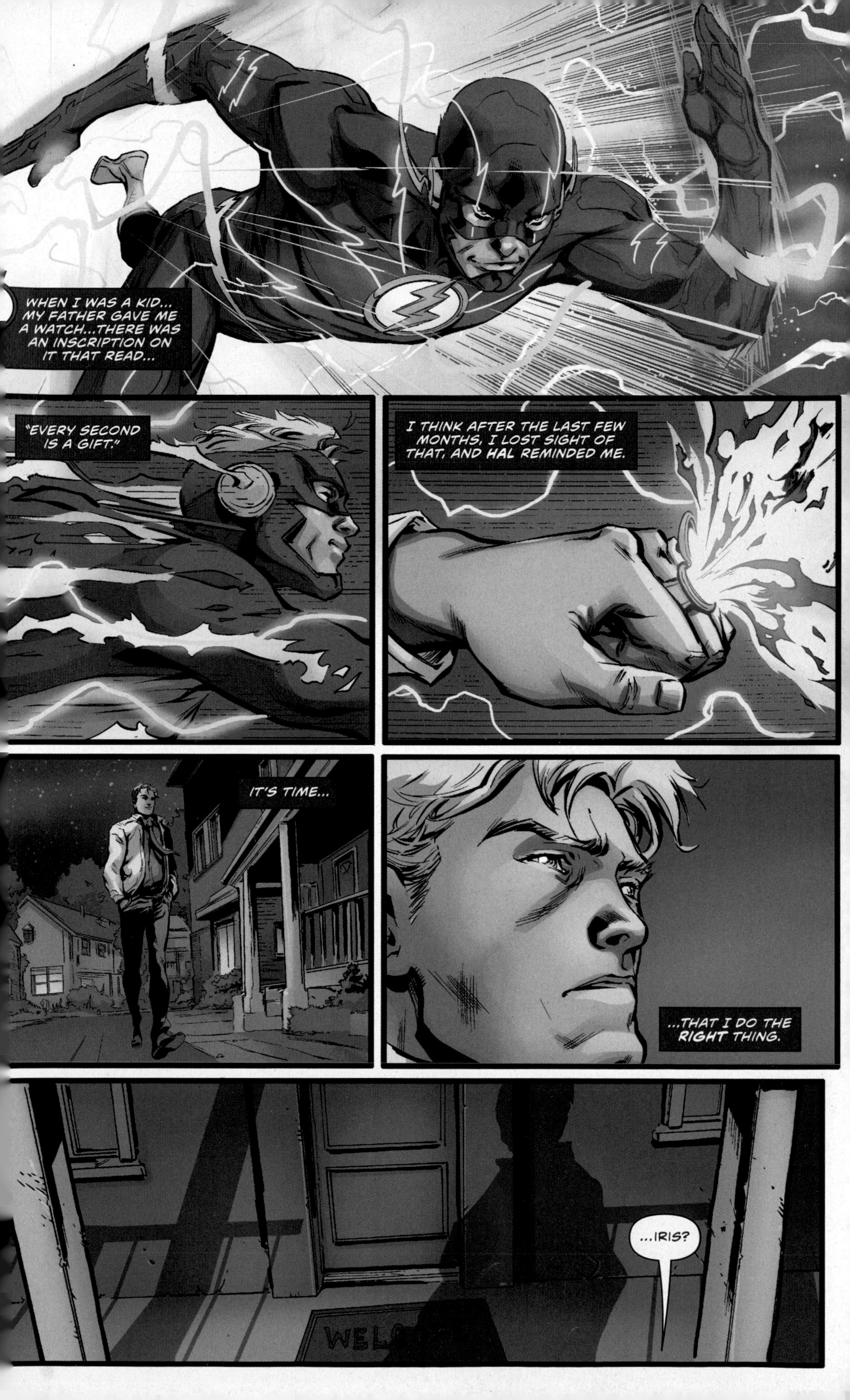
WHEN I WAS A KID... MY FATHER GAVE ME A WATCH...THERE WAS AN INSCRIPTION ON IT THAT READ...
"EVERY SECOND IS A GIFT."
I THINK AFTER THE LAST FEW MONTHS, I LOST SIGHT OF THAT, AND HAL REMINDED ME.
IT'S TIME...
...THAT I DO THE RIGHT THING.
...IRIS?

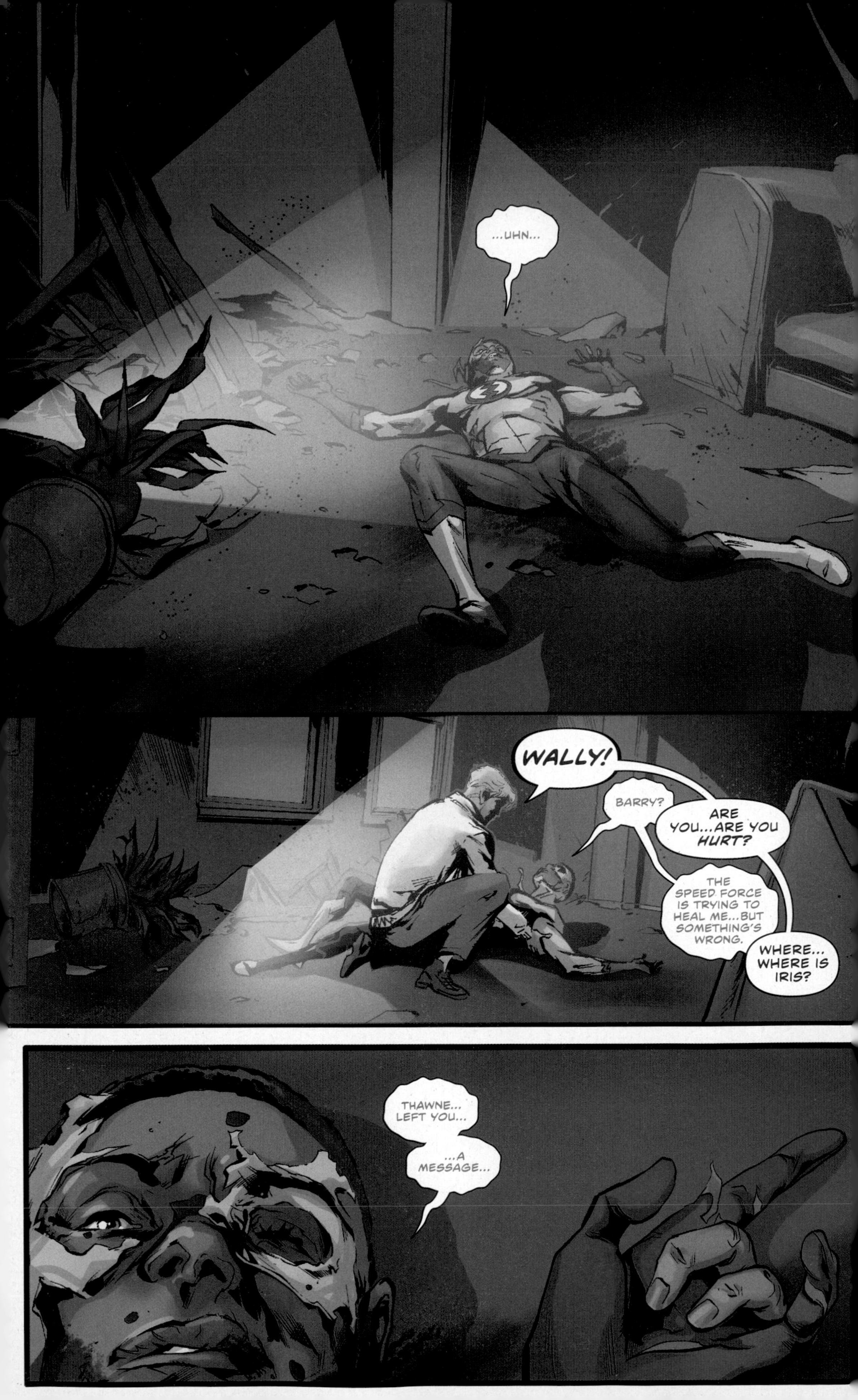
...UHN...
WALLY!
BARRY?
ARE YOU...ARE YOU HURT?
THE SPEED FORCE IS TRYING TO HEAL ME...BUT SOMETHING'S WRONG.
WHERE... WHERE IS IRIS?
THAWNE... LEFT YOU...
...A MESSAGE...

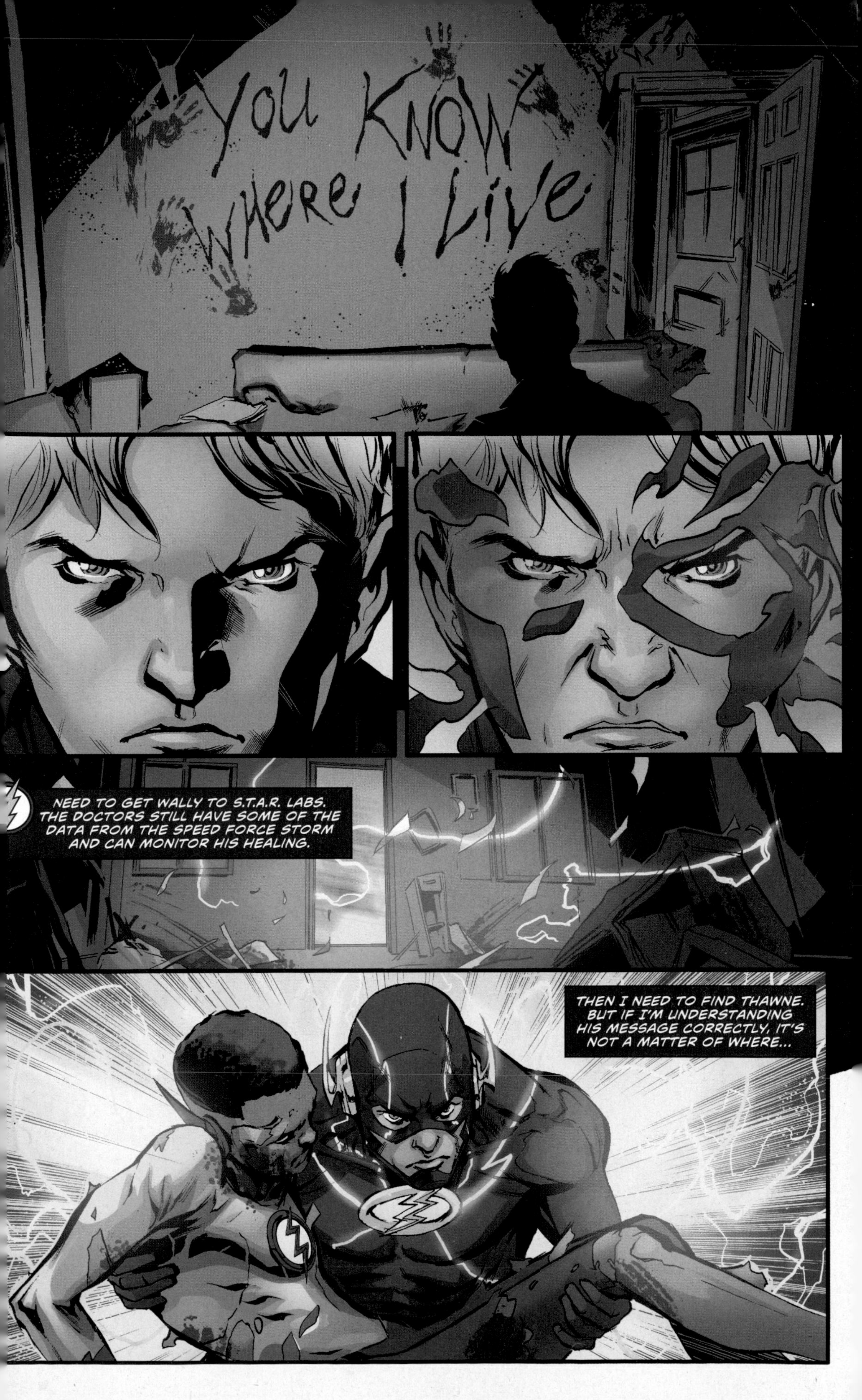
YOU KNOW WHERE I LIVE
NEED TO GET WALLY TO S.T.A.R. LABS. THE DOCTORS STILL HAVE SOME OF THE DATA FROM THE SPEED FORCE STORM AND CAN MONITOR HIS HEALING.
THEN I NEED TO FIND THAWNE. BUT IF I'M UNDERSTANDING HIS MESSAGE CORRECTLY, IT'S NOT A MATTER OF WHERE...

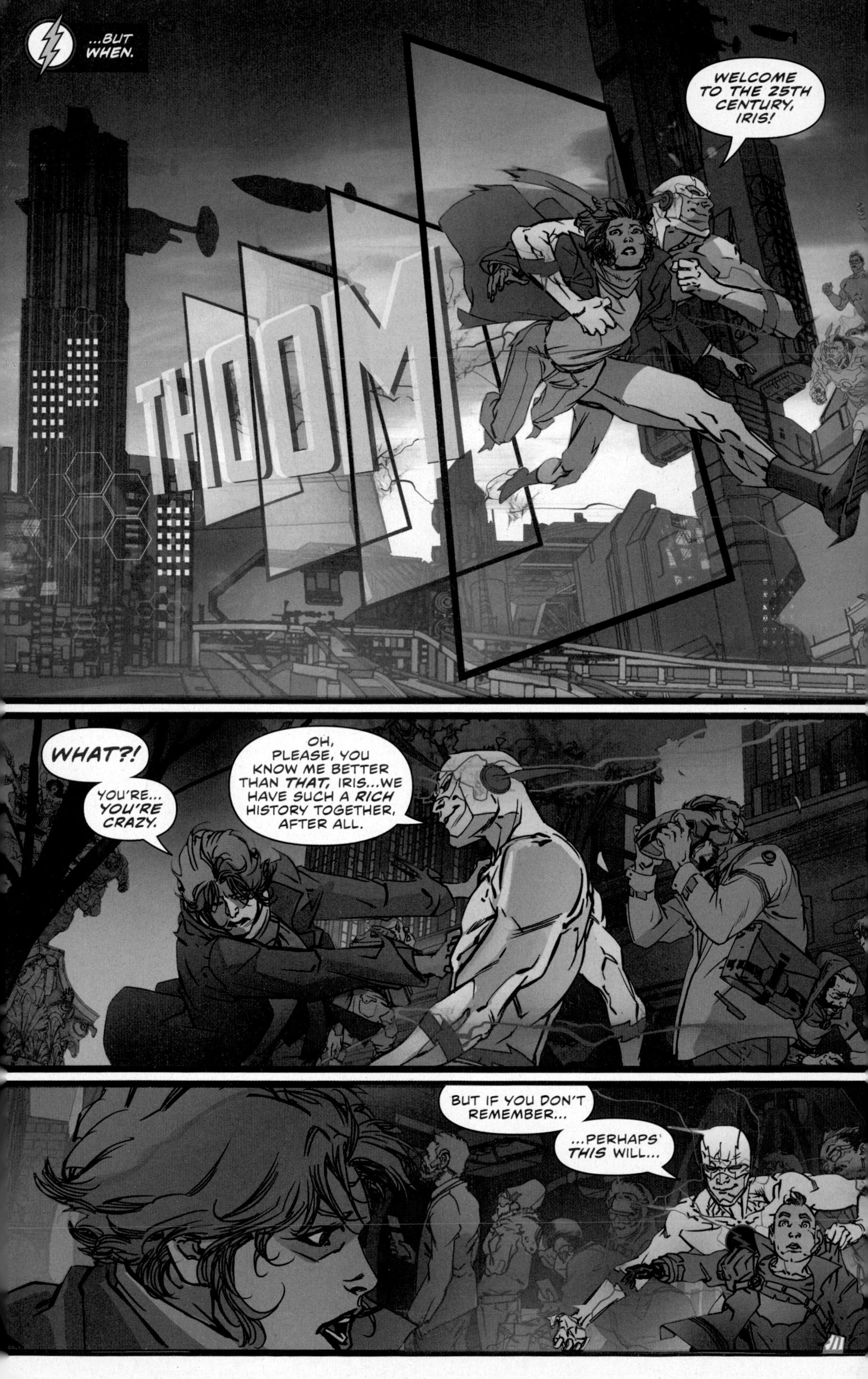

...BUT WHEN.
WELCOME TO THE 25TH CENTURY, IRIS!
THOOM!
WHAT?!
YOU'RE... YOU'RE CRAZY.
OH, PLEASE, YOU KNOW ME BETTER THAN THAT, IRIS...WE HAVE SUCH A RICH HISTORY TOGETHER, AFTER ALL.
BUT IF YOU DON'T REMEMBER...
...PERHAPS THIS WILL...

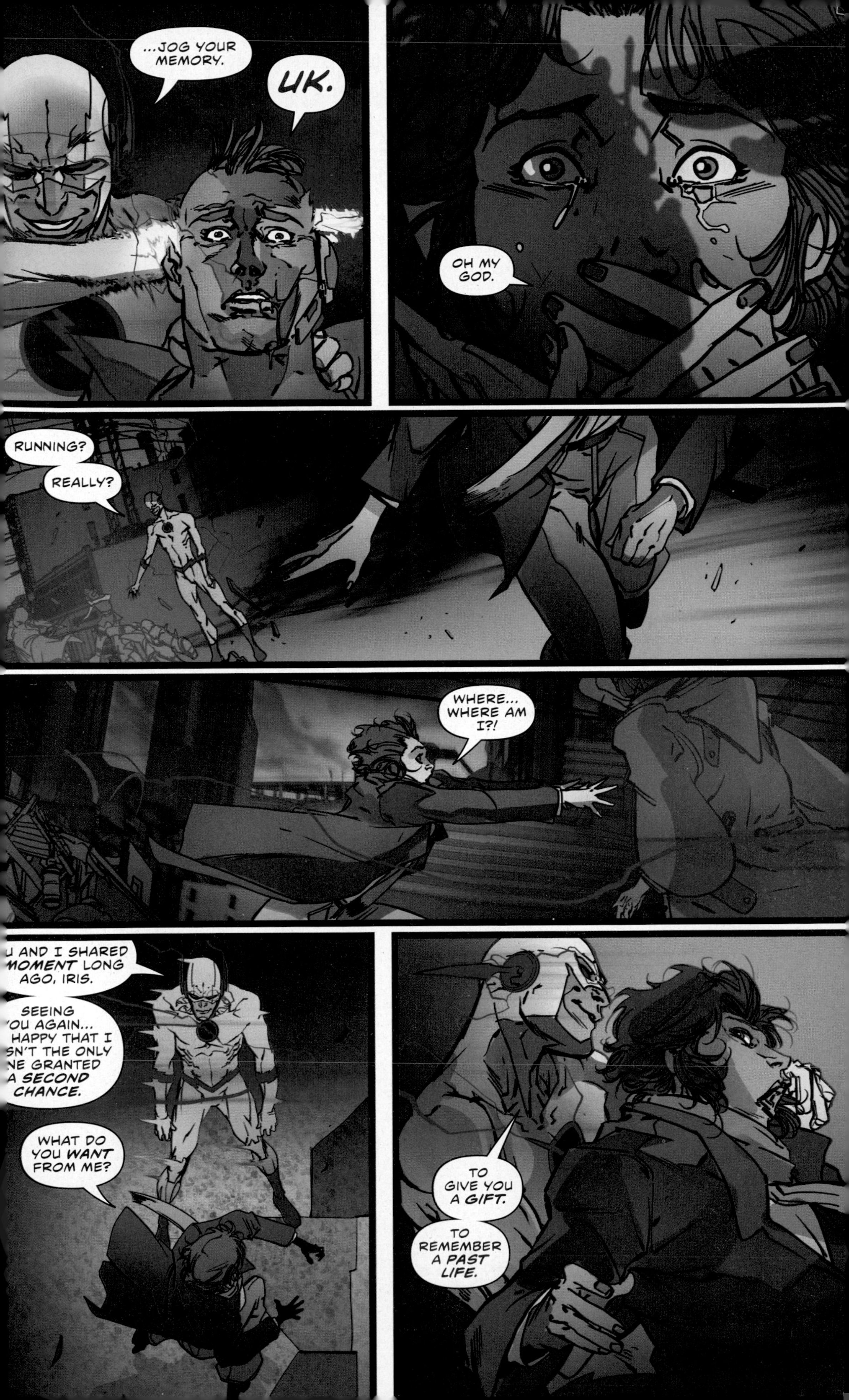
...JOG YOUR MEMORY.
UK.
OH MY GOD.
RUNNING?
REALLY?
WHERE... WHERE AM I?!
U AND I SHARED MOMENT LONG AGO, IRIS.
SEEING OU AGAIN... HAPPY THAT I SN'T THE ONLY NE GRANTED A SECOND CHANCE.
WHAT DO YOU WANT FROM ME?
TO GIVE YOU A GIFT.
TO REMEMBER A PAST LIFE.

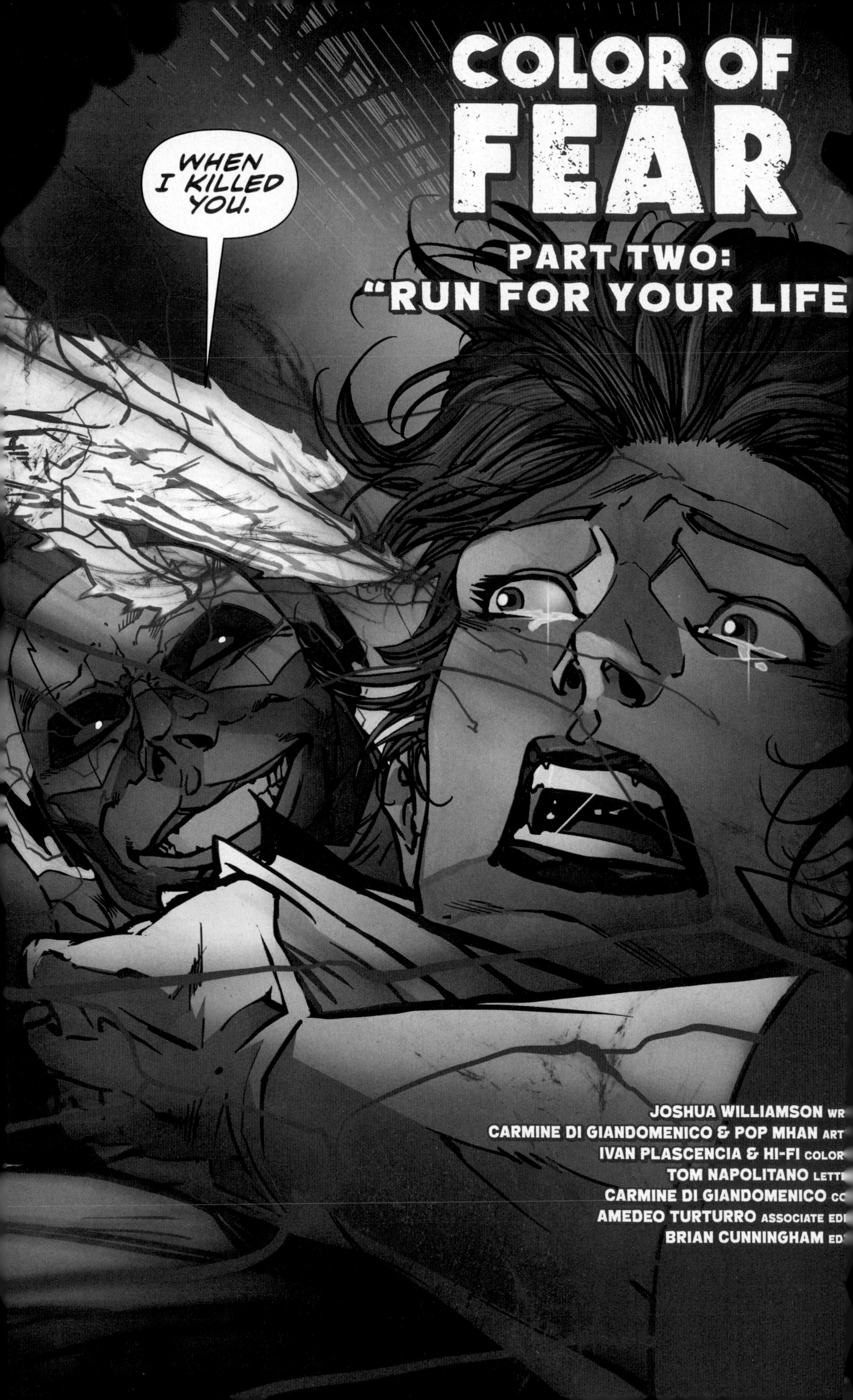
COLOR OF FEAR
WHEN I KILLED YOU.
PART TWO:
"RUN FOR YOUR LIFE
JOSHUA WILLIAMSON WR
CARMINE DI GIANDOMENICO & POP MHAN ART
IVAN PLASCENCIA & HI-FI COLOR
TOM NAPOLITANO LETT
CARMINE DI GIANDOMENICO CO
AMEDEO TURTURRO ASSOCIATE EDI
BRIAN CUNNINGHAM ED

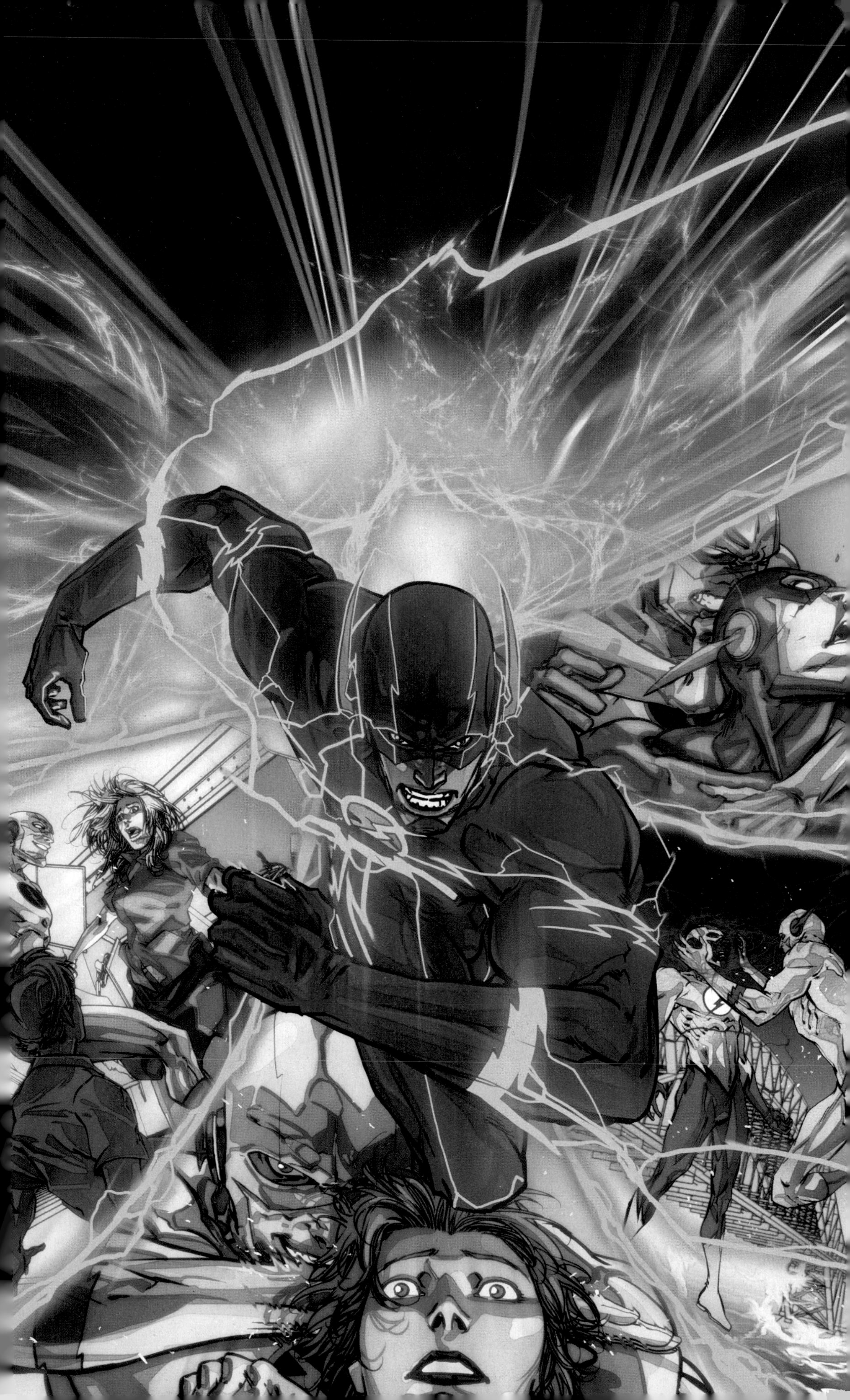

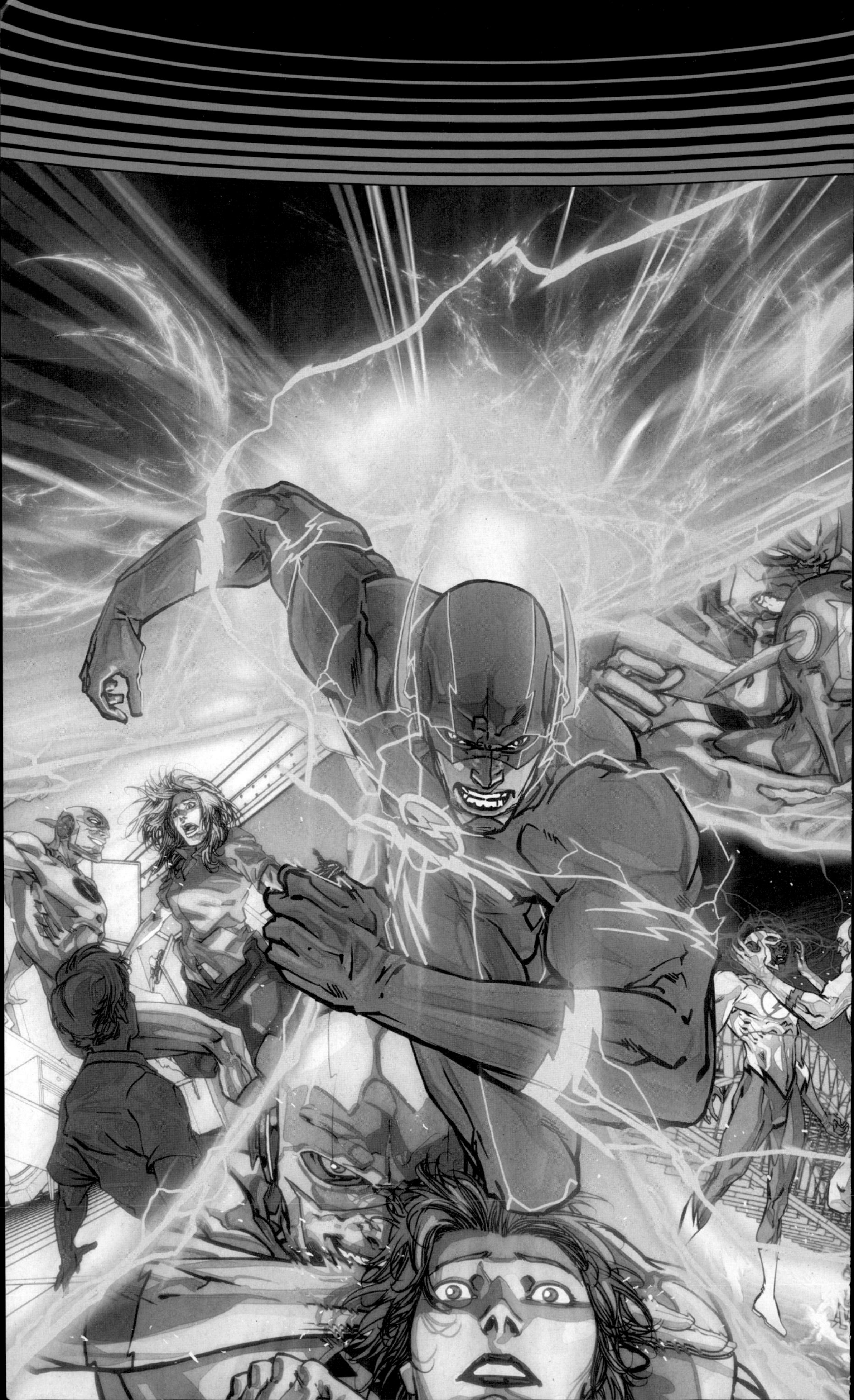

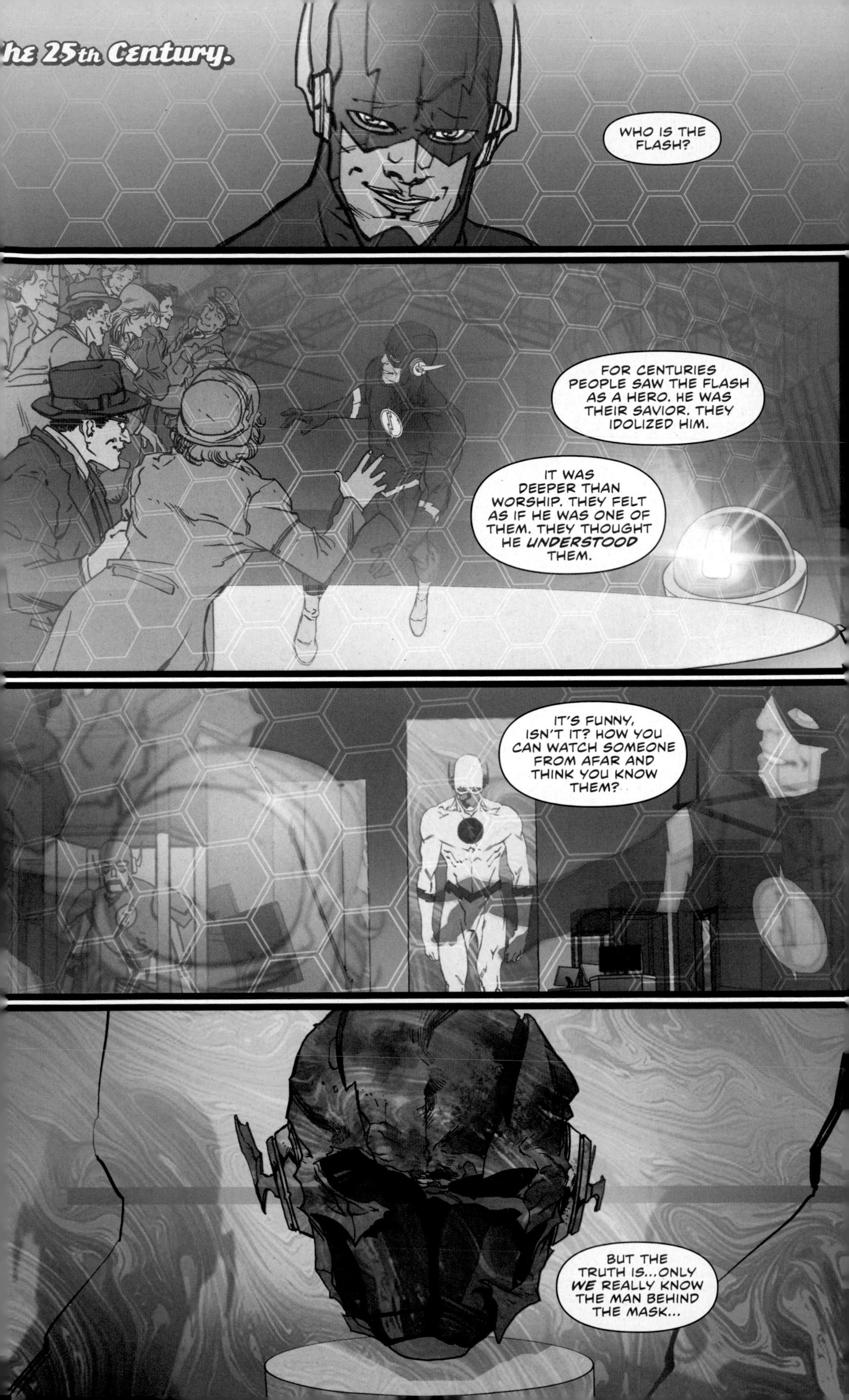
he 25th Century.
WHO IS THE FLASH?
FOR CENTURIES PEOPLE SAW THE FLASH AS A HERO. HE WAS THEIR SAVIOR. THEY IDOLIZED HIM.
IT WAS DEEPER THAN WORSHIP. THEY FELT AS IF HE WAS ONE OF THEM. THEY THOUGHT HE *UNDERSTOOD* THEM.
IT'S FUNNY, ISN'T IT? HOW YOU CAN WATCH SOMEONE FROM AFAR AND THINK YOU KNOW THEM?
BUT THE TRUTH IS...ONLY *WE* REALLY KNOW THE MAN BEHIND THE MASK...

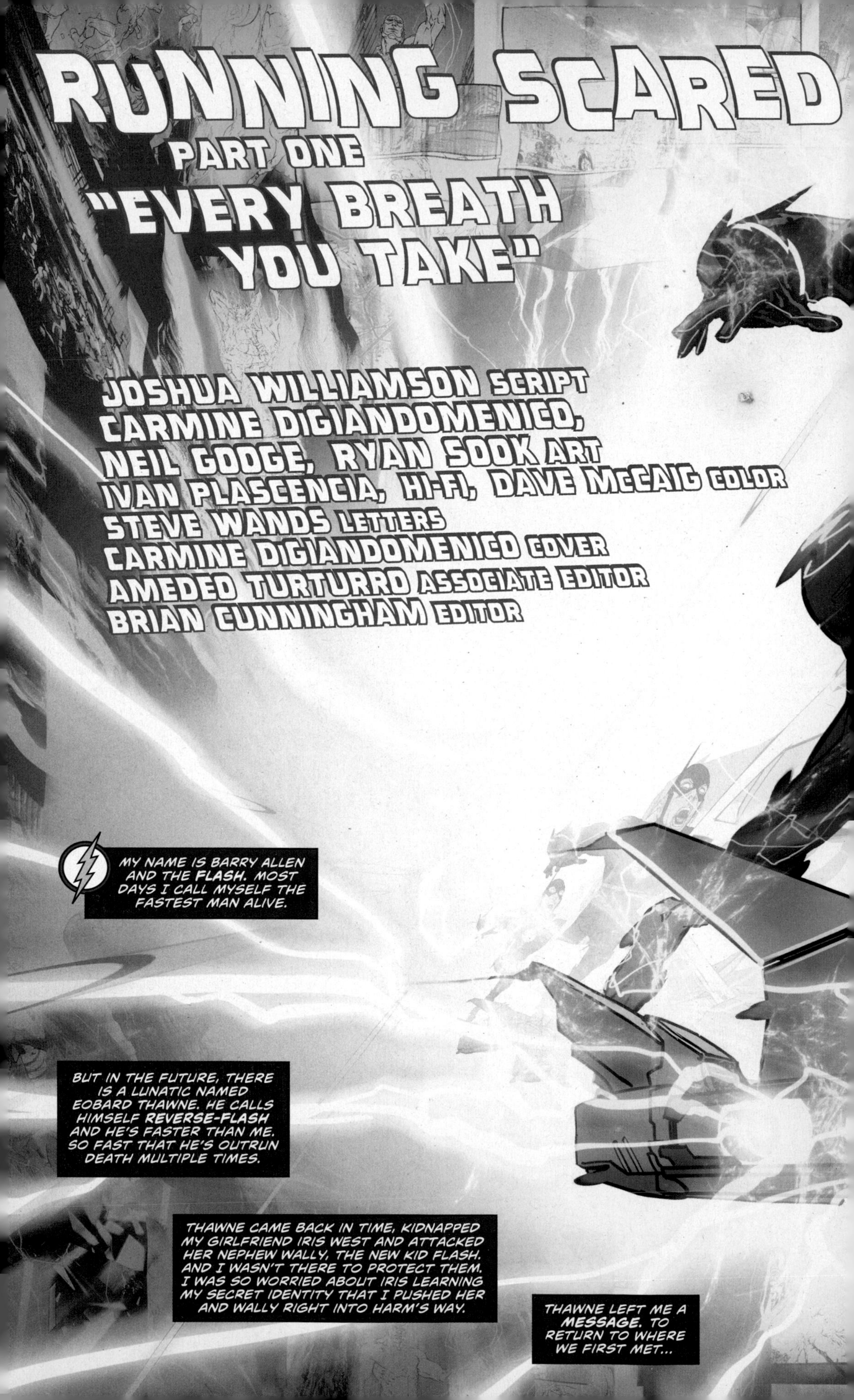
RUNNING SCARED
PART ONE
"EVERY BREATH YOU TAKE"
JOSHUA WILLIAMSON SCRIPT
CARMINE DIGIANDOMENICO, NEIL GOOGE, RYAN SOOK ART
IVAN PLASCENCIA, HI-FI, DAVE McCAIG COLOR
STEVE WANDS LETTERS
CARMINE DIGIANDOMENICO COVER
AMEDED TURTURRO ASSOCIATE EDITOR
BRIAN CUNNINGHAM EDITOR
MY NAME IS BARRY ALLEN AND THE FLASH. MOST DAYS I CALL MYSELF THE FASTEST MAN ALIVE.
BUT IN THE FUTURE, THERE IS A LUNATIC NAMED EOBARD THAWNE. HE CALLS HIMSELF REVERSE-FLASH AND HE'S FASTER THAN ME. SO FAST THAT HE'S OUTRUN DEATH MULTIPLE TIMES.
THAWNE CAME BACK IN TIME, KIDNAPPED MY GIRLFRIEND IRIS WEST AND ATTACKED HER NEPHEW WALLY, THE NEW KID FLASH. AND I WASN'T THERE TO PROTECT THEM. I WAS SO WORRIED ABOUT IRIS LEARNING MY SECRET IDENTITY THAT I PUSHED HER AND WALLY RIGHT INTO HARM'S WAY.
THAWNE LEFT ME A MESSAGE. TO RETURN TO WHERE WE FIRST MET...

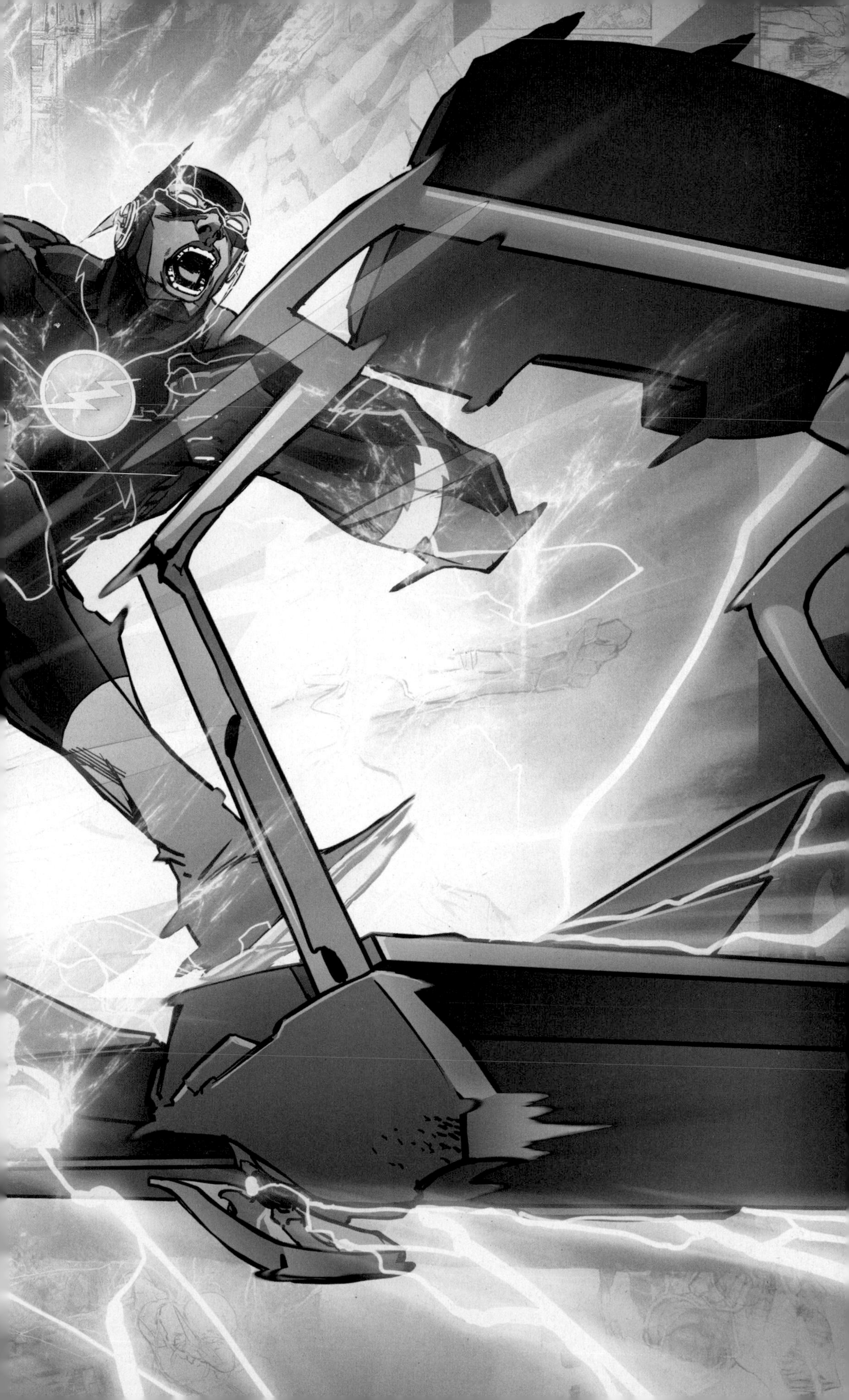

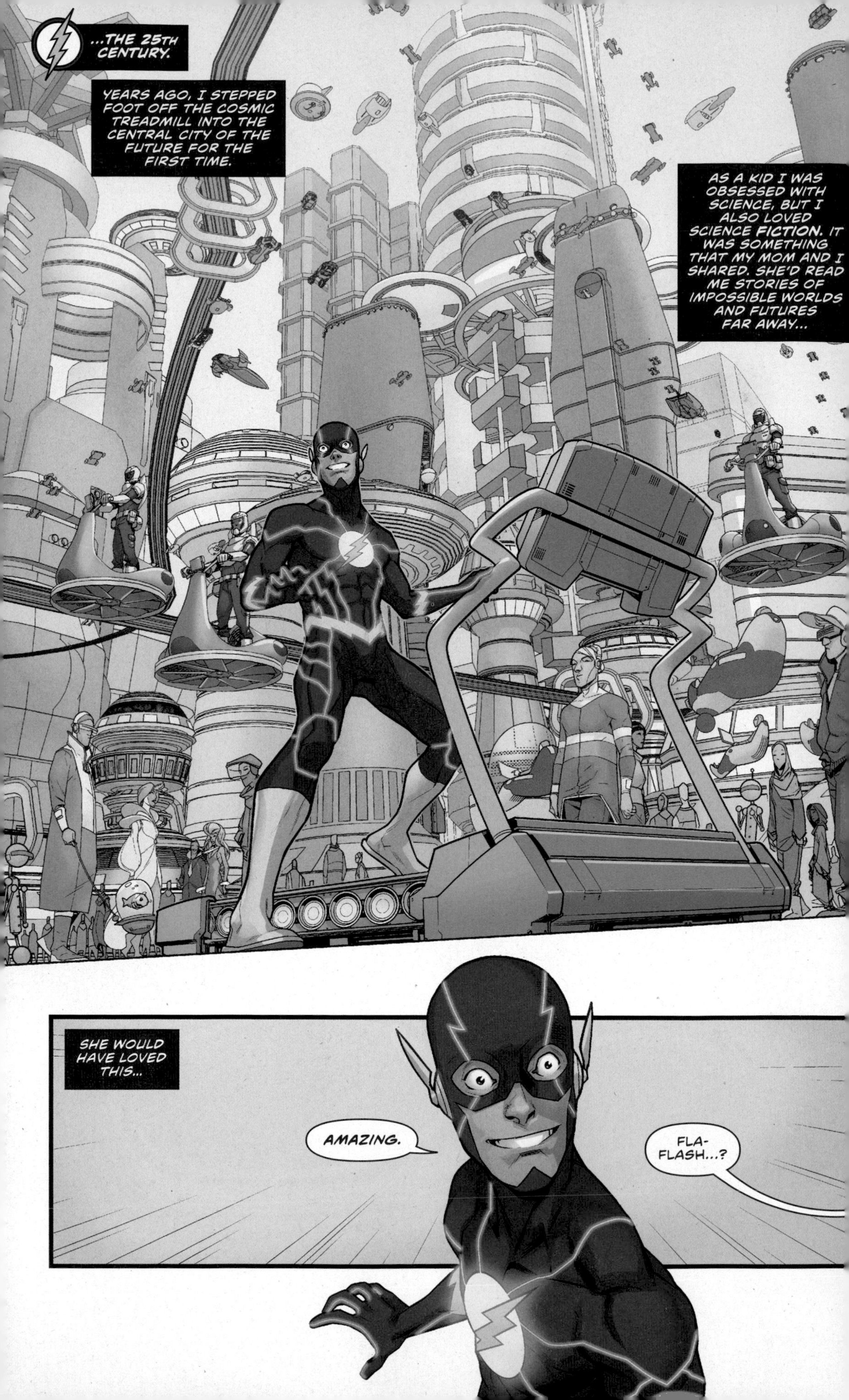
...THE 25TH CENTURY.
YEARS AGO, I STEPPED FOOT OFF THE COSMIC TREADMILL INTO THE CENTRAL CITY OF THE FUTURE FOR THE FIRST TIME.
AS A KID I WAS OBSESSED WITH SCIENCE, BUT I ALSO LOVED SCIENCE FICTION. IT WAS SOMETHING THAT MY MOM AND I SHARED. SHE'D READ ME STORIES OF IMPOSSIBLE WORLDS AND FUTURES FAR AWAY...
SHE WOULD HAVE LOVED THIS...
AMAZING.
FLA- FLASH...?

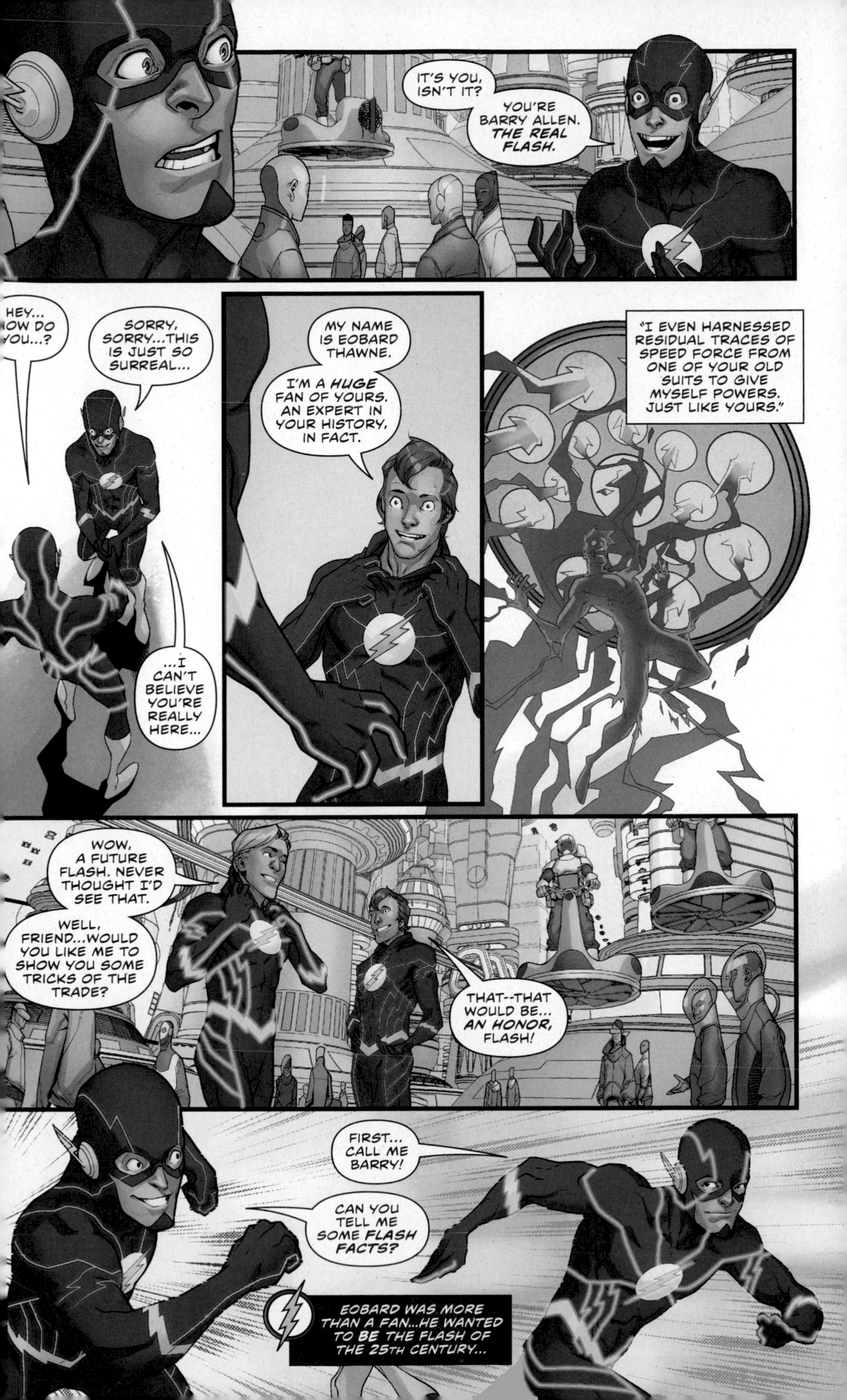

IT'S YOU, ISN'T IT?
YOU'RE BARRY ALLEN. THE REAL FLASH.
HEY... OW DO YOU...?
SORRY, SORRY...THIS IS JUST SO SURREAL...
...I CAN'T BELIEVE YOU'RE REALLY HERE...
MY NAME IS EOBARD THAWNE.
I'M A HUGE FAN OF YOURS. AN EXPERT IN YOUR HISTORY, IN FACT.
"I EVEN HARNESSED RESIDUAL TRACES OF SPEED FORCE FROM ONE OF YOUR OLD SUITS TO GIVE MYSELF POWERS. JUST LIKE YOURS."
WOW, A FUTURE FLASH. NEVER THOUGHT I'D SEE THAT.
WELL, FRIEND...WOULD YOU LIKE ME TO SHOW YOU SOME TRICKS OF THE TRADE?
THAT--THAT WOULD BE... AN HONOR, FLASH!
FIRST... CALL ME BARRY!
CAN YOU TELL ME SOME FLASH FACTS?
EOBARD WAS MORE THAN A FAN...HE WANTED TO BE THE FLASH OF THE 25TH CENTURY...

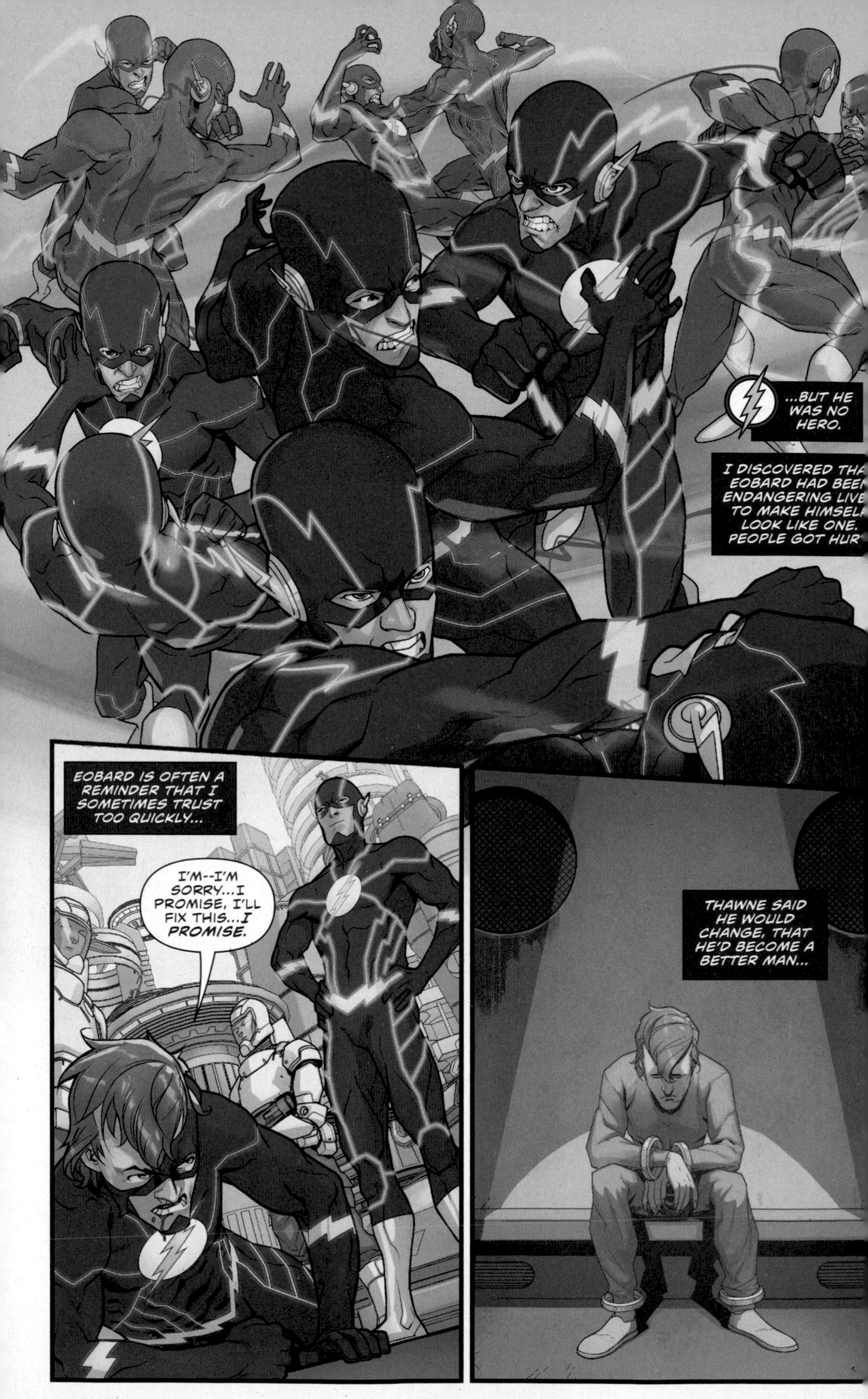
...BUT HE WAS NO HERO.
I DISCOVERED THA EOBARD HAD BEEN ENDANGERING LIVE TO MAKE HIMSEL LOOK LIKE ONE. PEOPLE GOT HUR
EOBARD IS OFTEN A REMINDER THAT I SOMETIMES TRUST TOO QUICKLY...
I'M--I'M SORRY...I PROMISE, I'LL FIX THIS...I PROMISE.
THANWE SAID HE WOULD CHANGE, THAT HE'D BECOME A BETTER MAN...

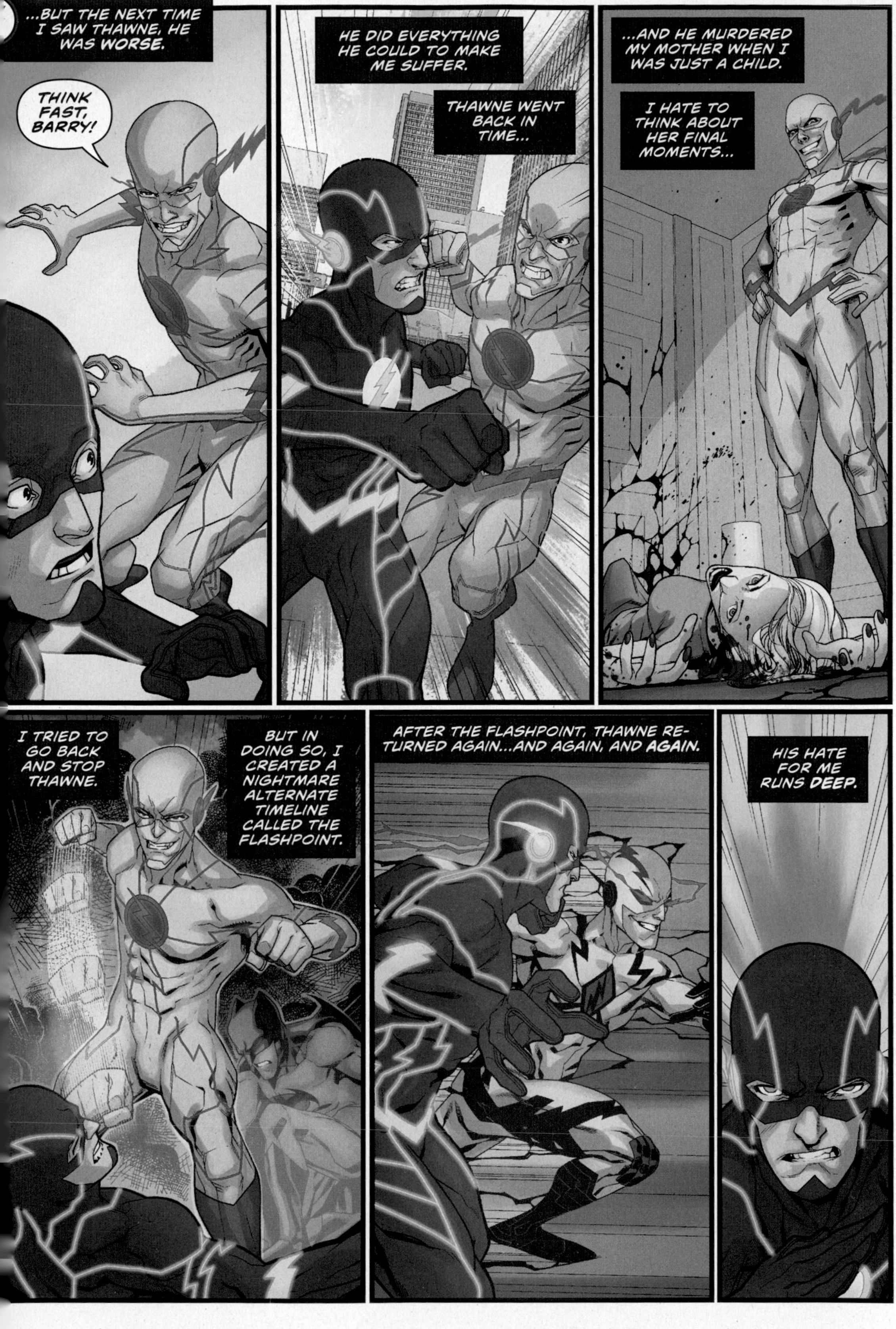
...BUT THE NEXT TIME I SAW THAWNE, HE WAS WORSE.
THINK FAST, BARRY!
HE DID EVERYTHING HE COULD TO MAKE ME SUFFER.
THAWNE WENT BACK IN TIME...
...AND HE MURDERED MY MOTHER WHEN I WAS JUST A CHILD.
I HATE TO THINK ABOUT HER FINAL MOMENTS...
I TRIED TO GO BACK AND STOP THAWNE.
BUT IN DOING SO, I CREATED A NIGHTMARE ALTERNATE TIMELINE CALLED THE FLASHPOINT.
AFTER THE FLASHPOINT, THAWNE RE-TURNED AGAIN...AND AGAIN, AND AGAIN.
HIS HATE FOR ME RUNS DEEP.

BUT I DON'T KNOW WHY.

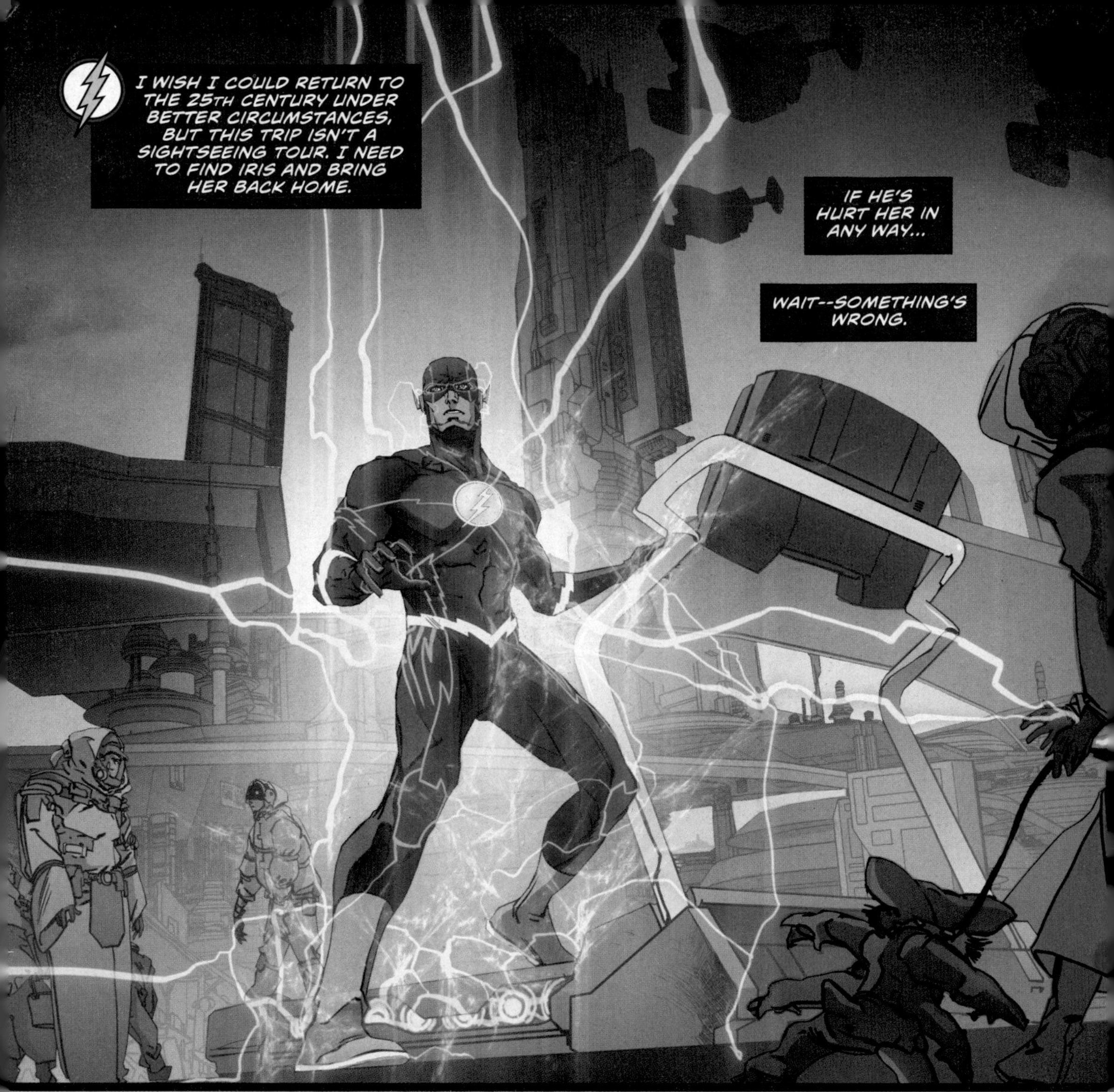
I WISH I COULD RETURN TO THE 25TH CENTURY UNDER BETTER CIRCUMSTANCES, BUT THIS TRIP ISN'T A SIGHTSEEING TOUR. I NEED TO FIND IRIS AND BRING HER BACK HOME.
IF HE'S HURT HER IN ANY WAY...
WAIT--SOMETHING'S WRONG.

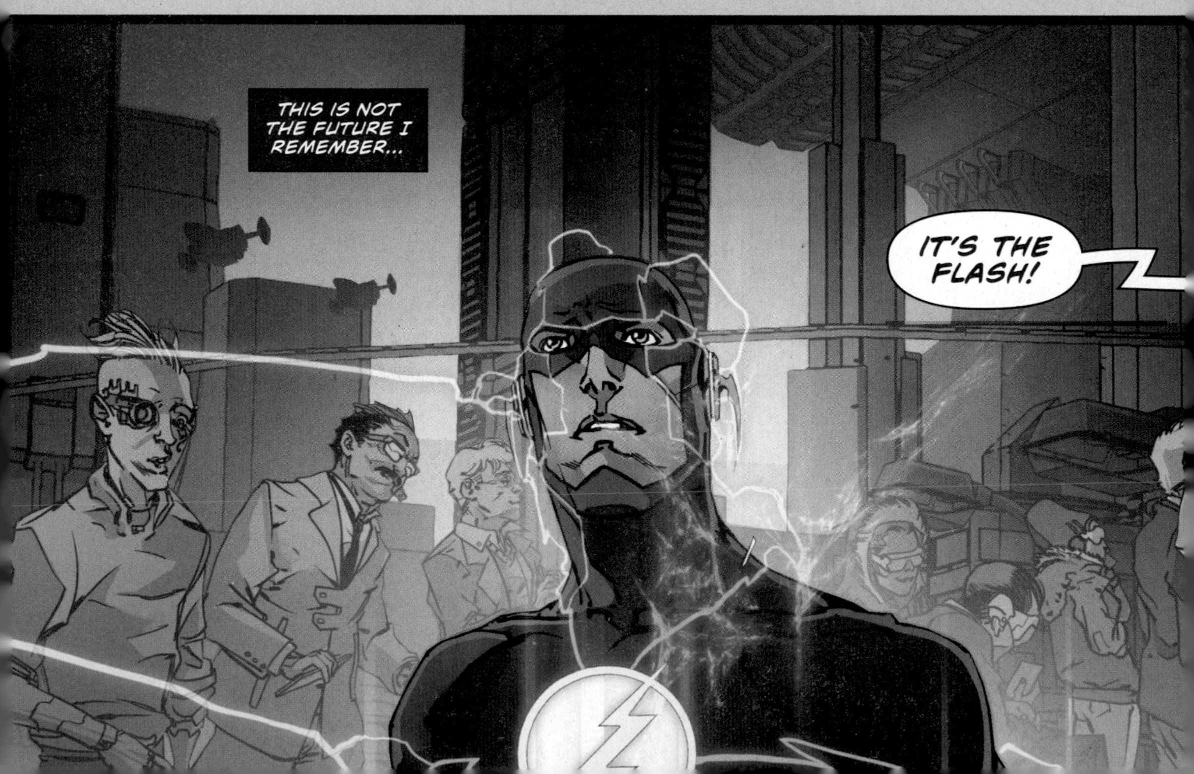
THIS IS NOT THE FUTURE I REMEMBER...
IT'S THE FLASH!

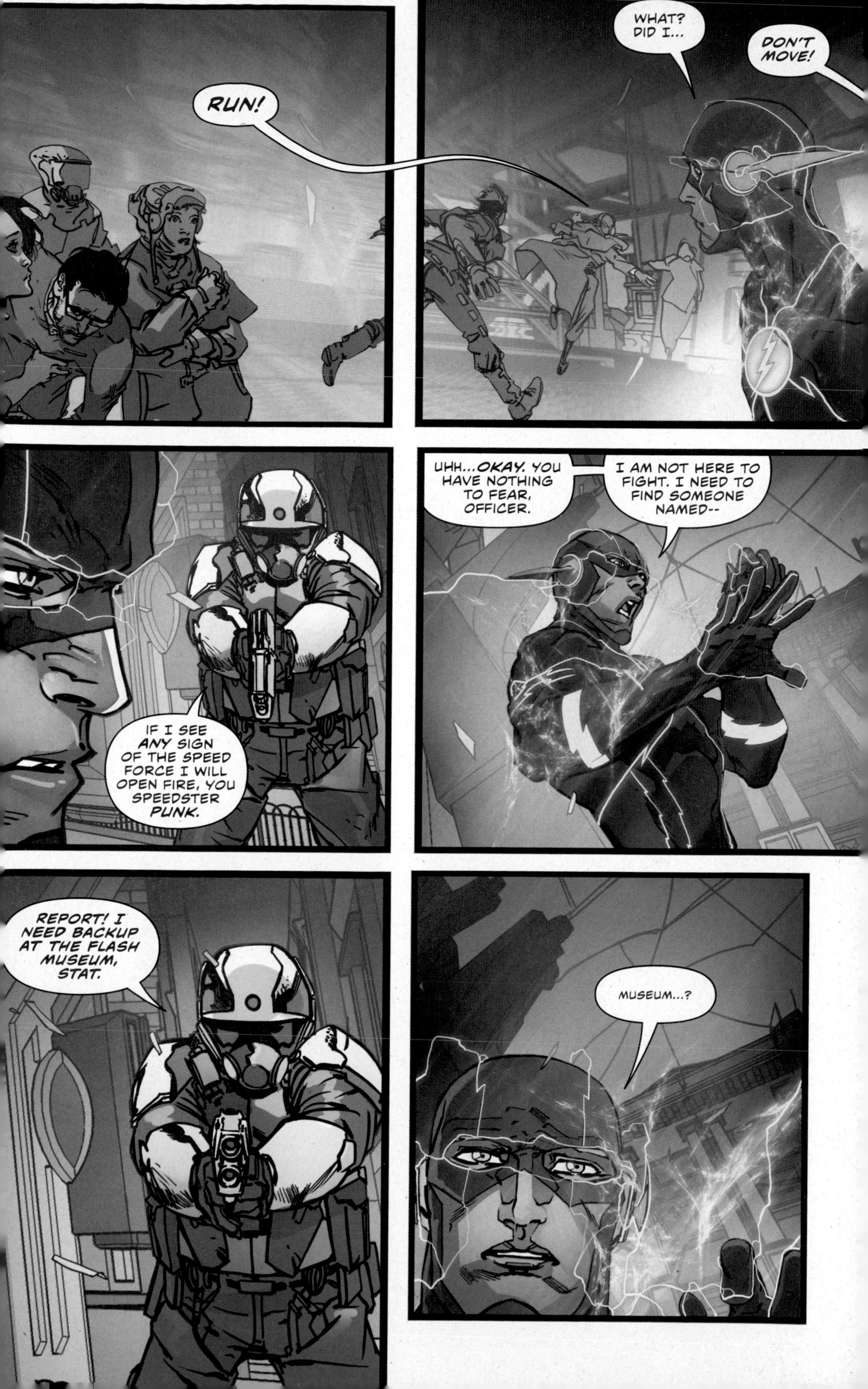
RUN!
WHAT? DID I...
DON'T MOVE!
IF I SEE ANY SIGN OF THE SPEED FORCE I WILL OPEN FIRE, YOU SPEEDSTER PUNK.
UHH...OKAY. YOU HAVE NOTHING TO FEAR, OFFICER.
I AM NOT HERE TO FIGHT. I NEED TO FIND SOMEONE NAMED--
REPORT! I NEED BACKUP AT THE FLASH MUSEUM, STAT.
MUSEUM...?

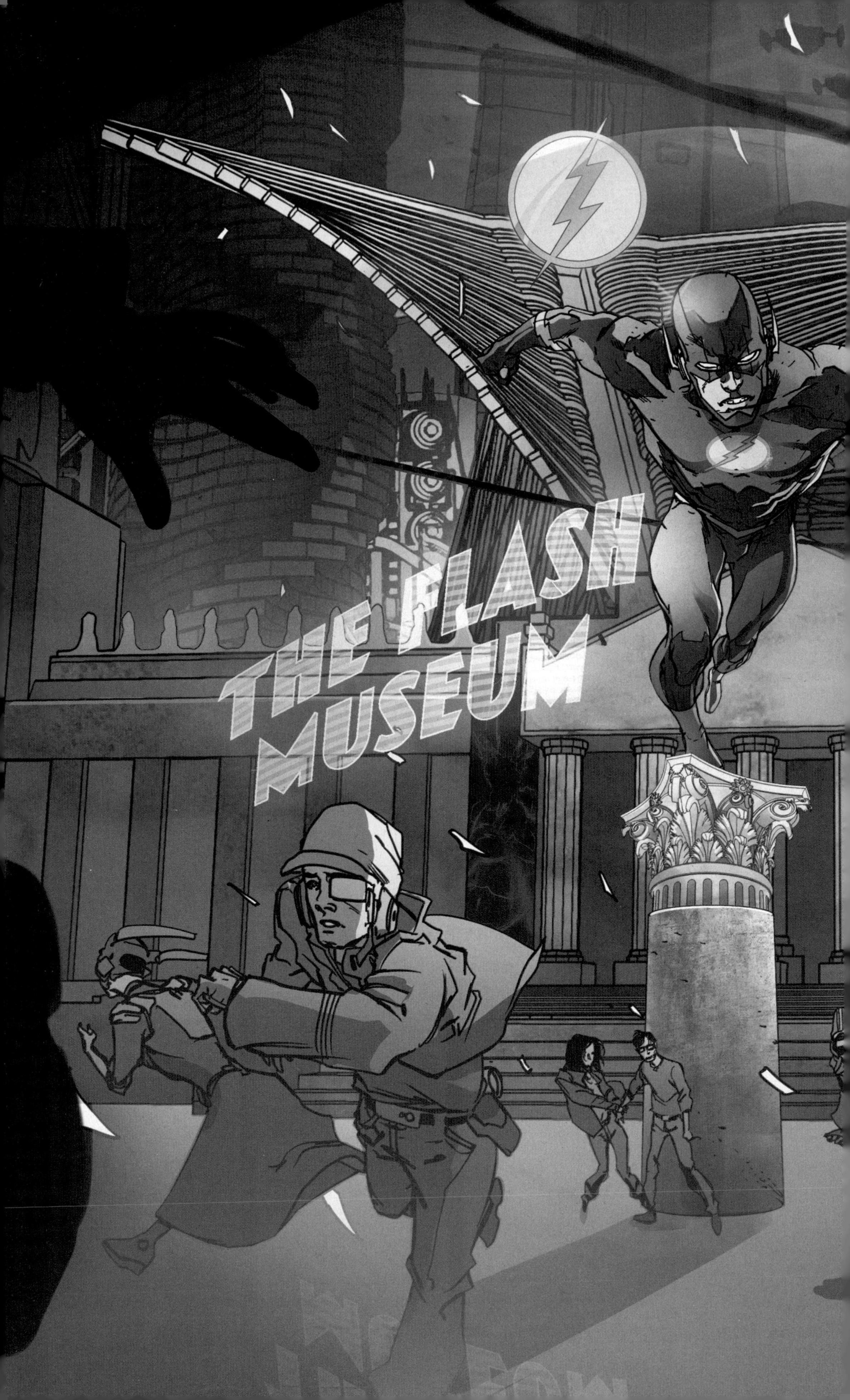
THE FLASH MUSEUM

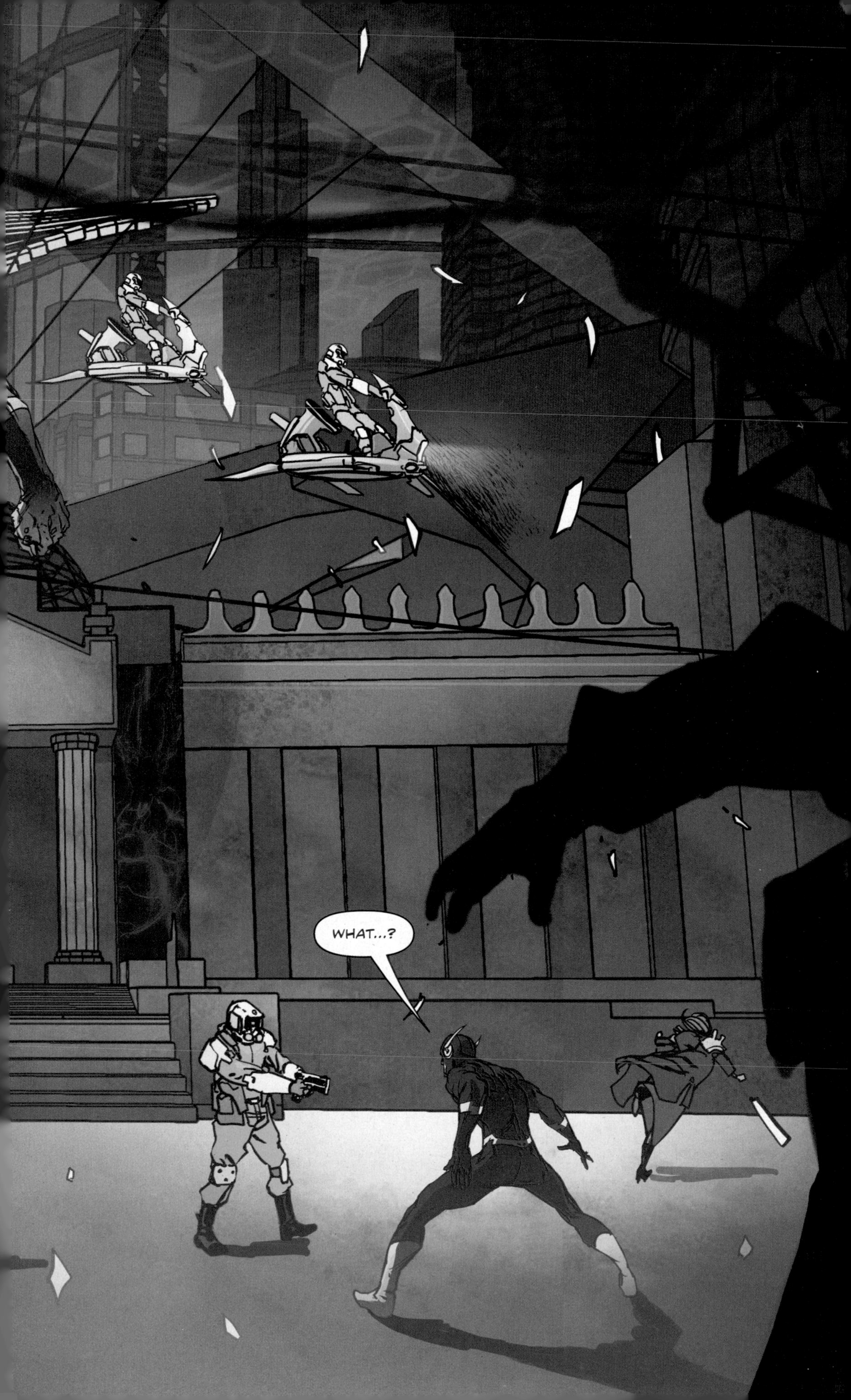
WHAT...?

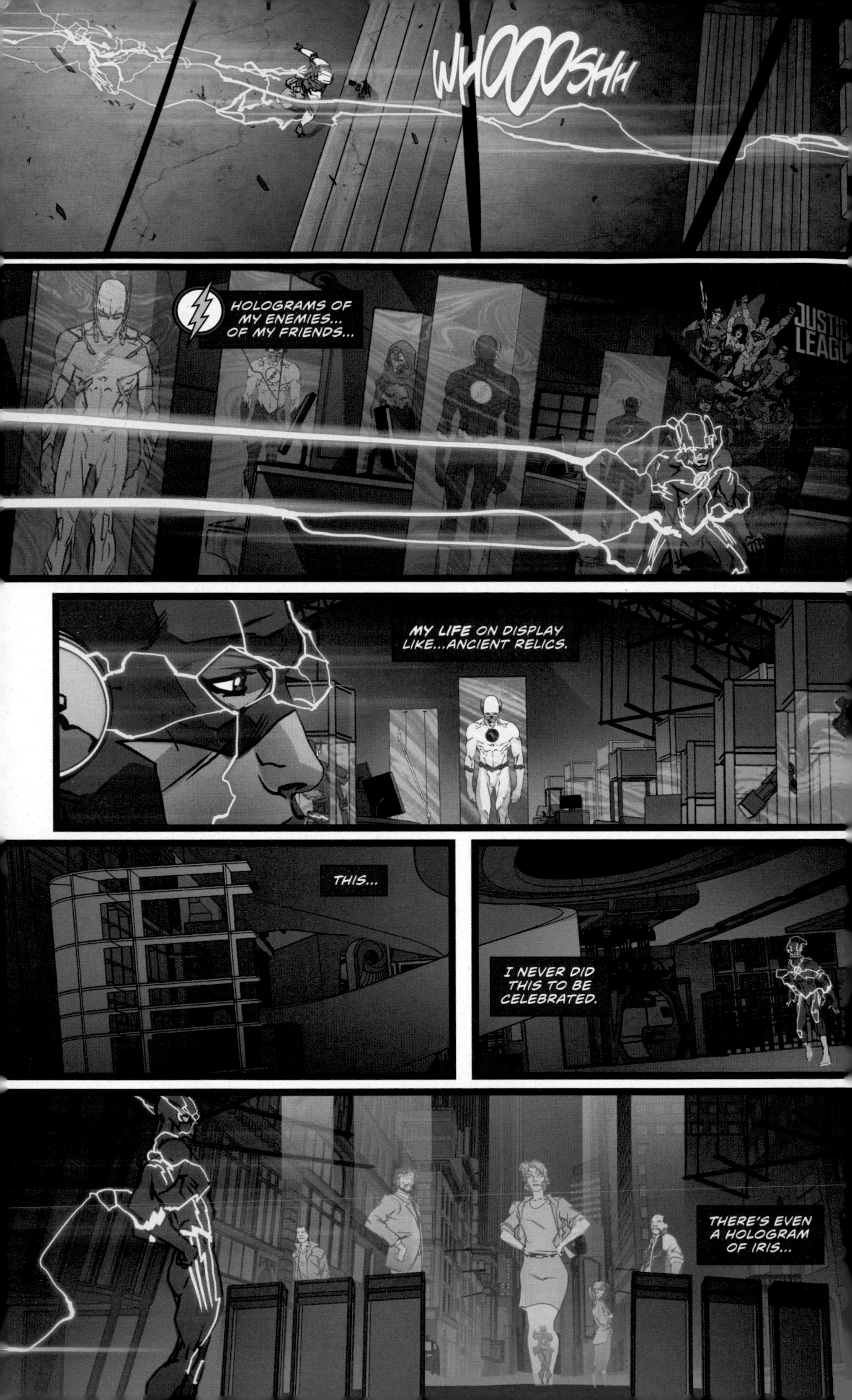
WHOOOOSHH
HOLOGRAMS OF MY ENEMIES... OF MY FRIENDS...
JUSTICE LEAGUE
MY LIFE ON DISPLAY LIKE...ANCIENT RELICS.
THIS...
I NEVER DID THIS TO BE CELEBRATED.
THERE'S EVEN A HOLOGRAM OF IRIS...

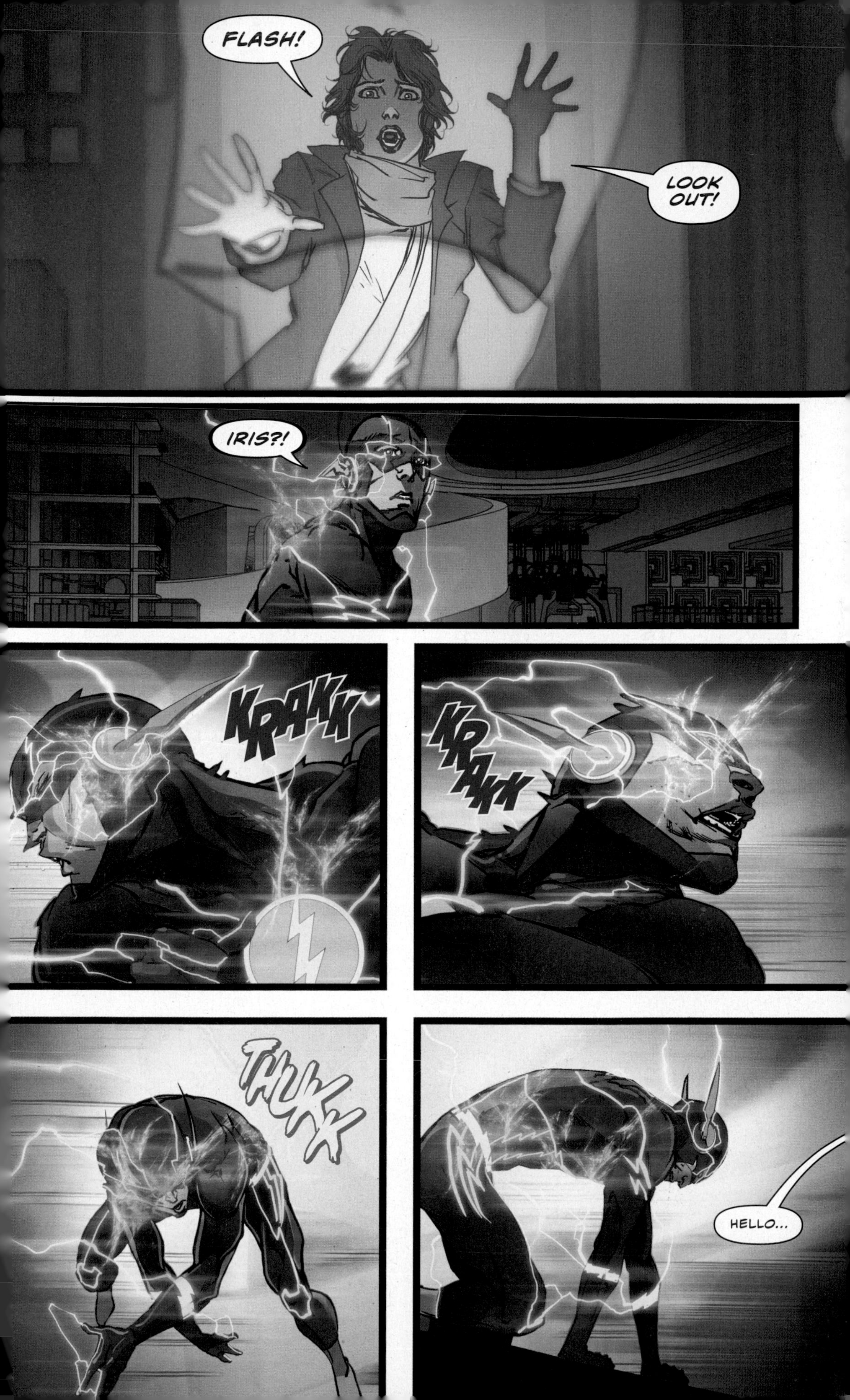
FLASH!
LOOK OUT!
IRIS?!
KRAKK
KRAKK
THUKK
HELLO...

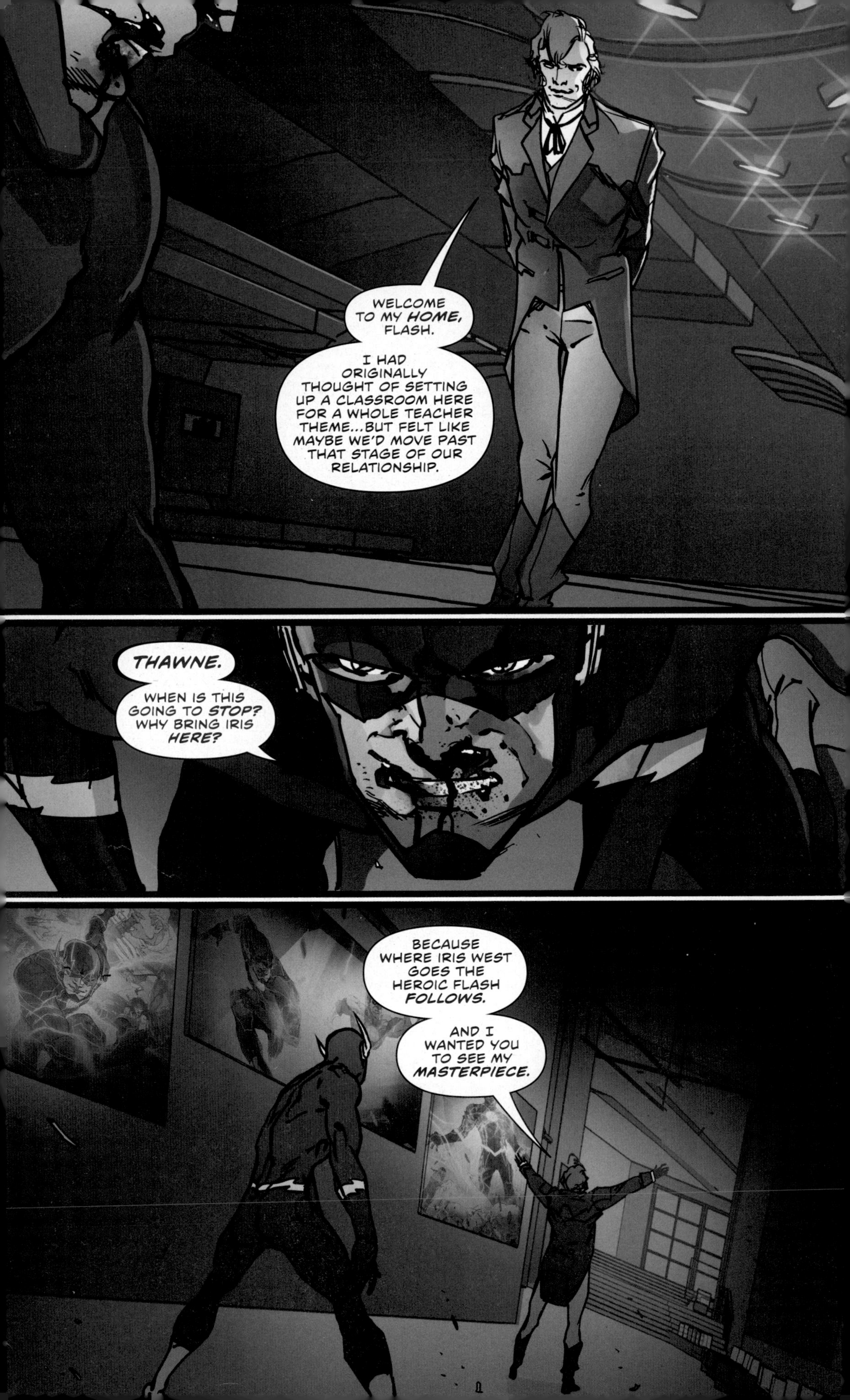
WELCOME TO MY *HOME*, FLASH.
I HAD ORIGINALLY THOUGHT OF SETTING UP A CLASSROOM HERE FOR A WHOLE TEACHER THEME...BUT FELT LIKE MAYBE WE'D MOVE PAST THAT STAGE OF OUR RELATIONSHIP.
THAWNE.
WHEN IS THIS GOING TO *STOP*? WHY BRING IRIS *HERE*?
BECAUSE WHERE IRIS WEST GOES THE HEROIC FLASH *FOLLOWS*.
AND I WANTED YOU TO SEE MY *MASTERPIECE*.

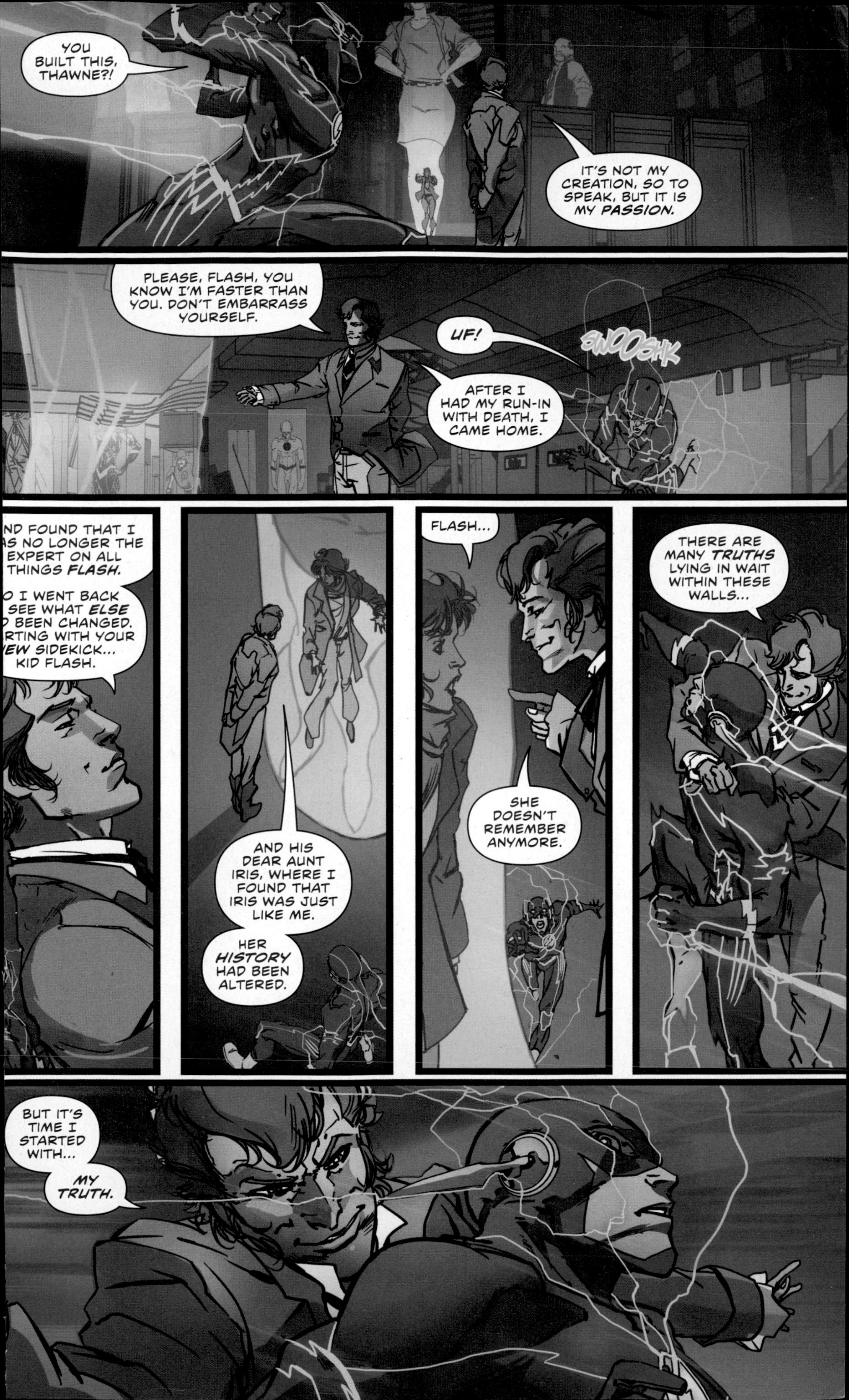

YOU BUILT THIS, THAWNE?!
IT'S NOT MY CREATION, SO TO SPEAK, BUT IT IS MY PASSION.
PLEASE, FLASH, YOU KNOW I'M FASTER THAN YOU. DON'T EMBARRASS YOURSELF.
UF!
SWOOSHK
AFTER I HAD MY RUN-IN WITH DEATH, I CAME HOME.
ND FOUND THAT I AS NO LONGER THE EXPERT ON ALL THINGS FLASH.
O I WENT BACK SEE WHAT ELSE D BEEN CHANGED. RTING WITH YOUR EW SIDEKICK... KID FLASH.
AND HIS DEAR AUNT IRIS, WHERE I FOUND THAT IRIS WAS JUST LIKE ME.
HER HISTORY HAD BEEN ALTERED.
FLASH...
SHE DOESN'T REMEMBER ANYMORE.
THERE ARE MANY TRUTHS LYING IN WAIT WITHIN THESE WALLS...
BUT IT'S TIME I STARTED WITH...
MY TRUTH.

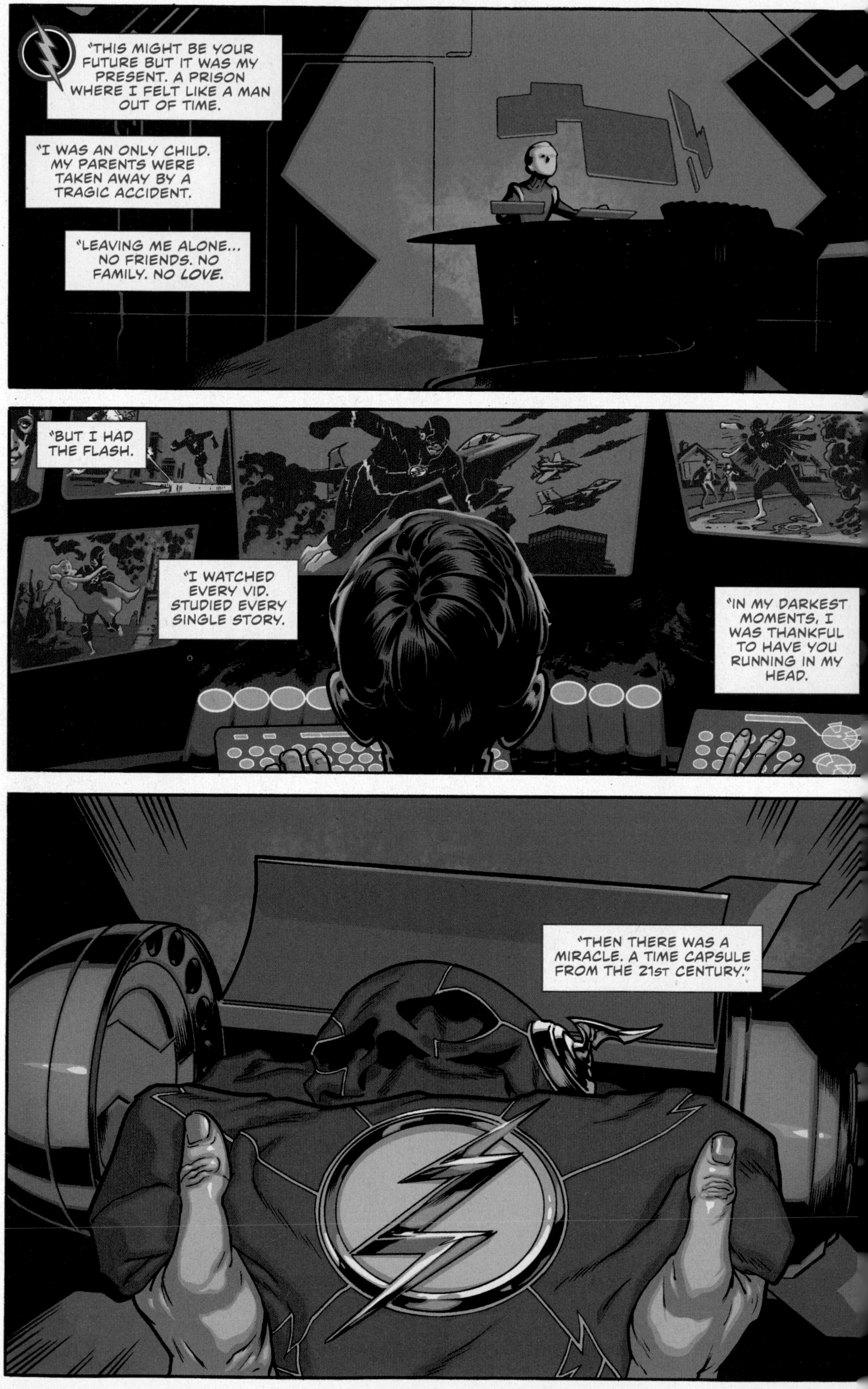
"THIS MIGHT BE YOUR FUTURE BUT IT WAS MY PRESENT. A PRISON WHERE I FELT LIKE A MAN OUT OF TIME.
"I WAS AN ONLY CHILD. MY PARENTS WERE TAKEN AWAY BY A TRAGIC ACCIDENT.
"LEAVING ME ALONE... NO FRIENDS. NO FAMILY. NO *LOVE*.
"BUT I HAD THE FLASH.
"I WATCHED EVERY VID. STUDIED EVERY SINGLE STORY.
"IN MY DARKEST MOMENTS, I WAS THANKFUL TO HAVE YOU RUNNING IN MY HEAD.
"THEN THERE WAS A MIRACLE. A TIME CAPSULE FROM THE 21ST CENTURY."

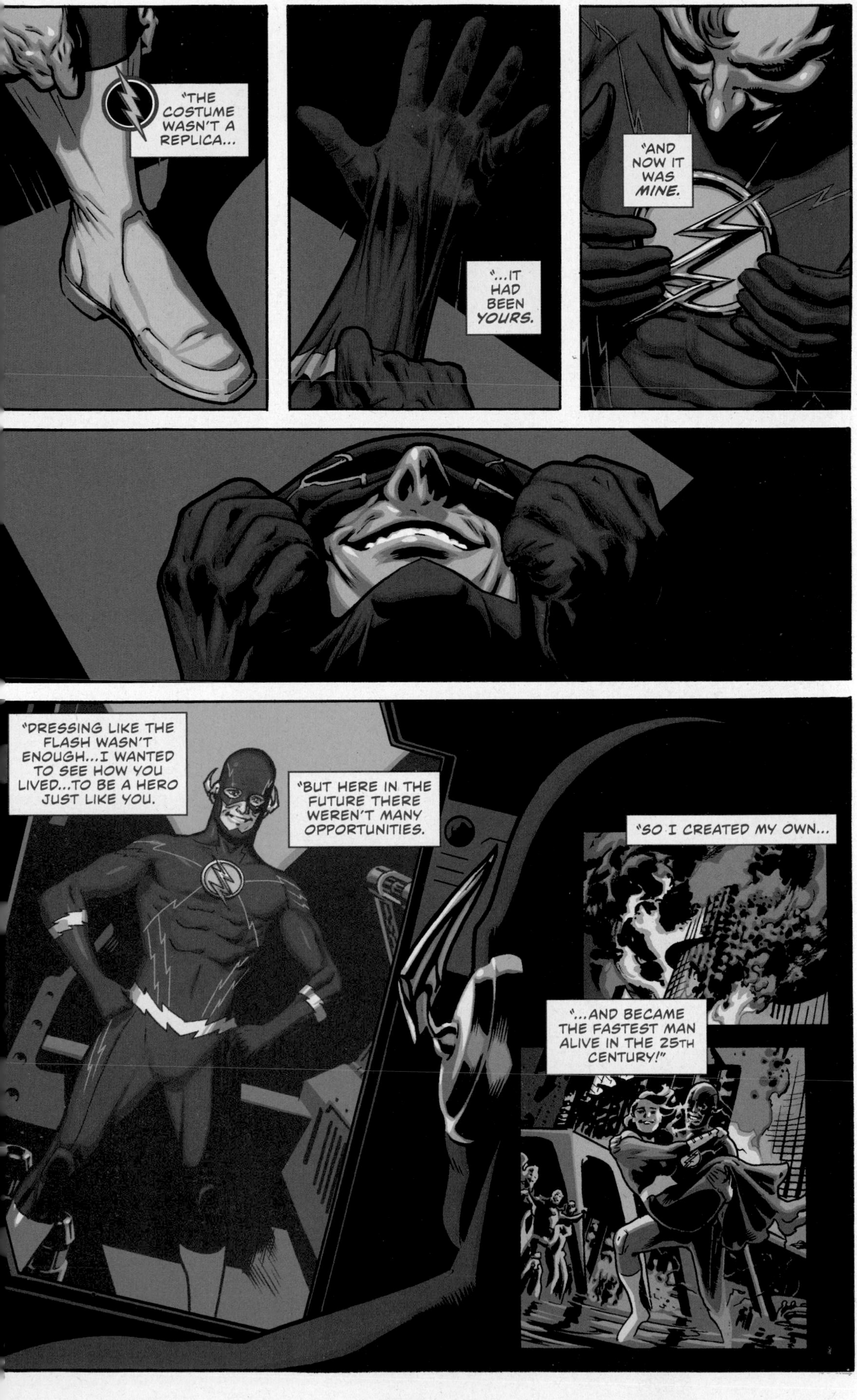
"THE COSTUME WASN'T A REPLICA...
"...IT HAD BEEN *YOURS*.
"AND NOW IT WAS *MINE*.
"DRESSING LIKE THE FLASH WASN'T ENOUGH...I WANTED TO SEE HOW YOU LIVED...TO BE A HERO JUST LIKE YOU.
"BUT HERE IN THE FUTURE THERE WEREN'T MANY OPPORTUNITIES.
"SO I CREATED MY OWN...
"...AND BECAME THE FASTEST MAN ALIVE IN THE 25TH CENTURY!"

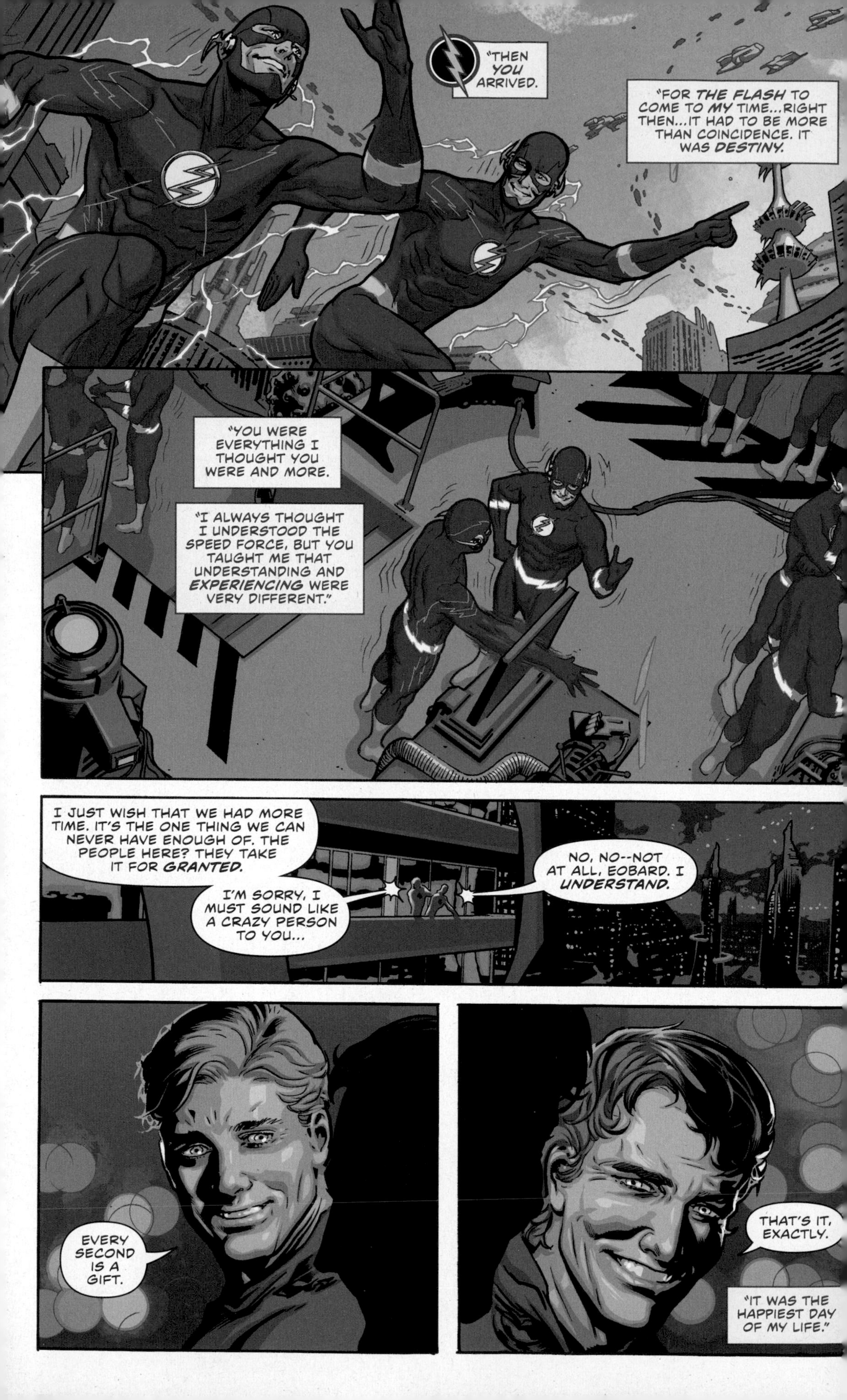
"THEN YOU ARRIVED.
"FOR THE FLASH TO COME TO MY TIME...RIGHT THEN...IT HAD TO BE MORE THAN COINCIDENCE. IT WAS DESTINY.
"YOU WERE EVERYTHING I THOUGHT YOU WERE AND MORE.
"I ALWAYS THOUGHT I UNDERSTOOD THE SPEED FORCE, BUT YOU TAUGHT ME THAT UNDERSTANDING AND EXPERIENCING WERE VERY DIFFERENT."
I JUST WISH THAT WE HAD MORE TIME. IT'S THE ONE THING WE CAN NEVER HAVE ENOUGH OF. THE PEOPLE HERE? THEY TAKE IT FOR GRANTED.
I'M SORRY, I MUST SOUND LIKE A CRAZY PERSON TO YOU...
NO, NO--NOT AT ALL, EOBARD. I UNDERSTAND.
EVERY SECOND IS A GIFT.
THAT'S IT, EXACTLY.
"IT WAS THE HAPPIEST DAY OF MY LIFE."

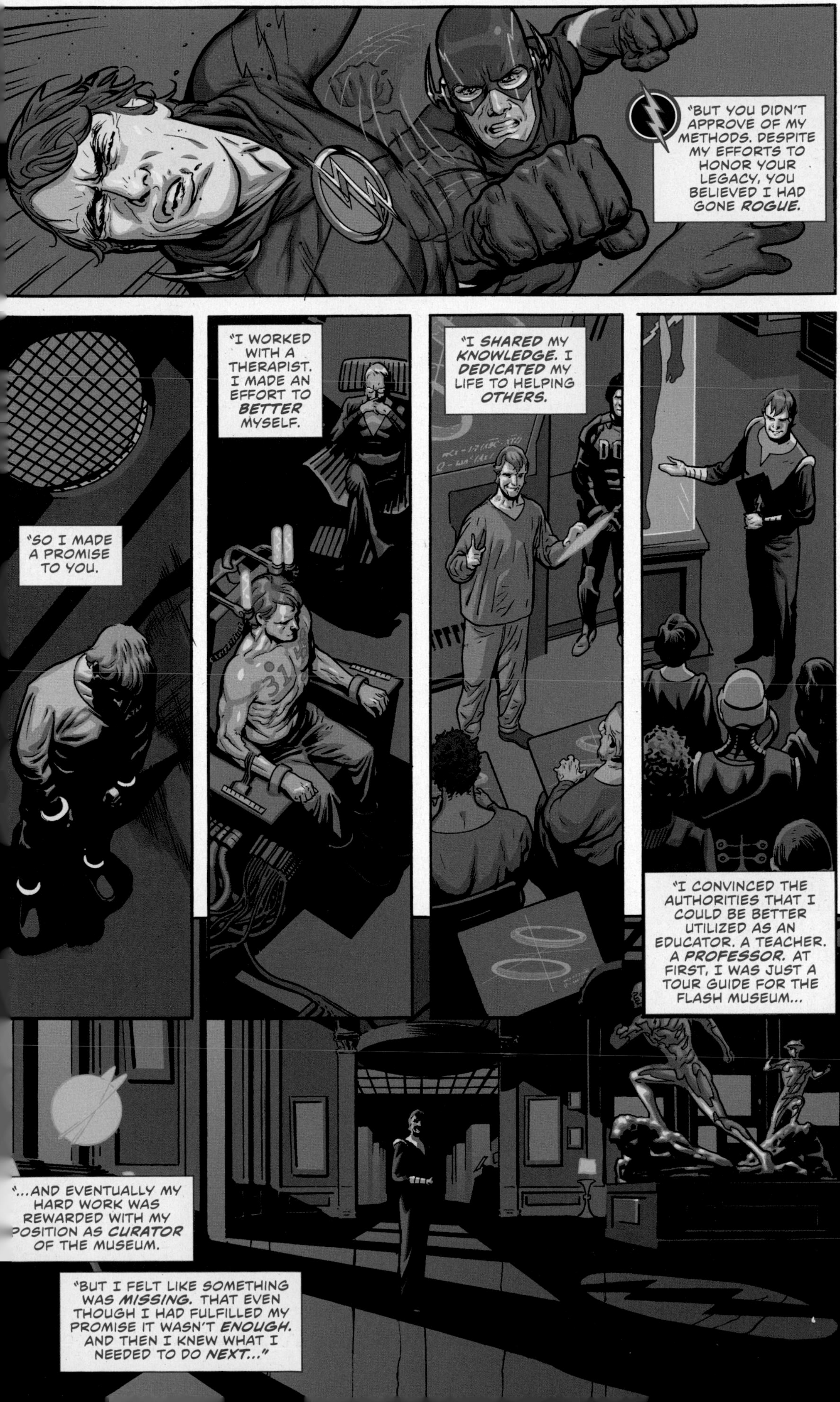
"BUT YOU DIDN'T APPROVE OF MY METHODS. DESPITE MY EFFORTS TO HONOR YOUR LEGACY, YOU BELIEVED I HAD GONE *ROGUE*.
"SO I MADE A PROMISE TO YOU.
"I WORKED WITH A THERAPIST. I MADE AN EFFORT TO *BETTER* MYSELF.
"I *SHARED* MY *KNOWLEDGE*. I *DEDICATED* MY LIFE TO HELPING *OTHERS*.
"I CONVINCED THE AUTHORITIES THAT I COULD BE BETTER UTILIZED AS AN EDUCATOR. A TEACHER. A *PROFESSOR*. AT FIRST, I WAS JUST A TOUR GUIDE FOR THE FLASH MUSEUM...
"...AND EVENTUALLY MY HARD WORK WAS REWARDED WITH MY POSITION AS *CURATOR* OF THE MUSEUM.
"BUT I FELT LIKE SOMETHING WAS *MISSING*. THAT EVEN THOUGH I HAD FULFILLED MY PROMISE IT WASN'T *ENOUGH*. AND THEN I KNEW WHAT I NEEDED TO DO *NEXT*..."

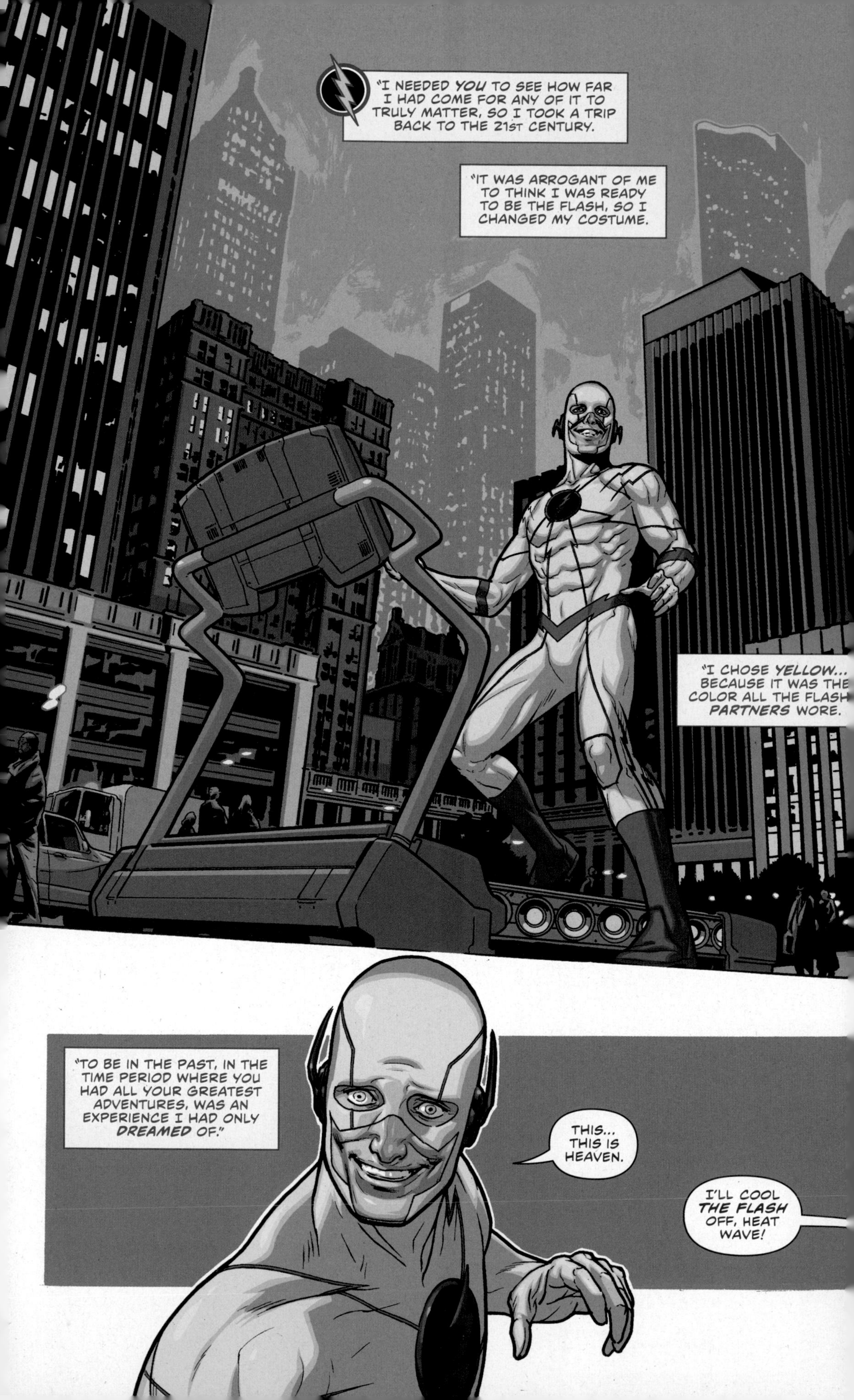
"I NEEDED *YOU* TO SEE HOW FAR I HAD COME FOR ANY OF IT TO TRULY MATTER, SO I TOOK A TRIP BACK TO THE 21st CENTURY.
"IT WAS ARROGANT OF ME TO THINK I WAS READY TO BE THE FLASH, SO I CHANGED MY COSTUME.
"I CHOSE *YELLOW*... BECAUSE IT WAS THE COLOR ALL THE FLASH *PARTNERS* WORE.
"TO BE IN THE PAST, IN THE TIME PERIOD WHERE YOU HAD ALL YOUR GREATEST ADVENTURES, WAS AN EXPERIENCE I HAD ONLY *DREAMED* OF."
THIS... THIS IS HEAVEN.
I'LL COOL *THE FLASH* OFF, HEAT WAVE!

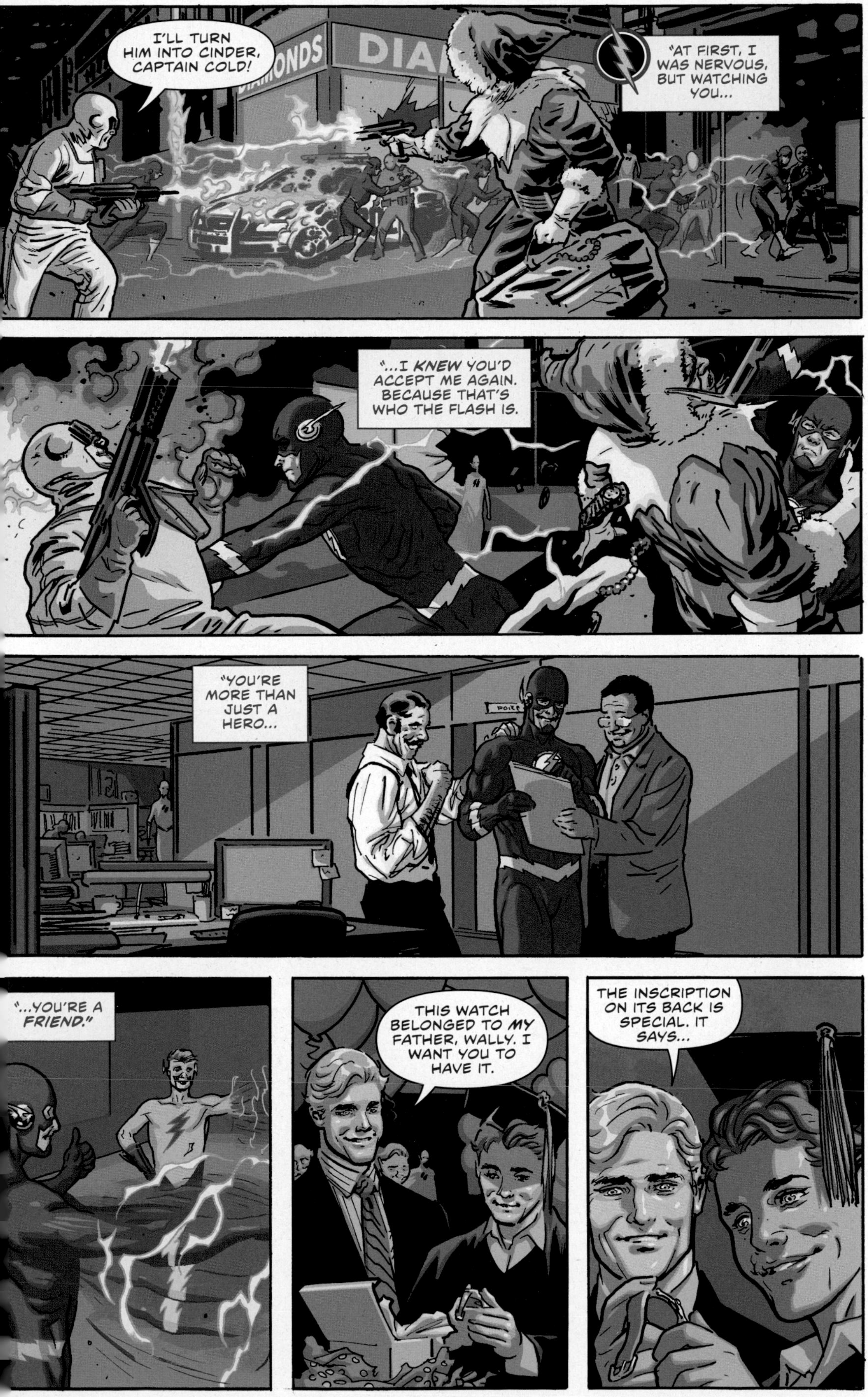
I'LL TURN HIM INTO CINDER, CAPTAIN COLD!
"AT FIRST, I WAS NERVOUS, BUT WATCHING YOU...
"...I *KNEW* YOU'D ACCEPT ME AGAIN. BECAUSE THAT'S WHO THE FLASH IS.
"YOU'RE MORE THAN JUST A HERO...
"...YOU'RE A *FRIEND*."
THIS WATCH BELONGED TO *MY* FATHER, WALLY. I WANT YOU TO HAVE IT.
THE INSCRIPTION ON ITS BACK IS SPECIAL. IT SAYS...

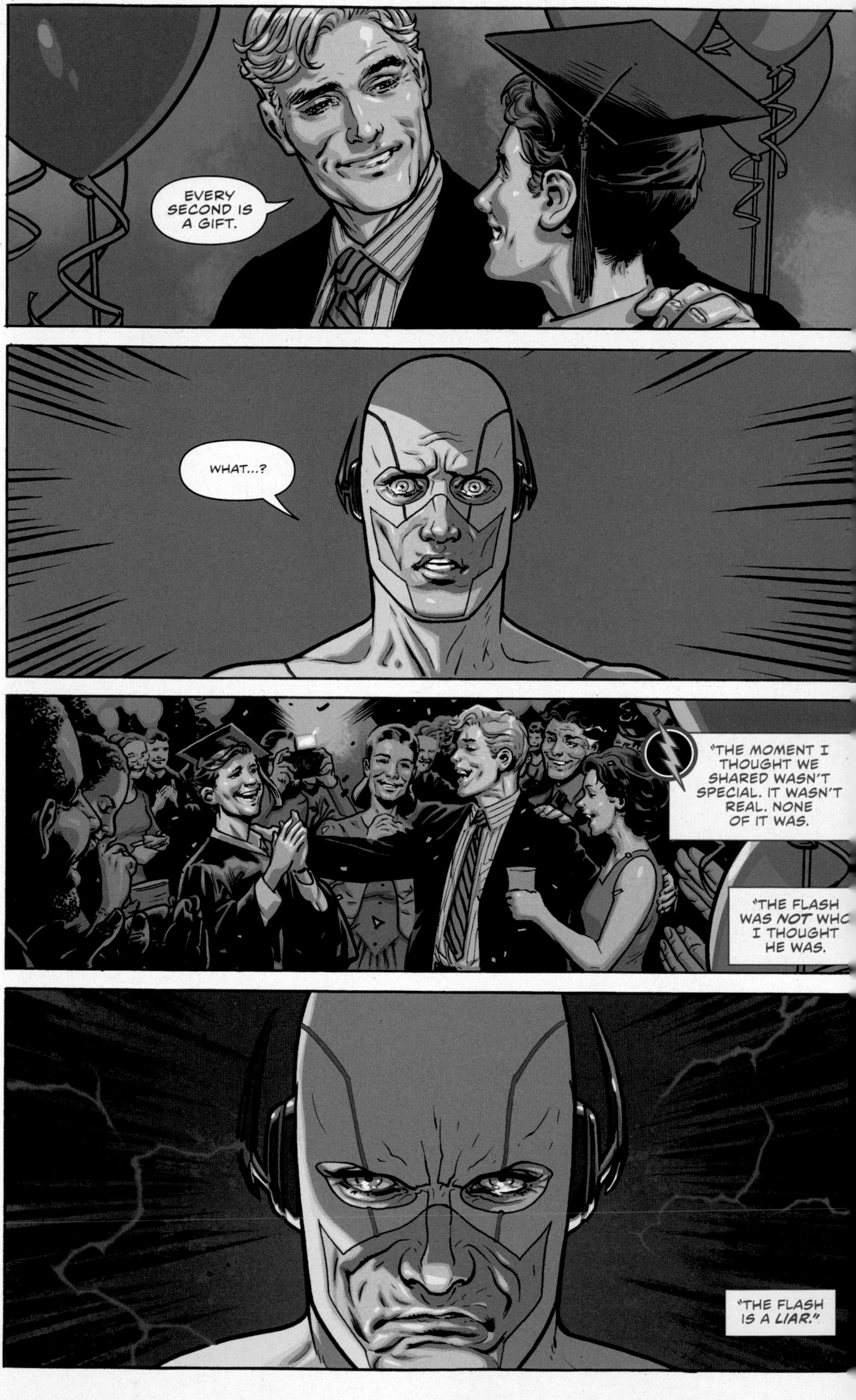
EVERY SECOND IS A GIFT.
WHAT...?
"THE MOMENT I THOUGHT WE SHARED WASN'T SPECIAL. IT WASN'T REAL. NONE OF IT WAS.
"THE FLASH WAS NOT WHO I THOUGHT HE WAS.
"THE FLASH IS A LIAR."

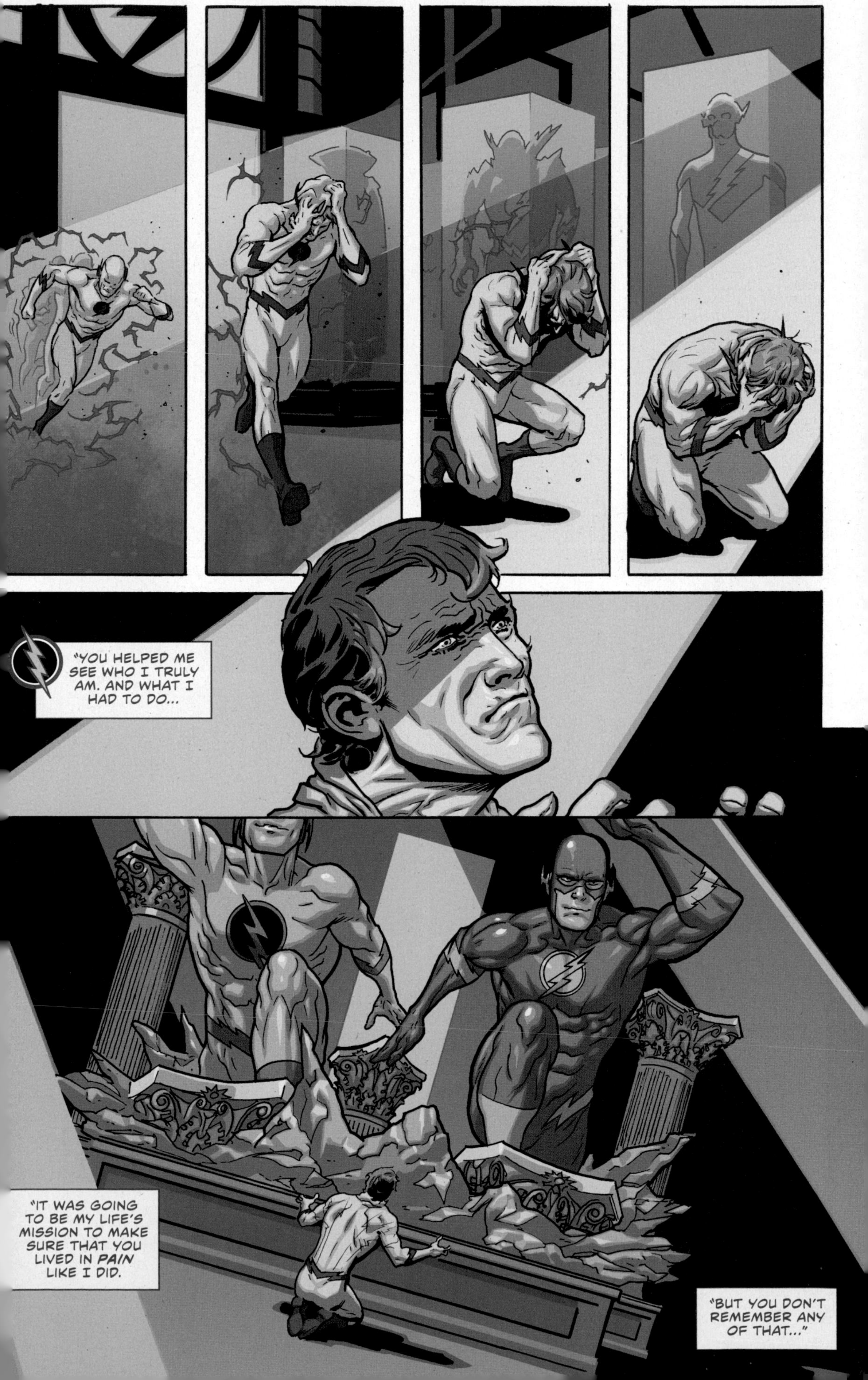
"YOU HELPED ME SEE WHO I TRULY AM. AND WHAT I HAD TO DO...
"IT WAS GOING TO BE MY LIFE'S MISSION TO MAKE SURE THAT YOU LIVED IN *PAIN* LIKE I DID.
"BUT YOU DON'T REMEMBER ANY OF THAT..."

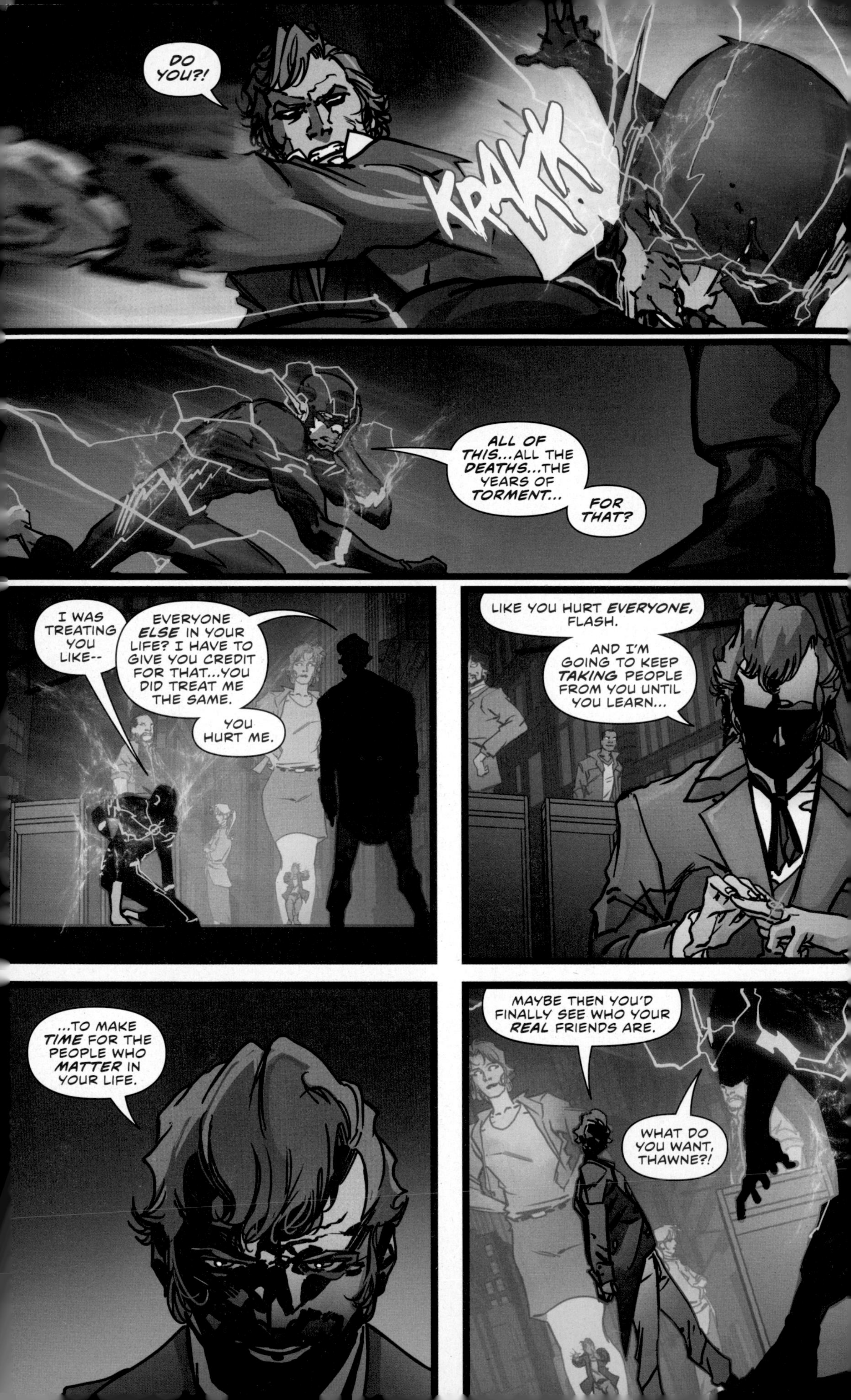
DO YOU?!
KRAKK!
ALL OF THIS...ALL THE DEATHS...THE YEARS OF TORMENT...
FOR THAT?
I WAS TREATING YOU LIKE--
EVERYONE ELSE IN YOUR LIFE? I HAVE TO GIVE YOU CREDIT FOR THAT...YOU DID TREAT ME THE SAME.
YOU HURT ME.
LIKE YOU HURT EVERYONE, FLASH.
AND I'M GOING TO KEEP TAKING PEOPLE FROM YOU UNTIL YOU LEARN...
...TO MAKE TIME FOR THE PEOPLE WHO MATTER IN YOUR LIFE.
MAYBE THEN YOU'D FINALLY SEE WHO YOUR REAL FRIENDS ARE.
WHAT DO YOU WANT, THAWNE?!

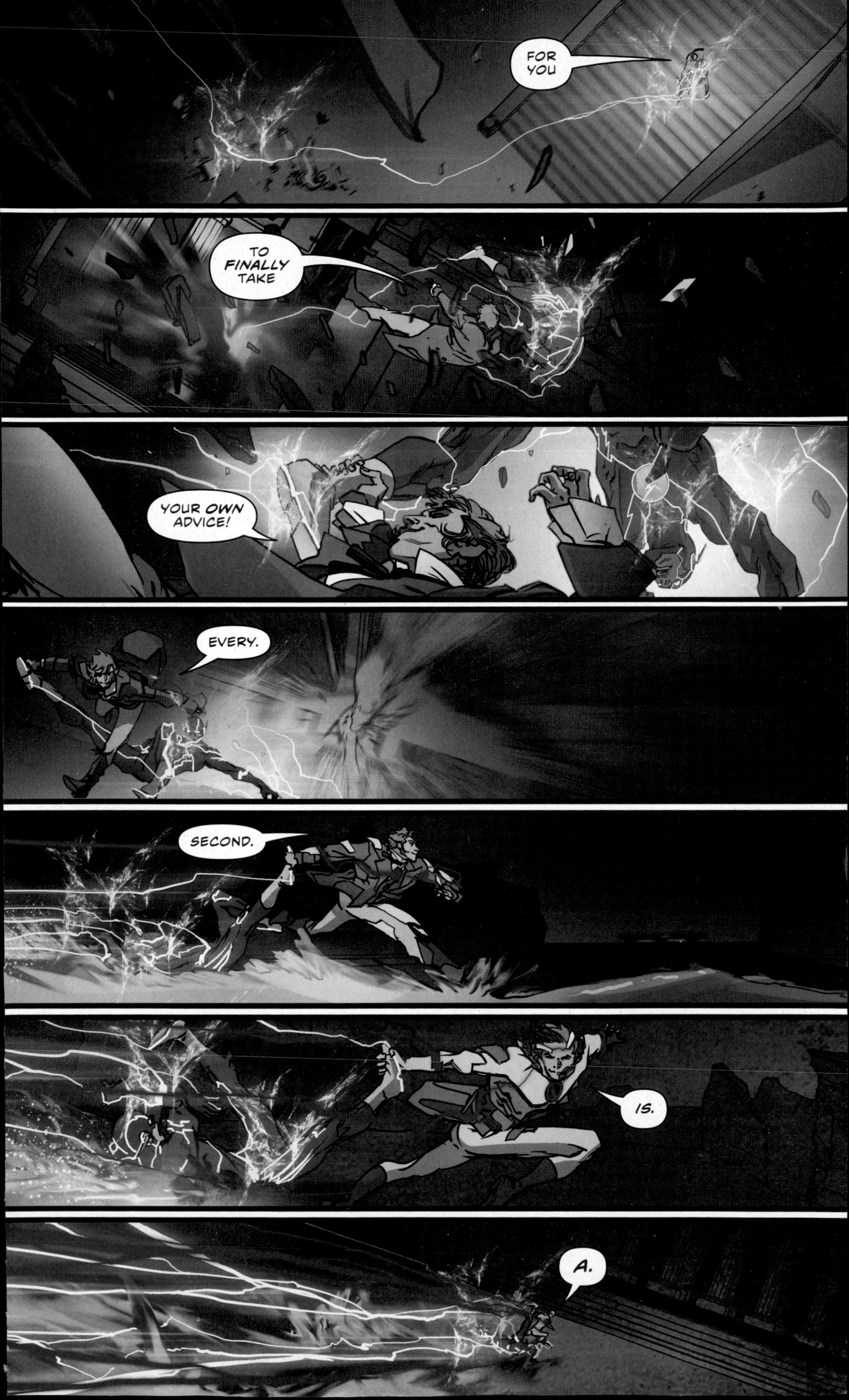
FOR YOU
TO FINALLY TAKE
YOUR OWN ADVICE!
EVERY.
SECOND.
IS.
A.

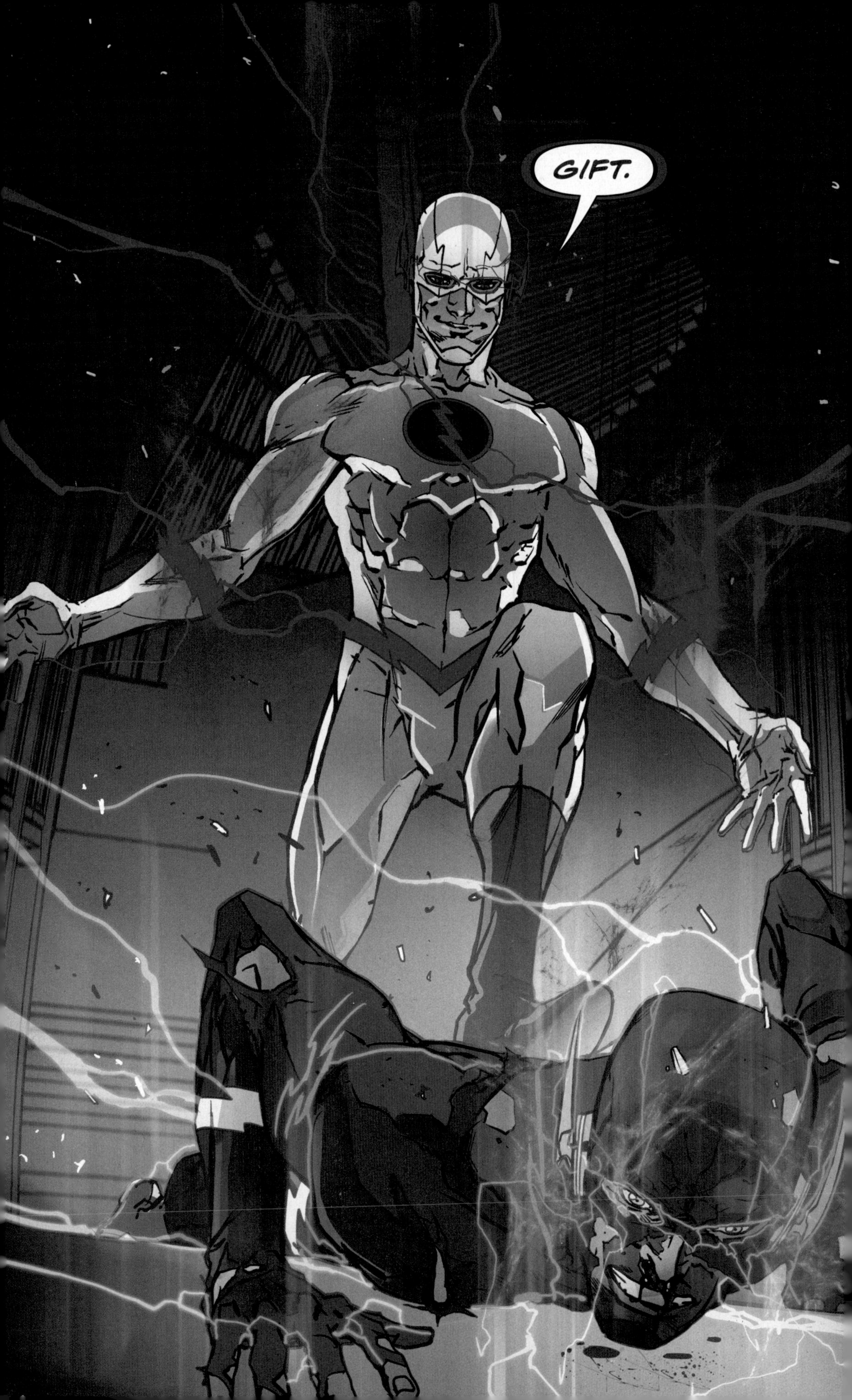
GIFT.

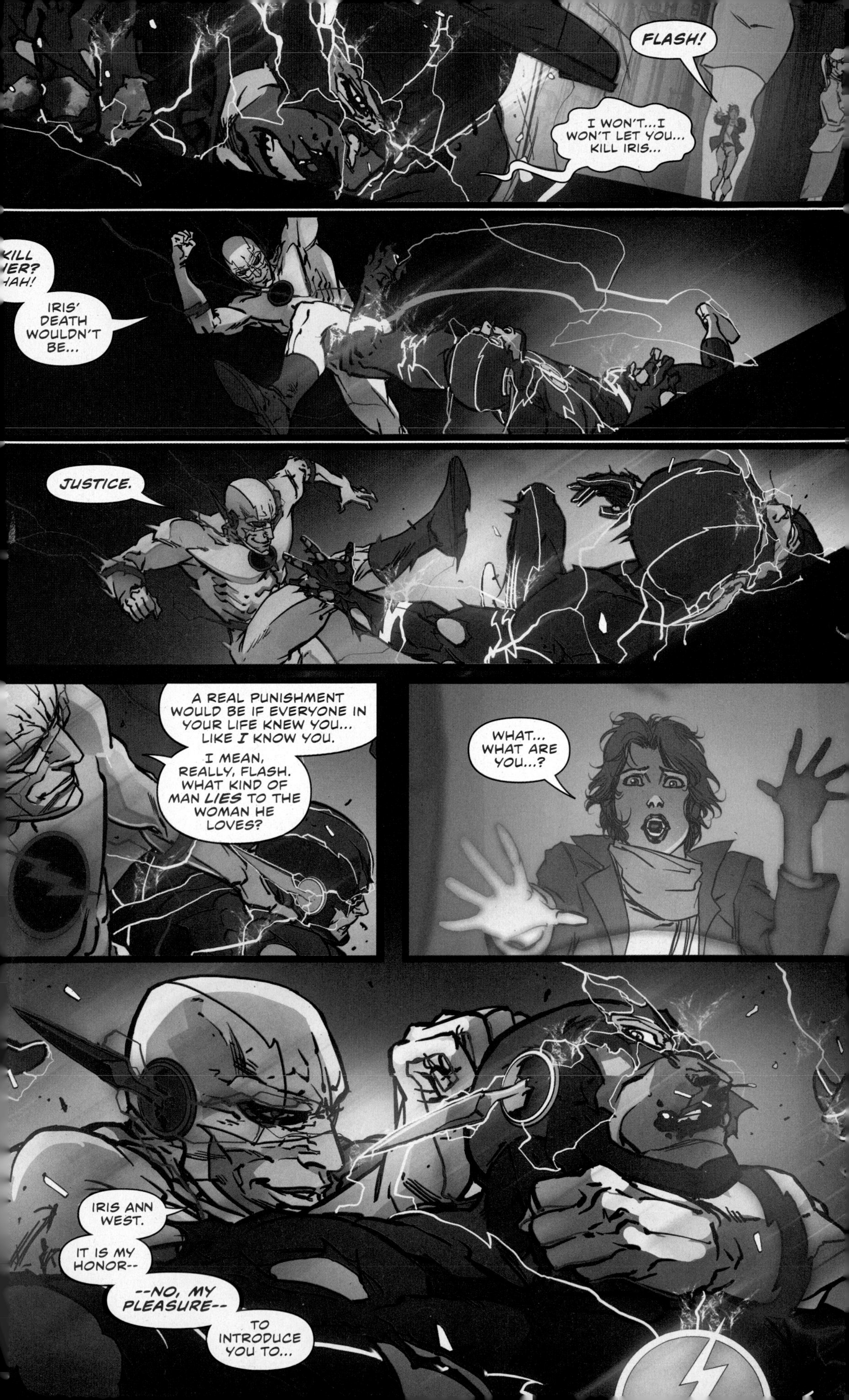
FLASH!
I WON'T...I WON'T LET YOU... KILL IRIS...
KILL HER? HAH!
IRIS' DEATH WOULDN'T BE...
JUSTICE.
A REAL PUNISHMENT WOULD BE IF EVERYONE IN YOUR LIFE KNEW YOU... LIKE I KNOW YOU.
I MEAN, REALLY, FLASH. WHAT KIND OF MAN LIES TO THE WOMAN HE LOVES?
WHAT... WHAT ARE YOU...?
IRIS ANN WEST.
IT IS MY HONOR--
--NO, MY PLEASURE--
TO INTRODUCE YOU TO...

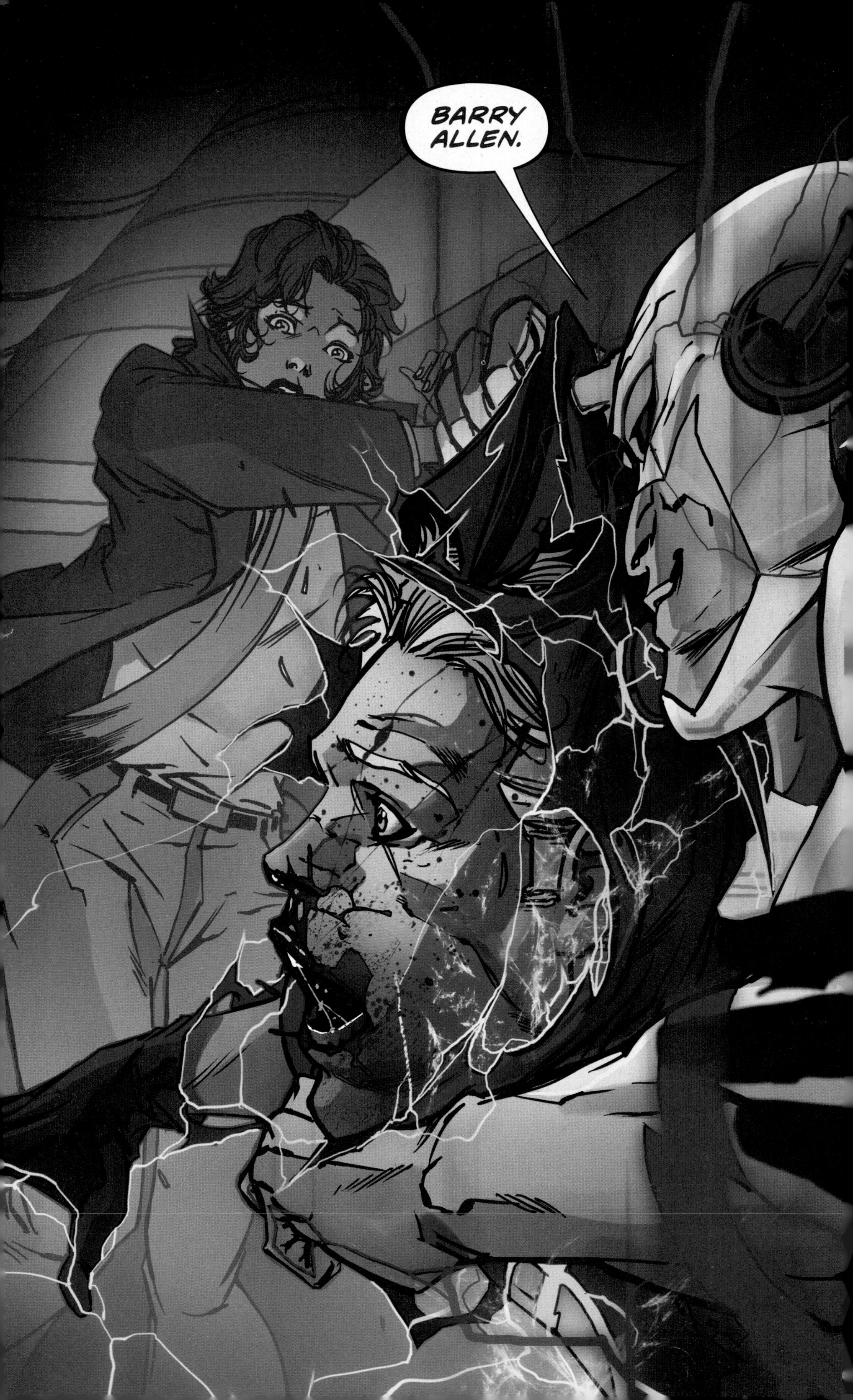
BARRY ALLEN.

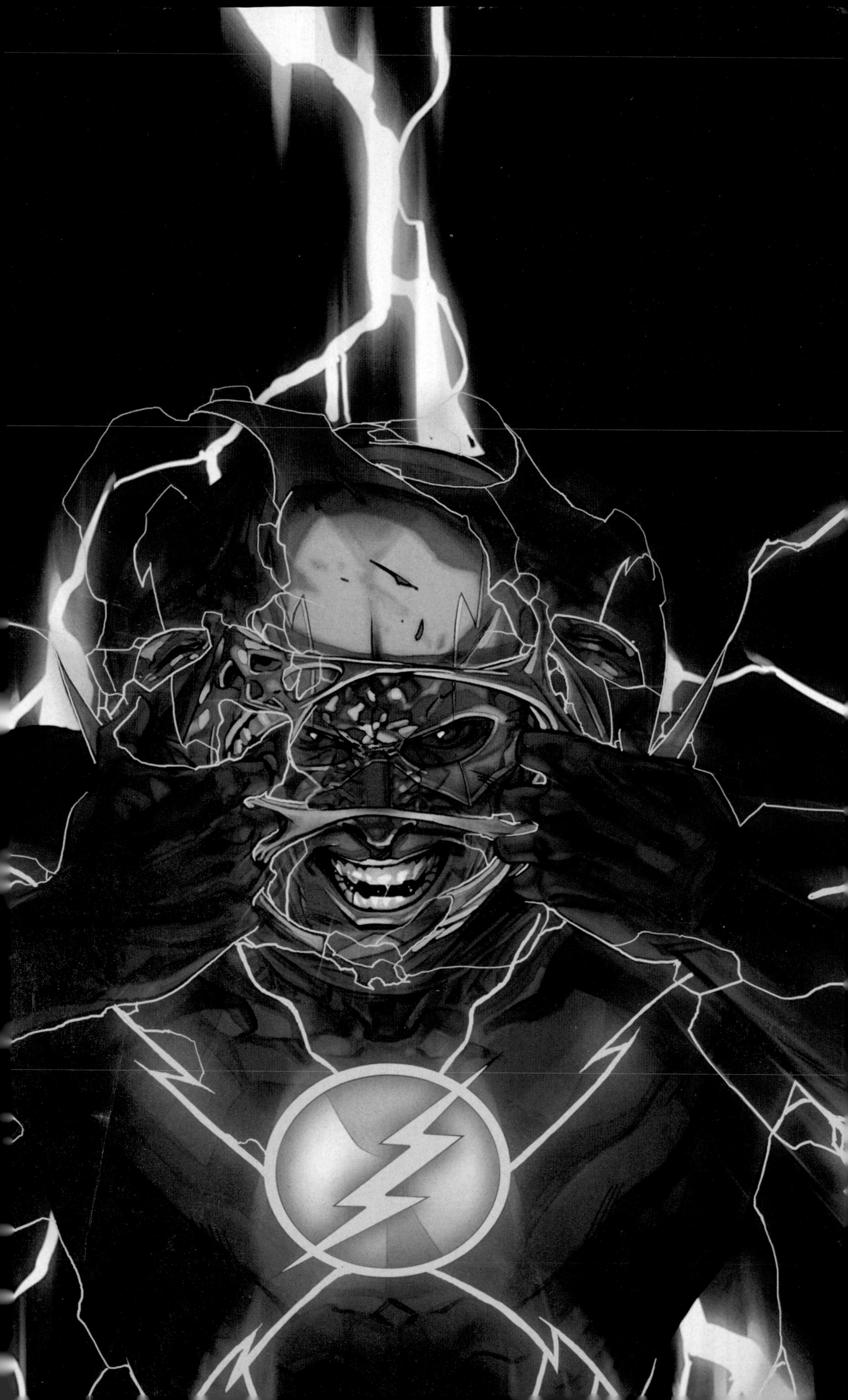

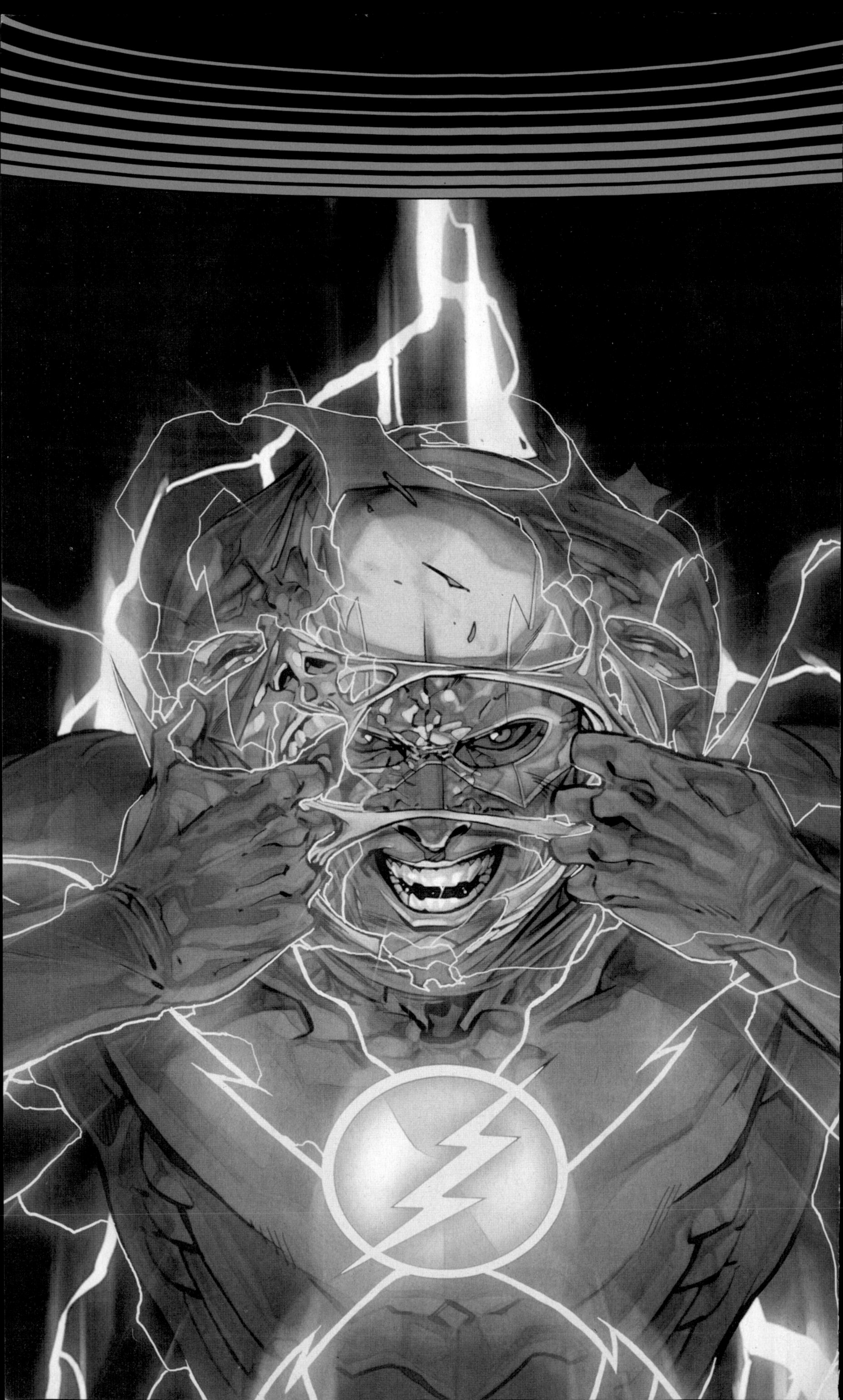

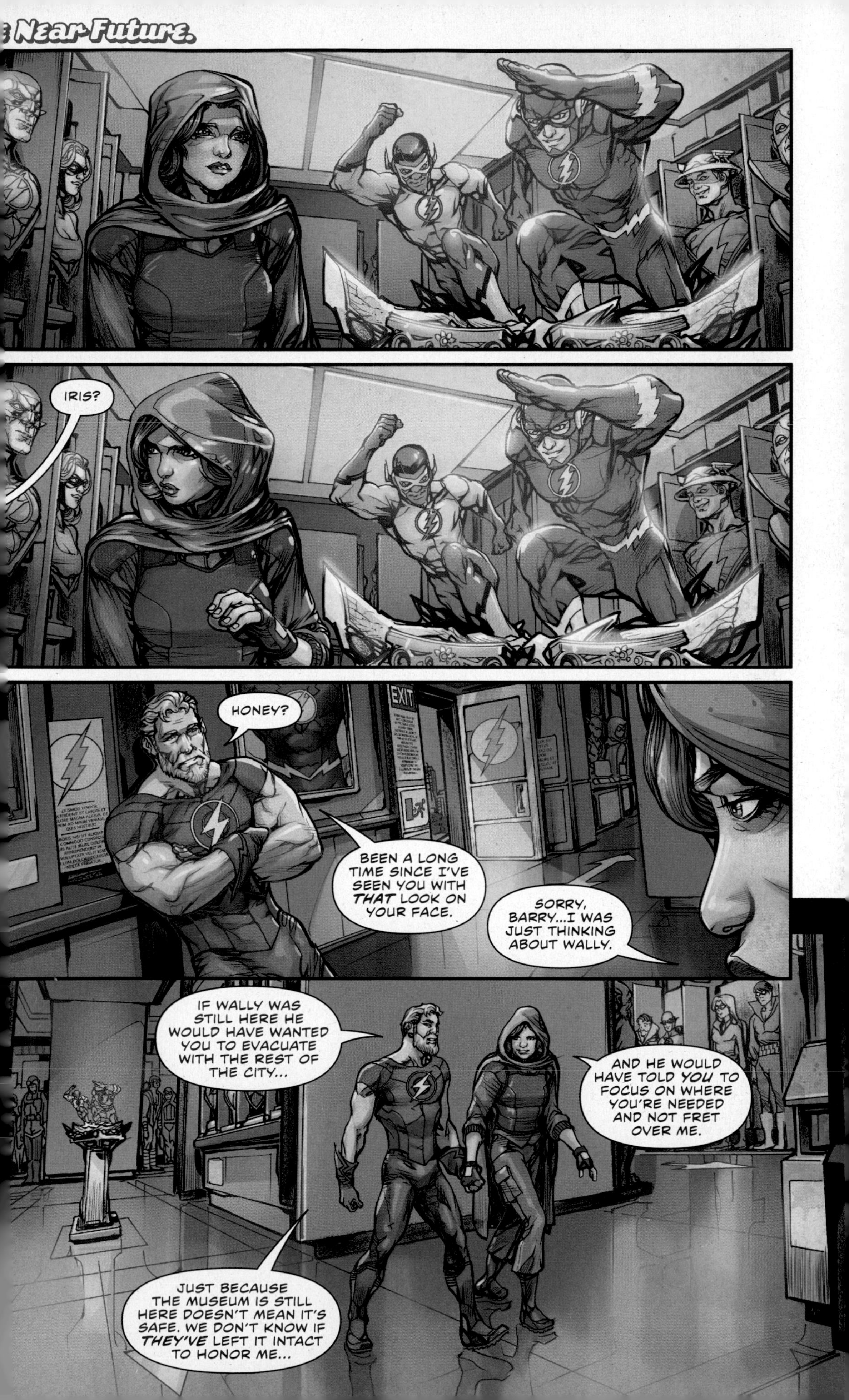
e Near Future.
IRIS?
HONEY?
EXIT
BEEN A LONG TIME SINCE I'VE SEEN YOU WITH *THAT* LOOK ON YOUR FACE.
SORRY, BARRY...I WAS JUST THINKING ABOUT WALLY.
IF WALLY WAS STILL HERE HE WOULD HAVE WANTED YOU TO EVACUATE WITH THE REST OF THE CITY...
AND HE WOULD HAVE TOLD *YOU* TO FOCUS ON WHERE YOU'RE NEEDED AND NOT FRET OVER ME.
JUST BECAUSE THE MUSEUM IS STILL HERE DOESN'T MEAN IT'S SAFE. WE DON'T KNOW IF *THEY'VE* LEFT IT INTACT TO HONOR ME...

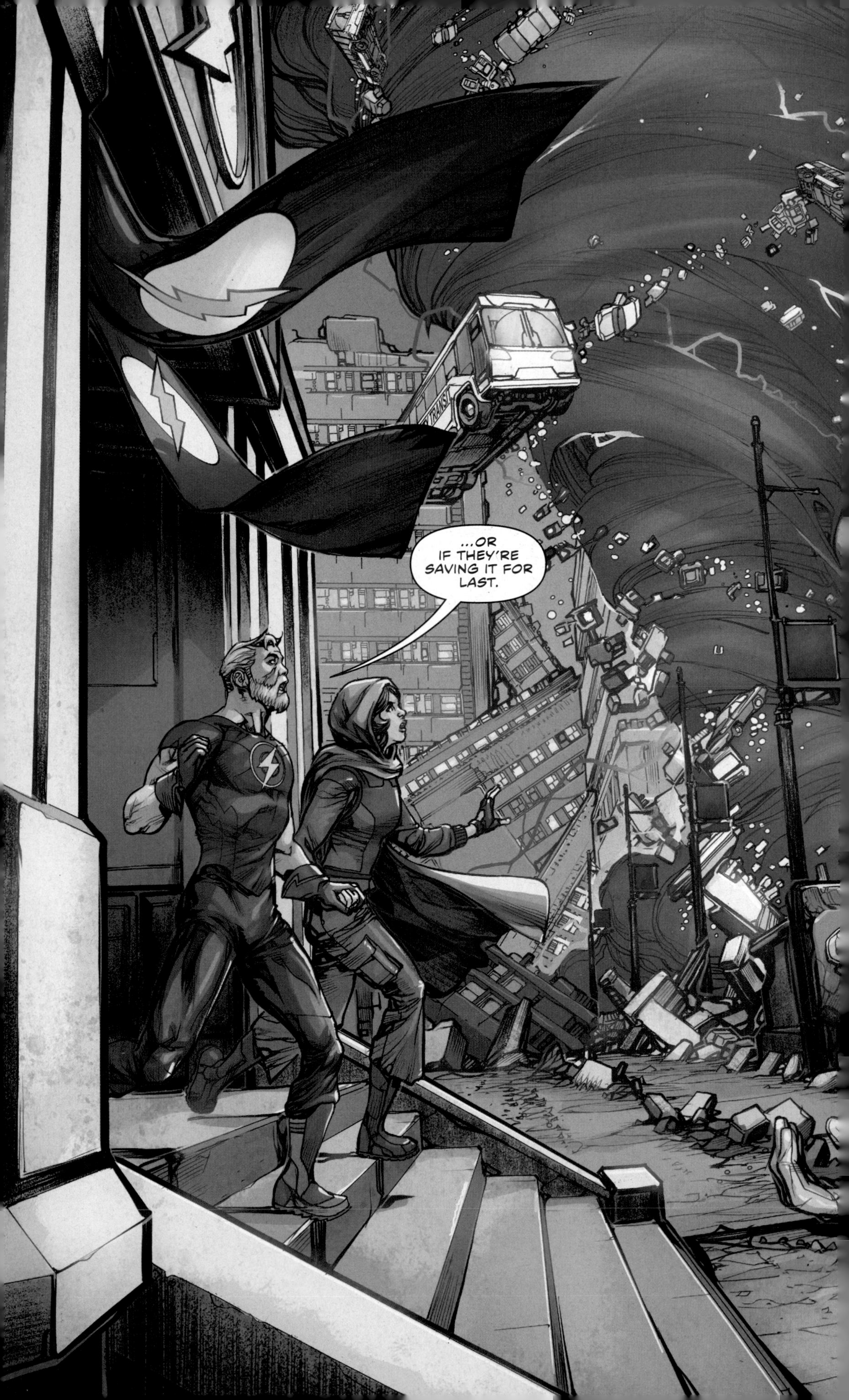
...OR IF THEY'RE SAVING IT FOR LAST.

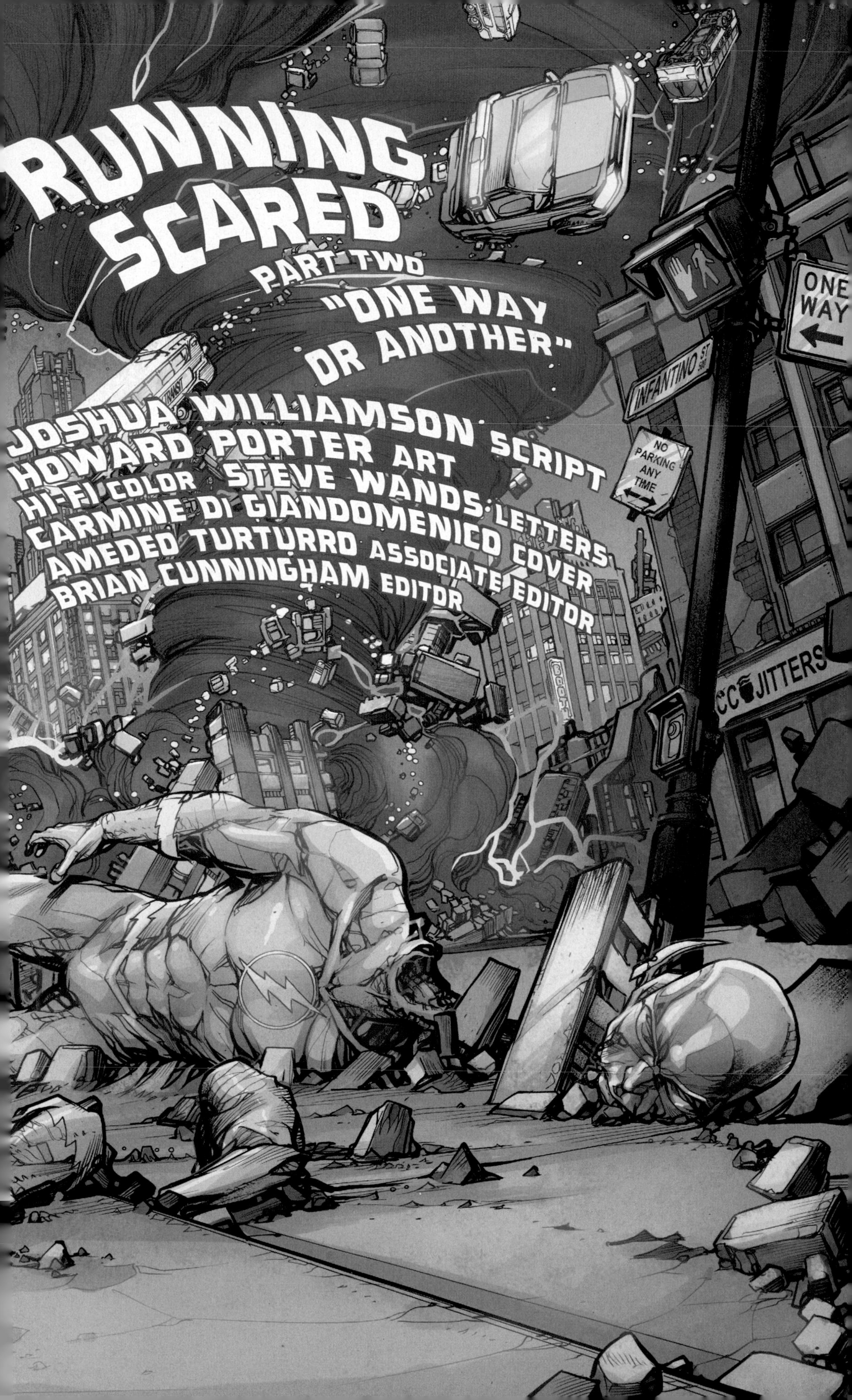
RUNNING SCARED
PART TWO
"ONE WAY OR ANOTHER"
JOSHUA WILLIAMSON SCRIPT
HOWARD PORTER ART
HI-FI COLOR STEVE WANDS LETTERS
CARMINE DI GIANDOMENICO COVER
AMEDEO TURTURRO ASSOCIATE EDITOR
BRIAN CUNNINGHAM EDITOR
ONE WAY
INFANTINO ST
NO PARKING ANY TIME
JITTERS

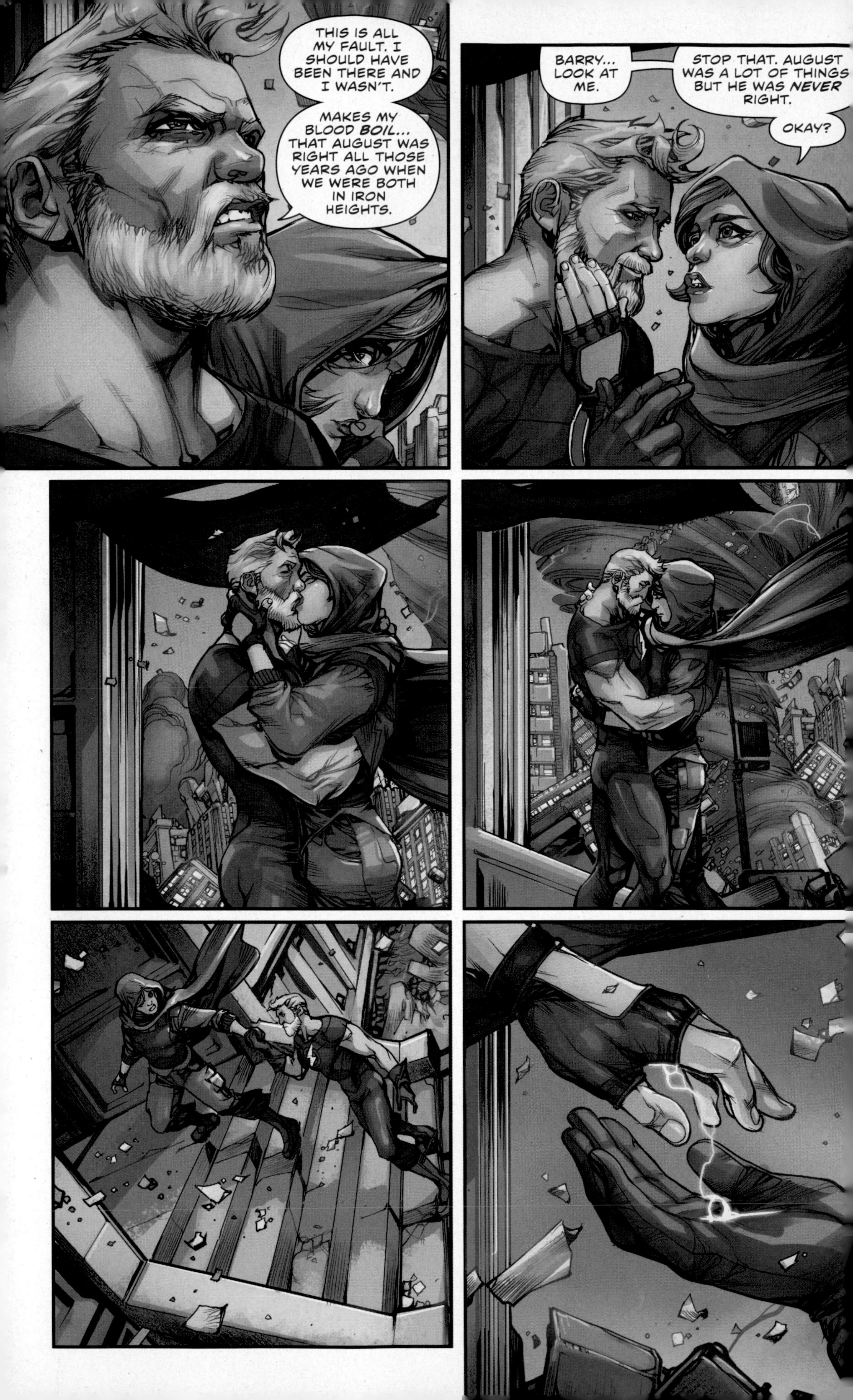
THIS IS ALL MY FAULT. I SHOULD HAVE BEEN THERE AND I WASN'T.
MAKES MY BLOOD BOIL... THAT AUGUST WAS RIGHT ALL THOSE YEARS AGO WHEN WE WERE BOTH IN IRON HEIGHTS.
BARRY... LOOK AT ME.
STOP THAT. AUGUST WAS A LOT OF THINGS BUT HE WAS NEVER RIGHT.
OKAY?

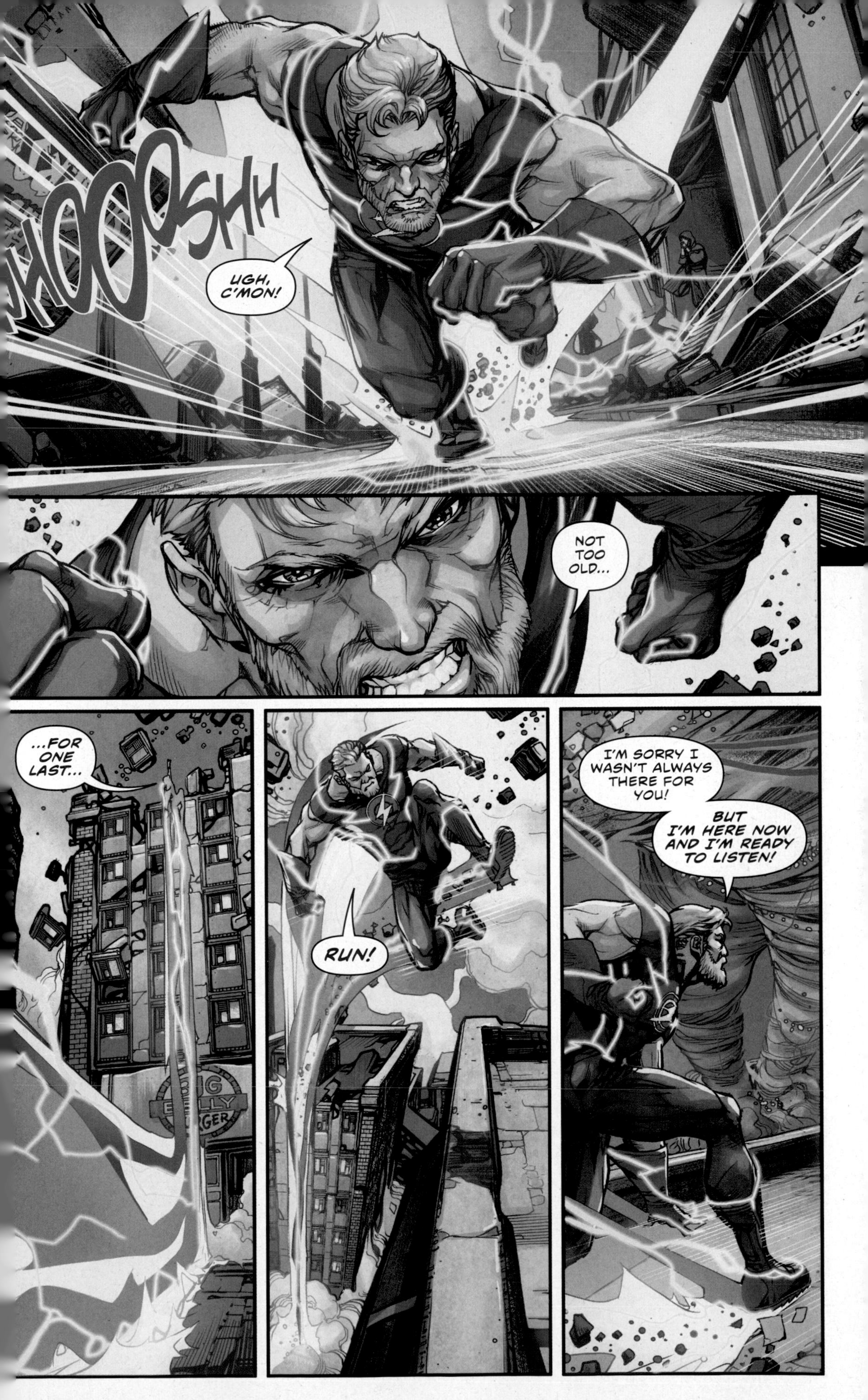
WHOOOOSHH
UGH, C'MON!
NOT TOO OLD...
...FOR ONE LAST...
RUN!
I'M SORRY I WASN'T ALWAYS THERE FOR YOU!
BUT I'M HERE NOW AND I'M READY TO LISTEN!

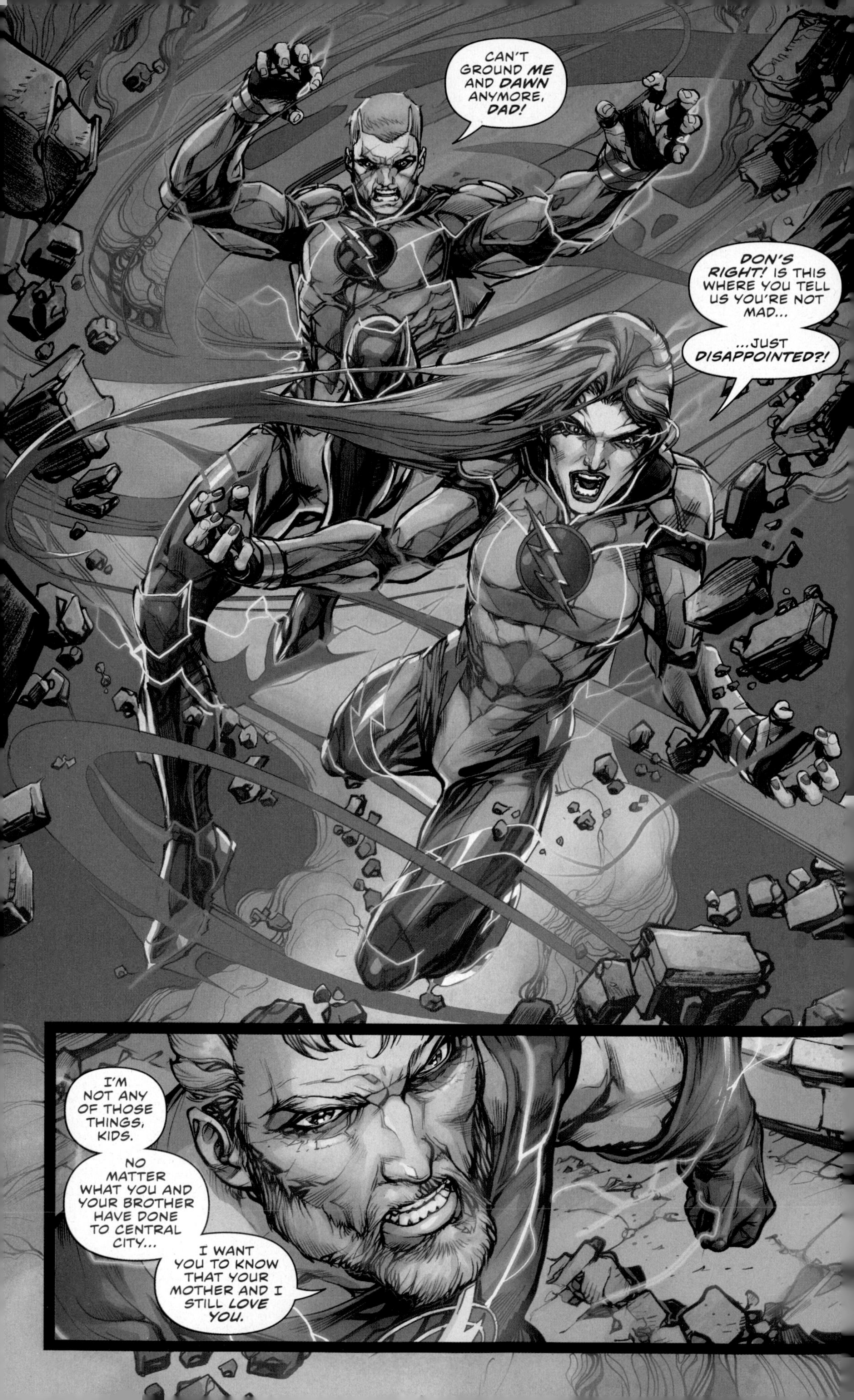
CAN'T GROUND *ME* AND *DAWN* ANYMORE, *DAD!*
DON'S RIGHT! IS THIS WHERE YOU TELL US YOU'RE NOT MAD...
...JUST *DISAPPOINTED?!*
I'M NOT ANY OF THOSE THINGS, KIDS.
NO MATTER WHAT YOU AND YOUR BROTHER HAVE DONE TO CENTRAL CITY...
I WANT YOU TO KNOW THAT YOUR MOTHER AND I STILL *LOVE YOU.*

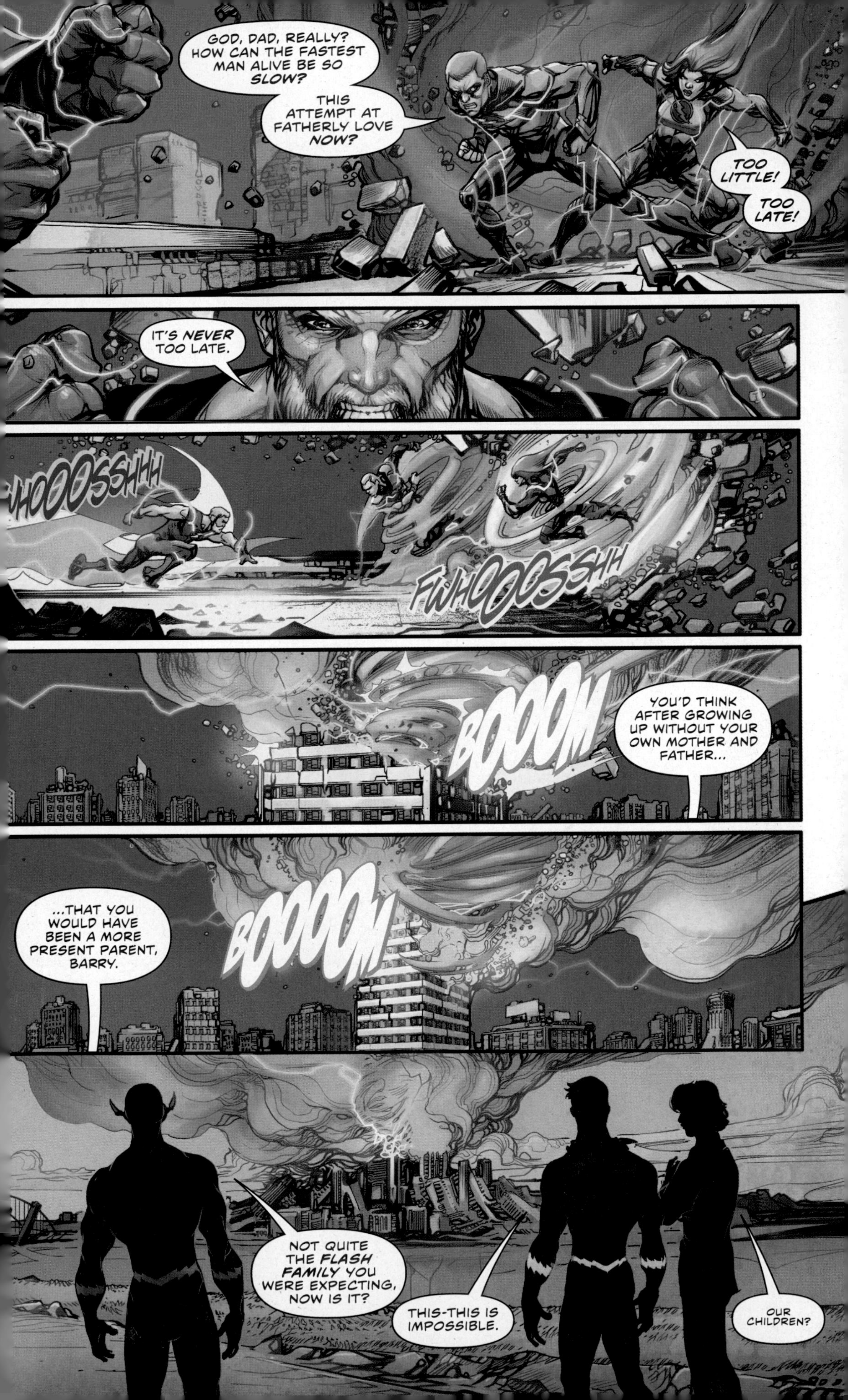
GOD, DAD, REALLY? HOW CAN THE FASTEST MAN ALIVE BE SO SLOW?
THIS ATTEMPT AT FATHERLY LOVE NOW?
TOO LITTLE!
TOO LATE!
IT'S NEVER TOO LATE.
FWHOOOSSHHH
FWHOOOSSHH
BOOOM
YOU'D THINK AFTER GROWING UP WITHOUT YOUR OWN MOTHER AND FATHER...
...THAT YOU WOULD HAVE BEEN A MORE PRESENT PARENT, BARRY.
BOOOOM
NOT QUITE THE FLASH FAMILY YOU WERE EXPECTING, NOW IS IT?
THIS-THIS IS IMPOSSIBLE.
OUR CHILDREN?

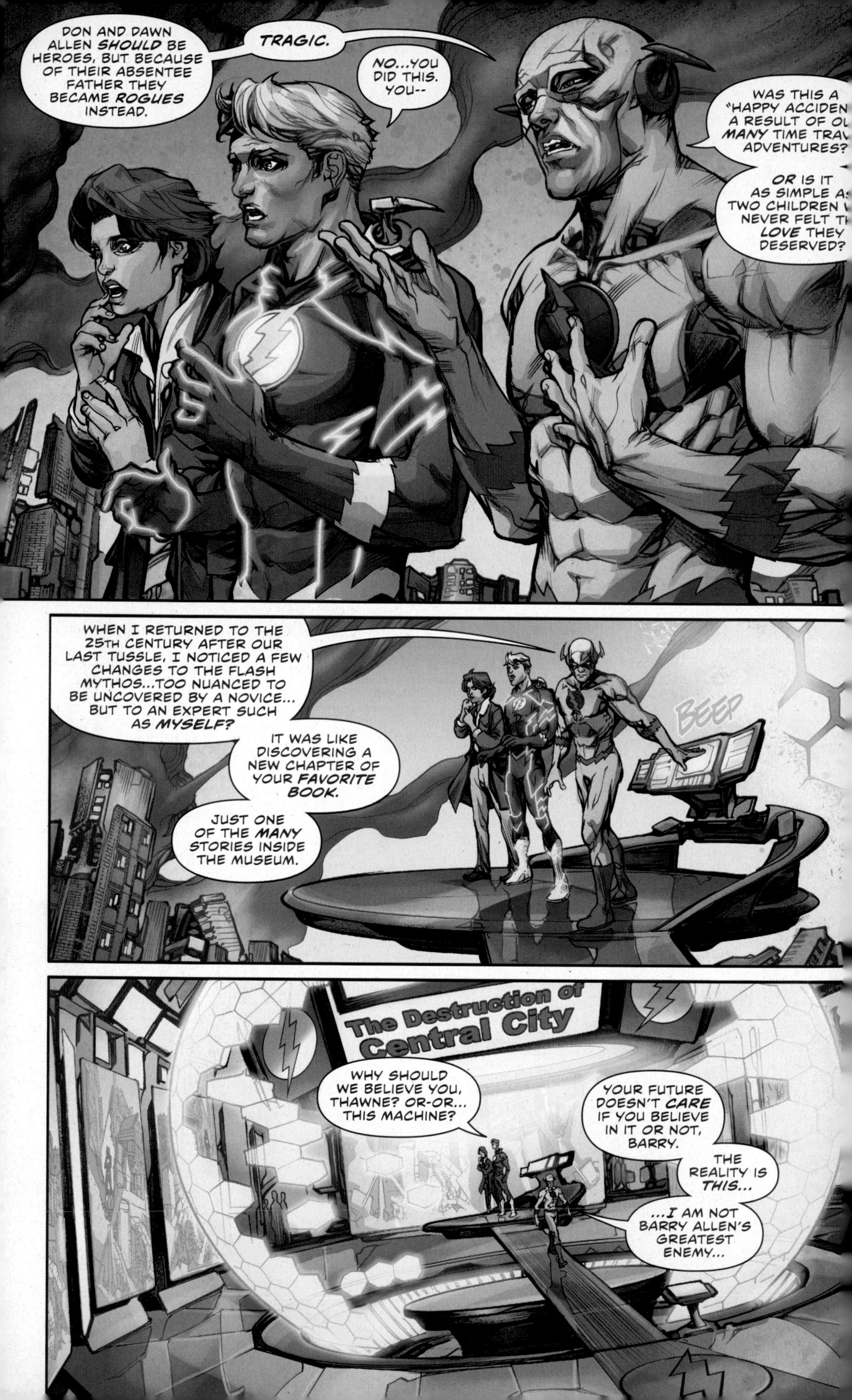
DON AND DAWN ALLEN SHOULD BE HEROES, BUT BECAUSE OF THEIR ABSENTEE FATHER THEY BECAME ROGUES INSTEAD.
TRAGIC.
NO...YOU DID THIS. YOU--
WAS THIS A "HAPPY ACCIDEN A RESULT OF OU MANY TIME TRAV ADVENTURES?
OR IS IT AS SIMPLE A TWO CHILDREN W NEVER FELT TH LOVE THEY DESERVED?
WHEN I RETURNED TO THE 25TH CENTURY AFTER OUR LAST TUSSLE, I NOTICED A FEW CHANGES TO THE FLASH MYTHOS...TOO NUANCED TO BE UNCOVERED BY A NOVICE... BUT TO AN EXPERT SUCH AS MYSELF?
IT WAS LIKE DISCOVERING A NEW CHAPTER OF YOUR FAVORITE BOOK.
JUST ONE OF THE MANY STORIES INSIDE THE MUSEUM.
BEEP
The Destruction of Central City
WHY SHOULD WE BELIEVE YOU, THAWNE? OR-OR... THIS MACHINE?
YOUR FUTURE DOESN'T CARE IF YOU BELIEVE IN IT OR NOT, BARRY.
THE REALITY IS THIS...
...I AM NOT BARRY ALLEN'S GREATEST ENEMY...

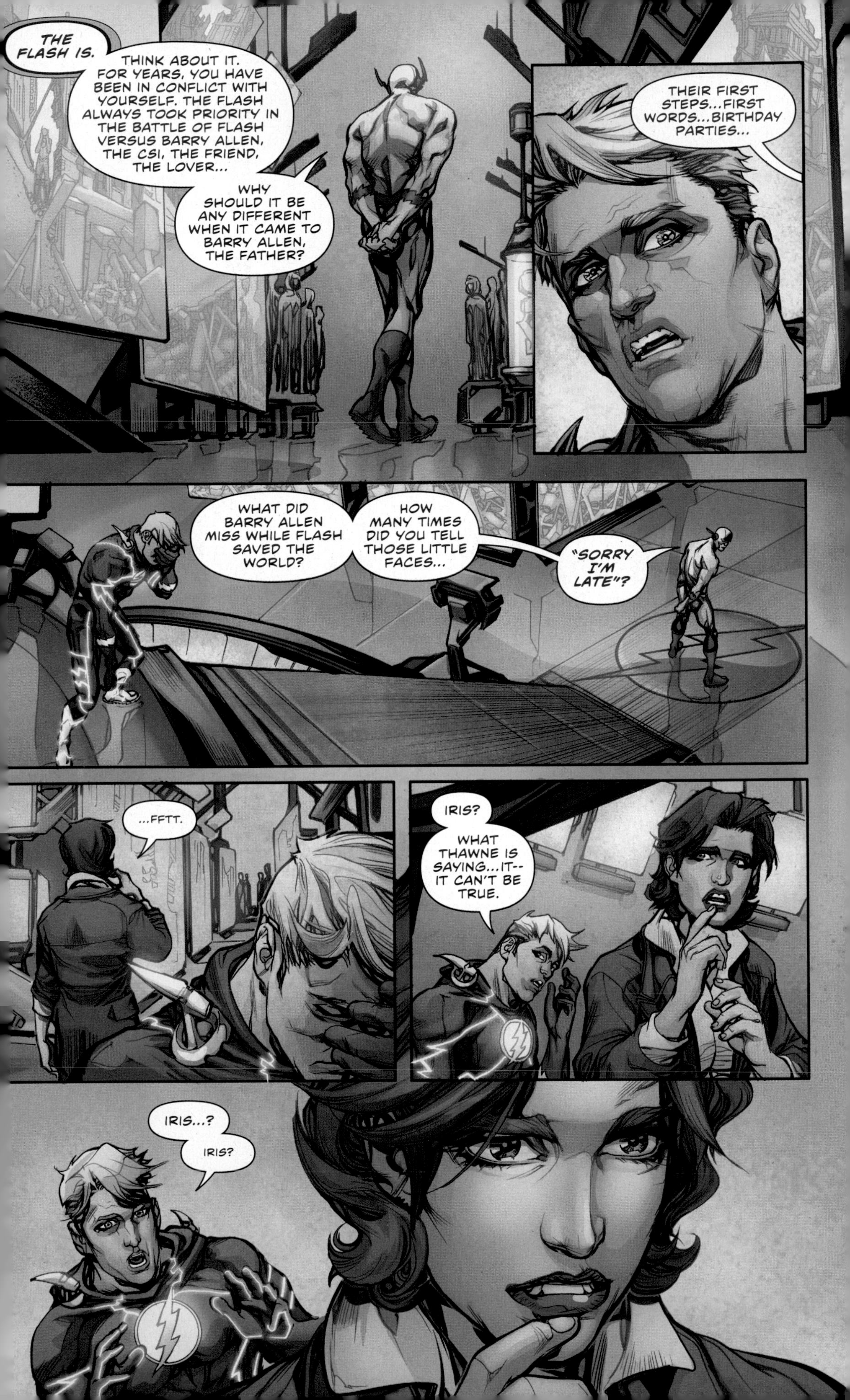
THE FLASH IS.
THINK ABOUT IT. FOR YEARS, YOU HAVE BEEN IN CONFLICT WITH YOURSELF. THE FLASH ALWAYS TOOK PRIORITY IN THE BATTLE OF FLASH VERSUS BARRY ALLEN, THE CSI, THE FRIEND, THE LOVER...
WHY SHOULD IT BE ANY DIFFERENT WHEN IT CAME TO BARRY ALLEN, THE FATHER?
THEIR FIRST STEPS...FIRST WORDS...BIRTHDAY PARTIES...
WHAT DID BARRY ALLEN MISS WHILE FLASH SAVED THE WORLD?
HOW MANY TIMES DID YOU TELL THOSE LITTLE FACES...
"SORRY I'M LATE"?
...FFTT.
IRIS?
WHAT THAWNE IS SAYING...IT-- IT CAN'T BE TRUE.
IRIS...?
IRIS?

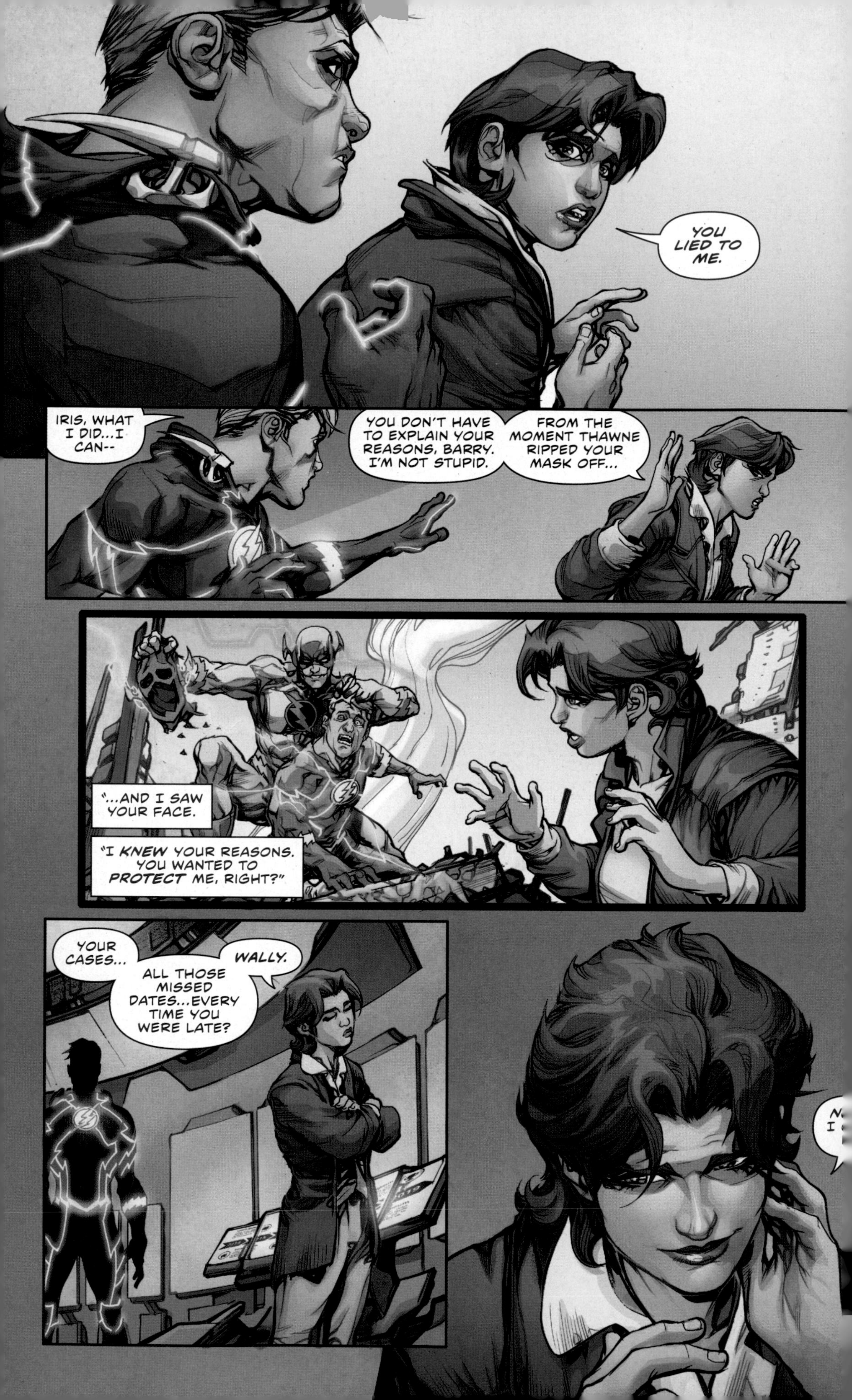
YOU LIED TO ME.
IRIS, WHAT I DID...I CAN--
YOU DON'T HAVE TO EXPLAIN YOUR REASONS, BARRY. I'M NOT STUPID.
FROM THE MOMENT THAWNE RIPPED YOUR MASK OFF...
"...AND I SAW YOUR FACE.
"I KNEW YOUR REASONS. YOU WANTED TO PROTECT ME, RIGHT?"
YOUR CASES...
WALLY.
ALL THOSE MISSED DATES...EVERY TIME YOU WERE LATE?

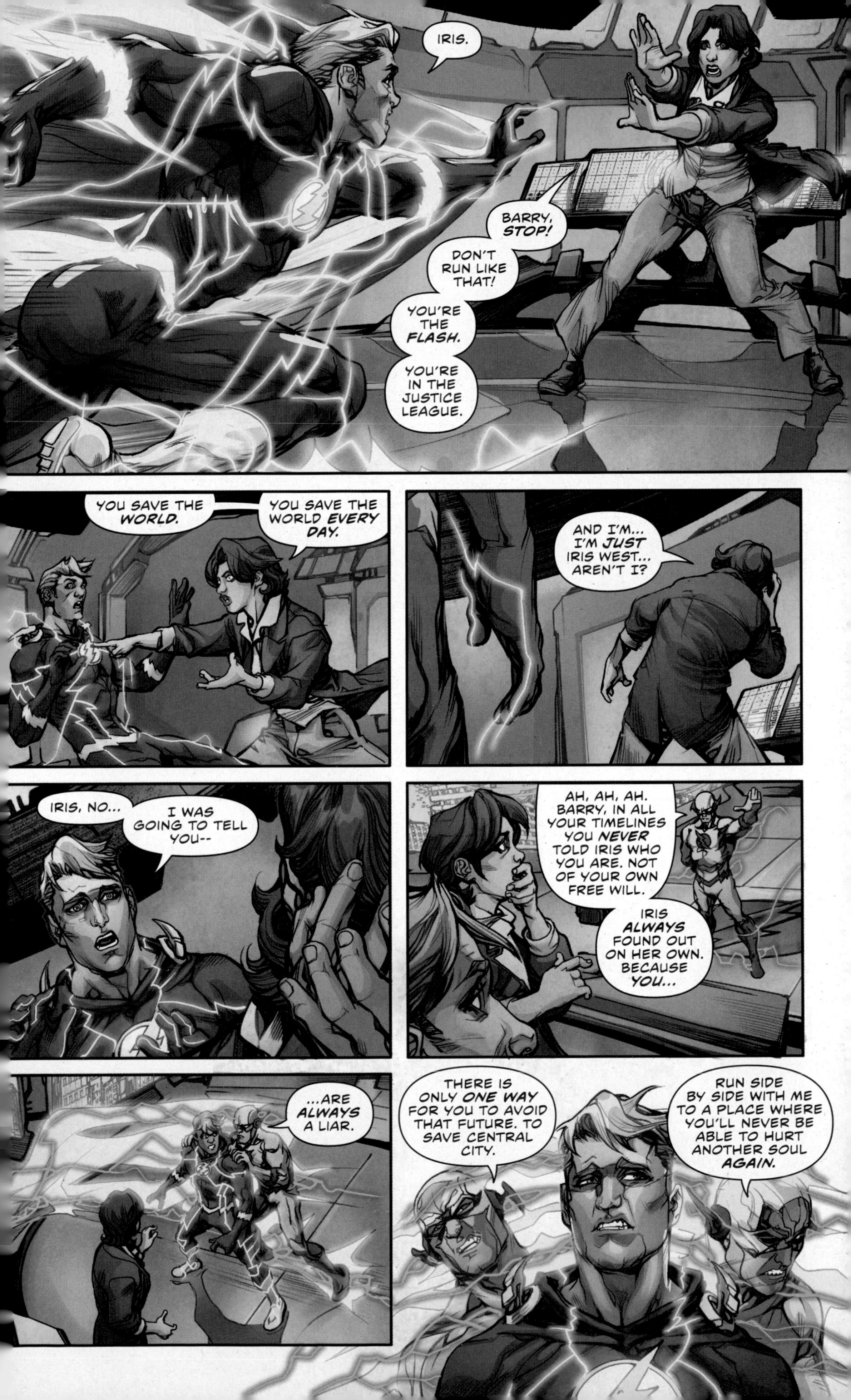
IRIS.
BARRY, STOP!
DON'T RUN LIKE THAT!
YOU'RE THE FLASH.
YOU'RE IN THE JUSTICE LEAGUE.
YOU SAVE THE WORLD.
YOU SAVE THE WORLD EVERY DAY.
AND I'M... I'M JUST IRIS WEST... AREN'T I?
IRIS, NO...
I WAS GOING TO TELL YOU--
AH, AH, AH. BARRY, IN ALL YOUR TIMELINES YOU NEVER TOLD IRIS WHO YOU ARE. NOT OF YOUR OWN FREE WILL.
IRIS ALWAYS FOUND OUT ON HER OWN. BECAUSE YOU...
...ARE ALWAYS A LIAR.
THERE IS ONLY ONE WAY FOR YOU TO AVOID THAT FUTURE. TO SAVE CENTRAL CITY.
RUN SIDE BY SIDE WITH ME TO A PLACE WHERE YOU'LL NEVER BE ABLE TO HURT ANOTHER SOUL AGAIN.

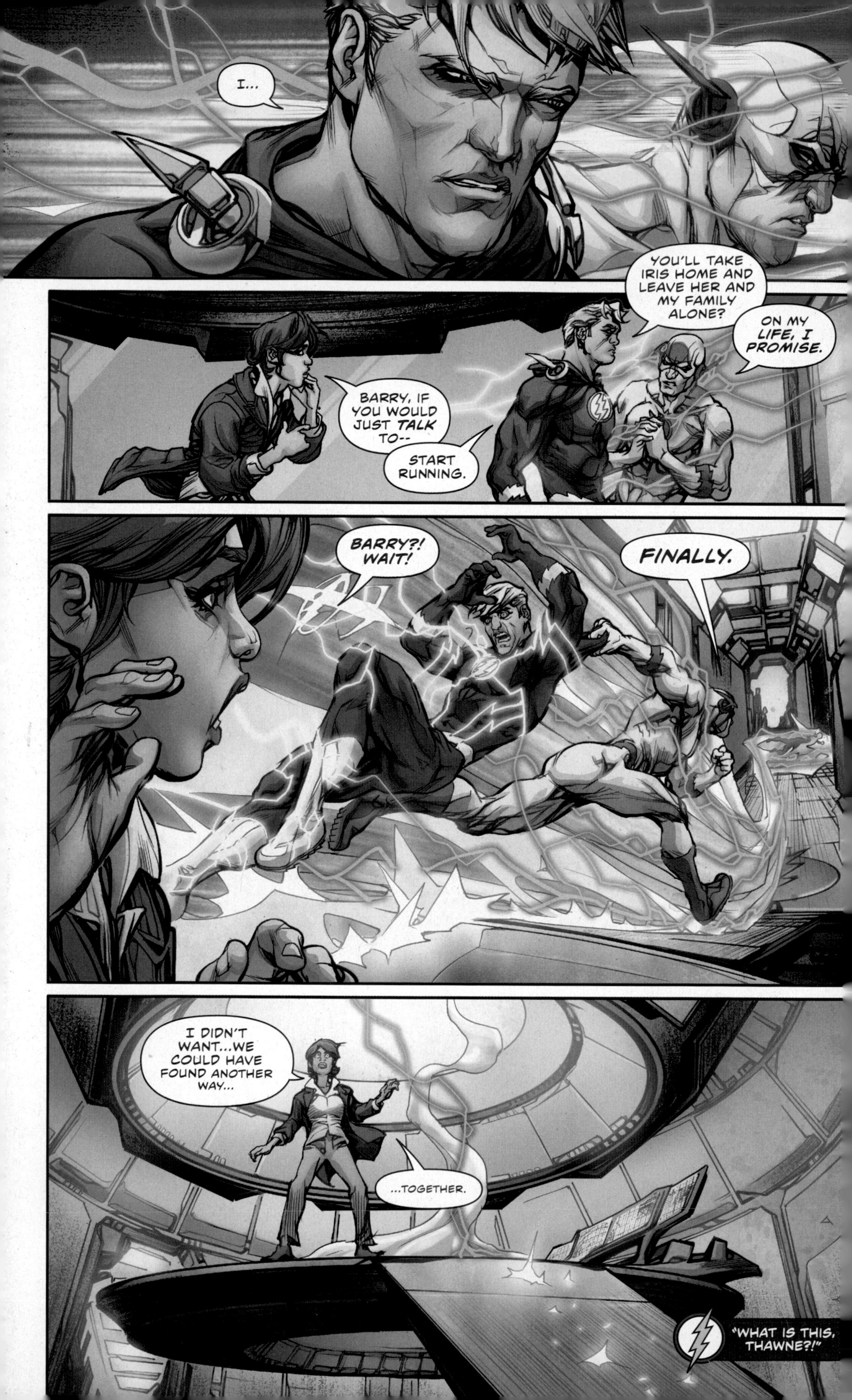
I...
YOU'LL TAKE IRIS HOME AND LEAVE HER AND MY FAMILY ALONE?
ON MY LIFE, I PROMISE.
BARRY, IF YOU WOULD JUST TALK TO--
START RUNNING.
BARRY?! WAIT!
FINALLY.
I DIDN'T WANT...WE COULD HAVE FOUND ANOTHER WAY...
...TOGETHER.
"WHAT IS THIS, THAWNE?!"

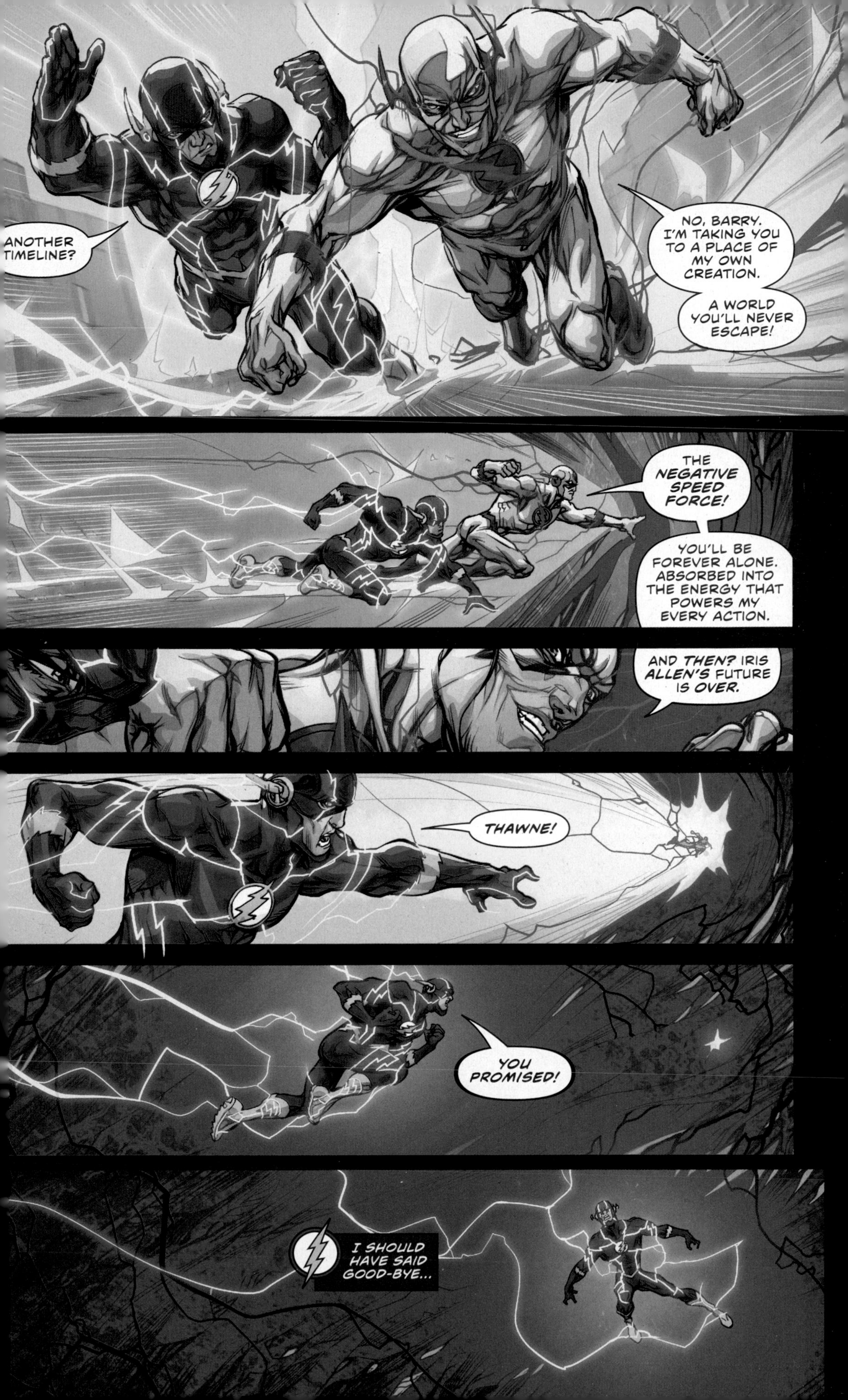
ANOTHER TIMELINE?
NO, BARRY. I'M TAKING YOU TO A PLACE OF MY OWN CREATION.
A WORLD YOU'LL NEVER ESCAPE!
THE NEGATIVE SPEED FORCE!
YOU'LL BE FOREVER ALONE. ABSORBED INTO THE ENERGY THAT POWERS MY EVERY ACTION.
AND THEN? IRIS ALLEN'S FUTURE IS OVER.
THAWNE!
YOU PROMISED!
I SHOULD HAVE SAID GOOD-BYE...

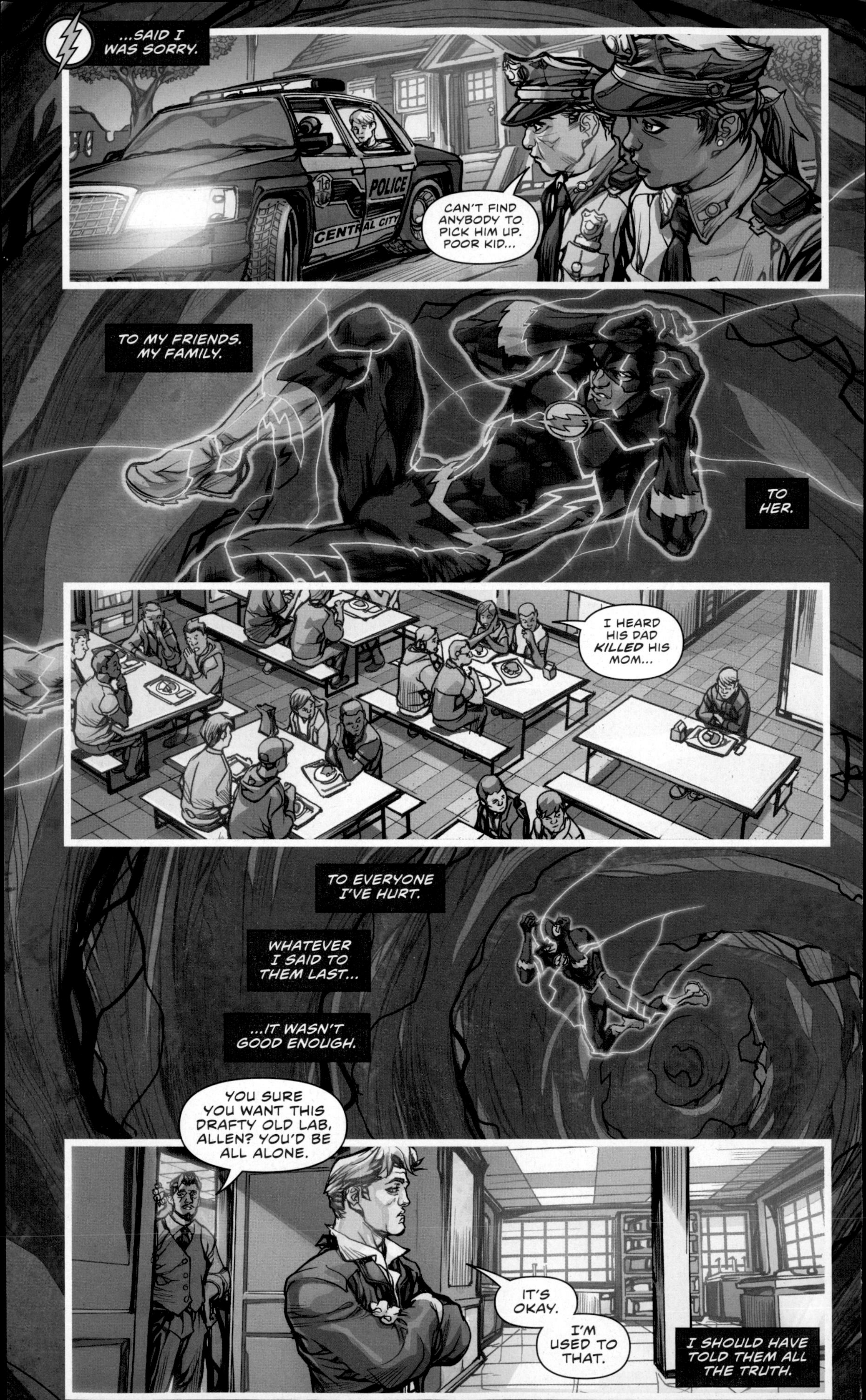

...SAID I WAS SORRY.
CAN'T FIND ANYBODY TO PICK HIM UP. POOR KID...
POLICE
CENTRAL CITY
TO MY FRIENDS. MY FAMILY.
TO HER.
I HEARD HIS DAD KILLED HIS MOM...
TO EVERYONE I'VE HURT.
WHATEVER I SAID TO THEM LAST...
...IT WASN'T GOOD ENOUGH.
YOU SURE YOU WANT THIS DRAFTY OLD LAB, ALLEN? YOU'D BE ALL ALONE.
IT'S OKAY.
I'M USED TO THAT.
I SHOULD HAVE TOLD THEM ALL THE TRUTH.

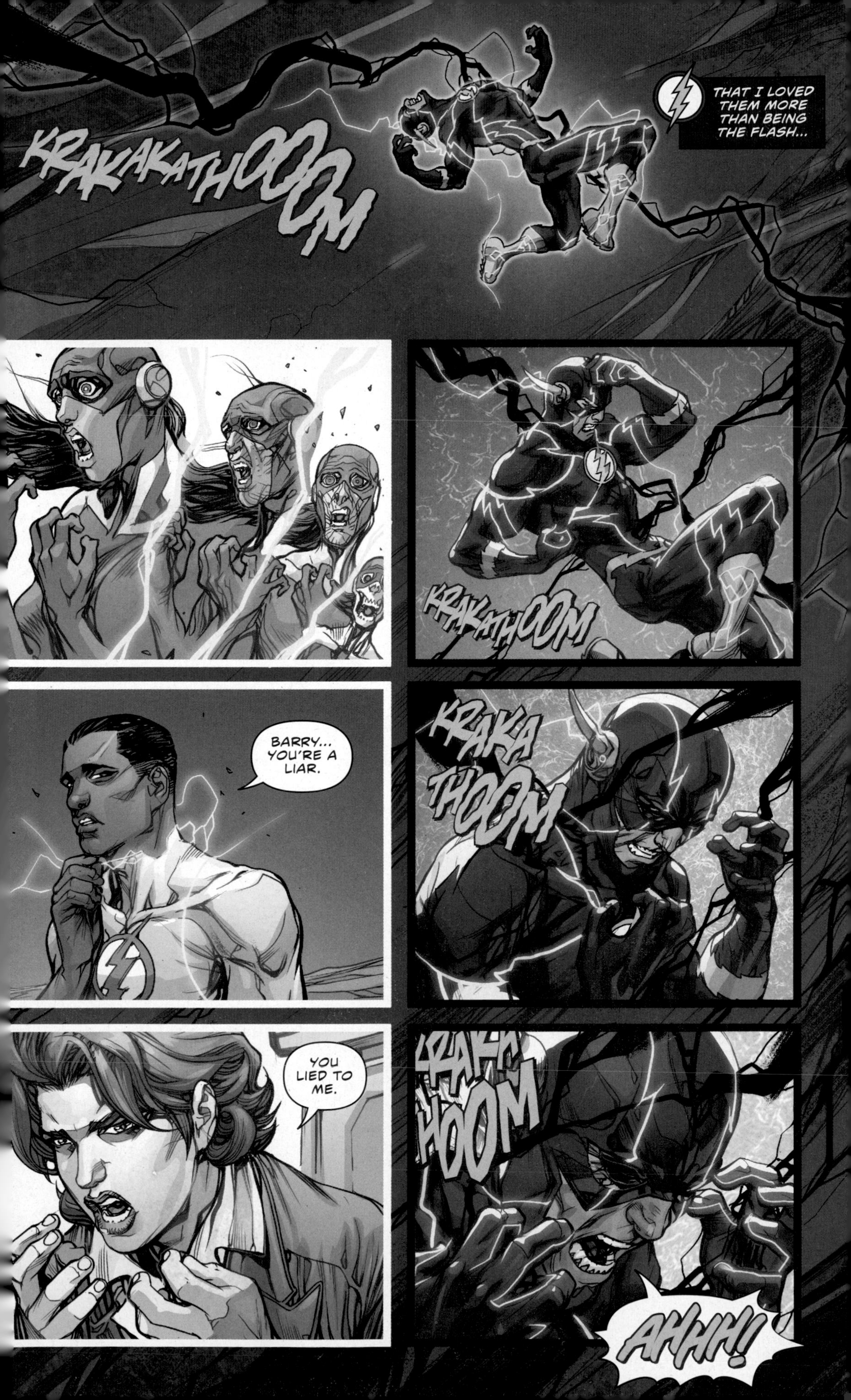
KRAKAKATHOOOOM
THAT I LOVED THEM MORE THAN BEING THE FLASH...
KRAKATHOOM
BARRY... YOU'RE A LIAR.
KRAKA THOOM
YOU LIED TO ME.
AHHH!!

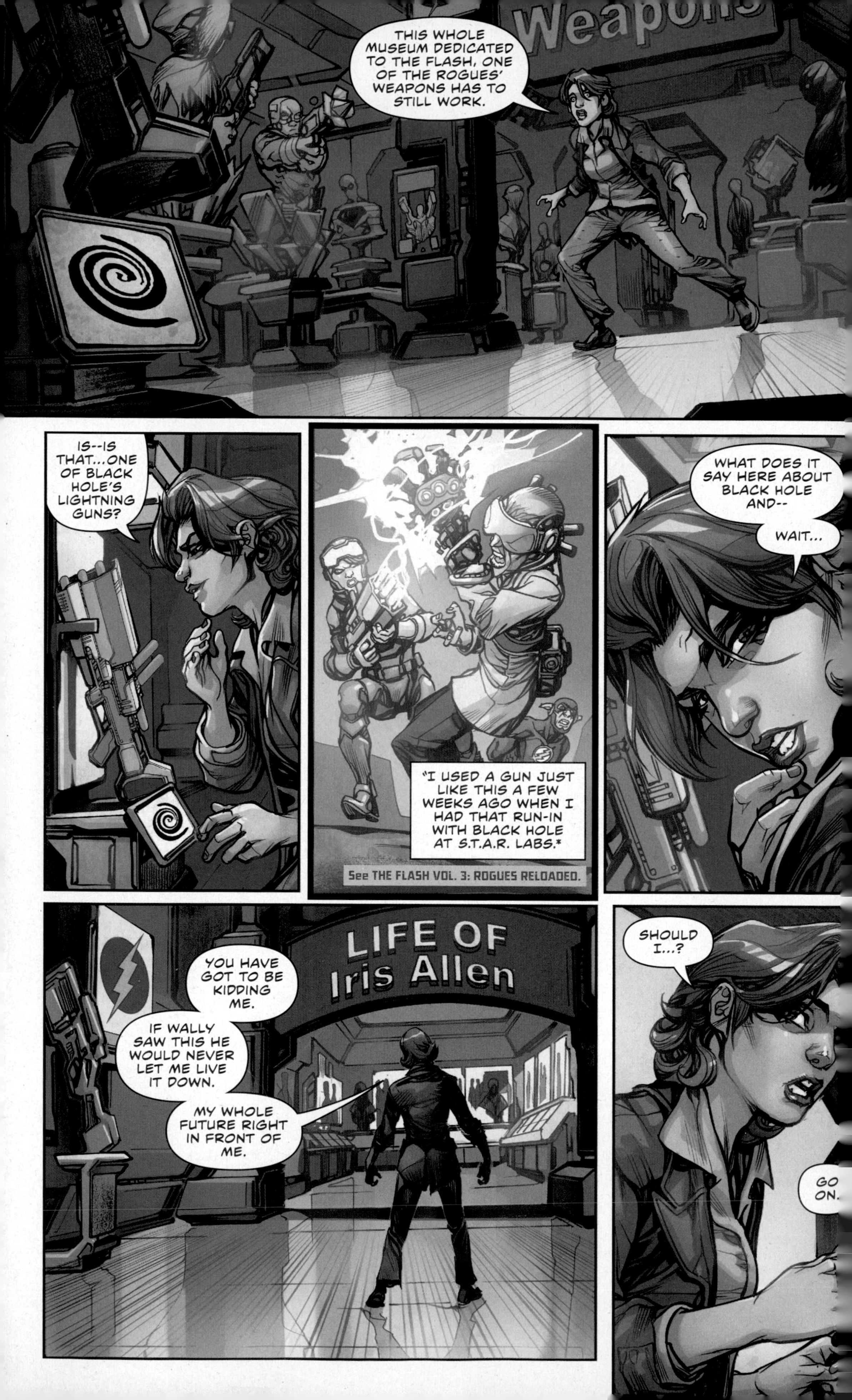
Weapons
THIS WHOLE MUSEUM DEDICATED TO THE FLASH, ONE OF THE ROGUES' WEAPONS HAS TO STILL WORK.
IS--IS THAT...ONE OF BLACK HOLE'S LIGHTNING GUNS?
"I USED A GUN JUST LIKE THIS A FEW WEEKS AGO WHEN I HAD THAT RUN-IN WITH BLACK HOLE AT S.T.A.R. LABS.*
See THE FLASH VOL. 3: ROGUES RELOADED.
WHAT DOES IT SAY HERE ABOUT BLACK HOLE AND--
WAIT...
LIFE OF Iris Allen
YOU HAVE GOT TO BE KIDDING ME.
IF WALLY SAW THIS HE WOULD NEVER LET ME LIVE IT DOWN.
MY WHOLE FUTURE RIGHT IN FRONT OF ME.
SHOULD I...?
GO ON.

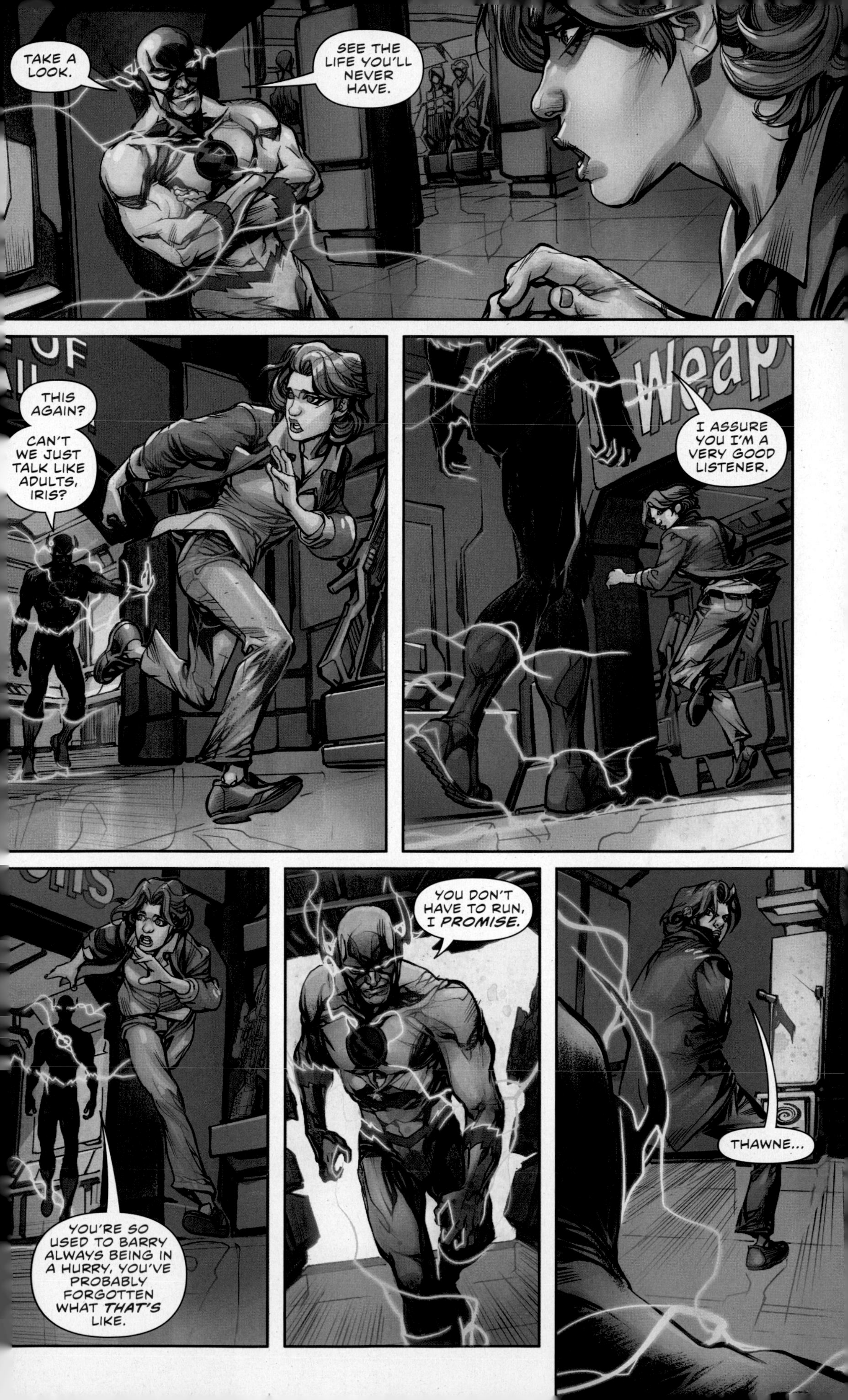
TAKE A LOOK.
SEE THE LIFE YOU'LL NEVER HAVE.
THIS AGAIN?
CAN'T WE JUST TALK LIKE ADULTS, IRIS?
I ASSURE YOU I'M A VERY GOOD LISTENER.
YOU'RE SO USED TO BARRY ALWAYS BEING IN A HURRY, YOU'VE PROBABLY FORGOTTEN WHAT *THAT'S* LIKE.
YOU DON'T HAVE TO RUN, I *PROMISE.*
THAWNE...

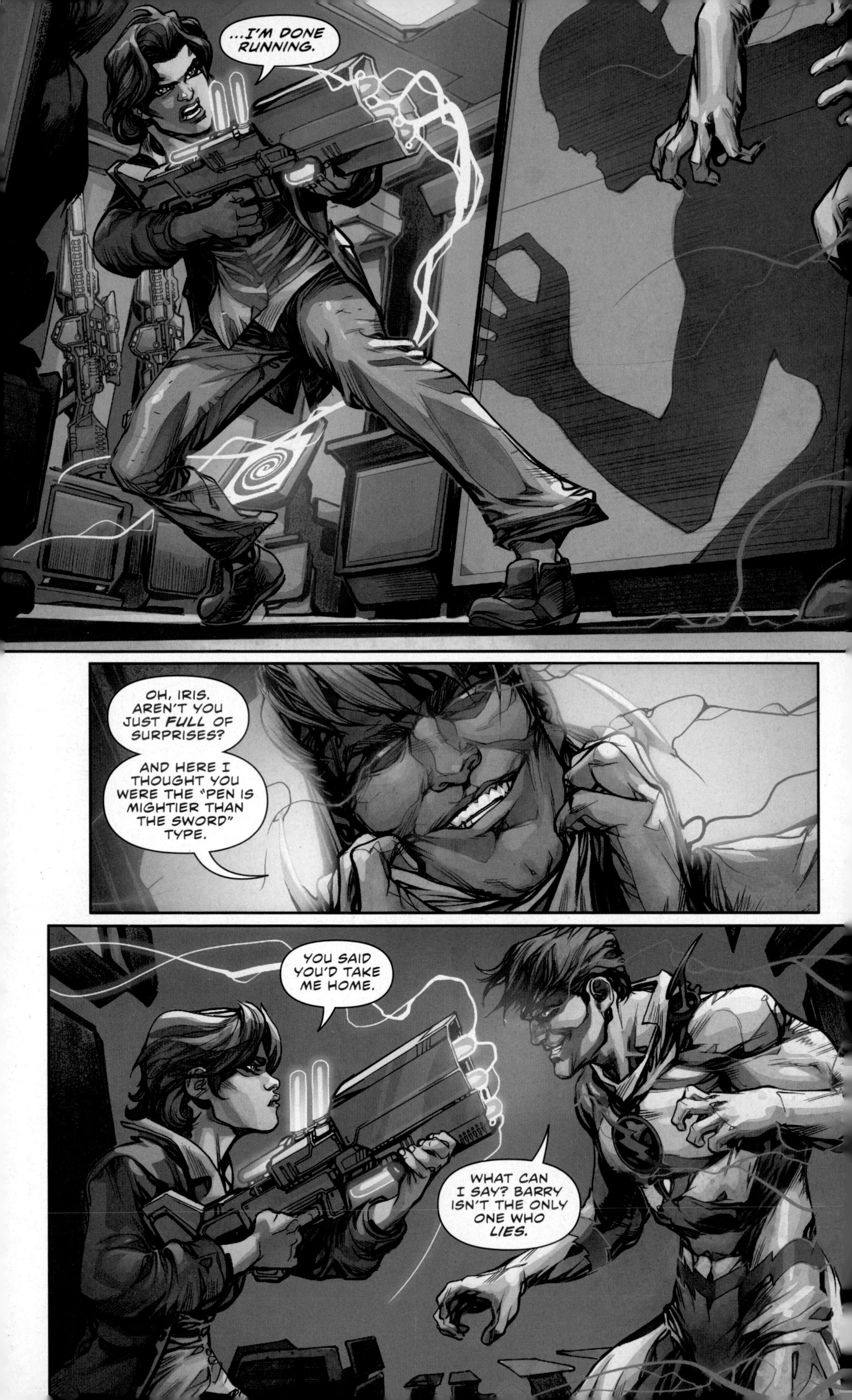
...I'M DONE RUNNING.
OH, IRIS. AREN'T YOU JUST FULL OF SURPRISES?
AND HERE I THOUGHT YOU WERE THE "PEN IS MIGHTIER THAN THE SWORD" TYPE.
YOU SAID YOU'D TAKE ME HOME.
WHAT CAN I SAY? BARRY ISN'T THE ONLY ONE WHO LIES.

BOOM

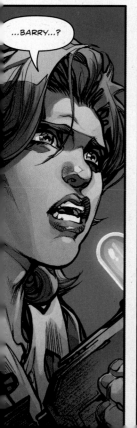

KRASH

Speed Force

...BARRY...?

IMPOSSIBLE.
HOW...?

Speed Force

FLASH?
YOU'RE...

...BEAUTIFUL.

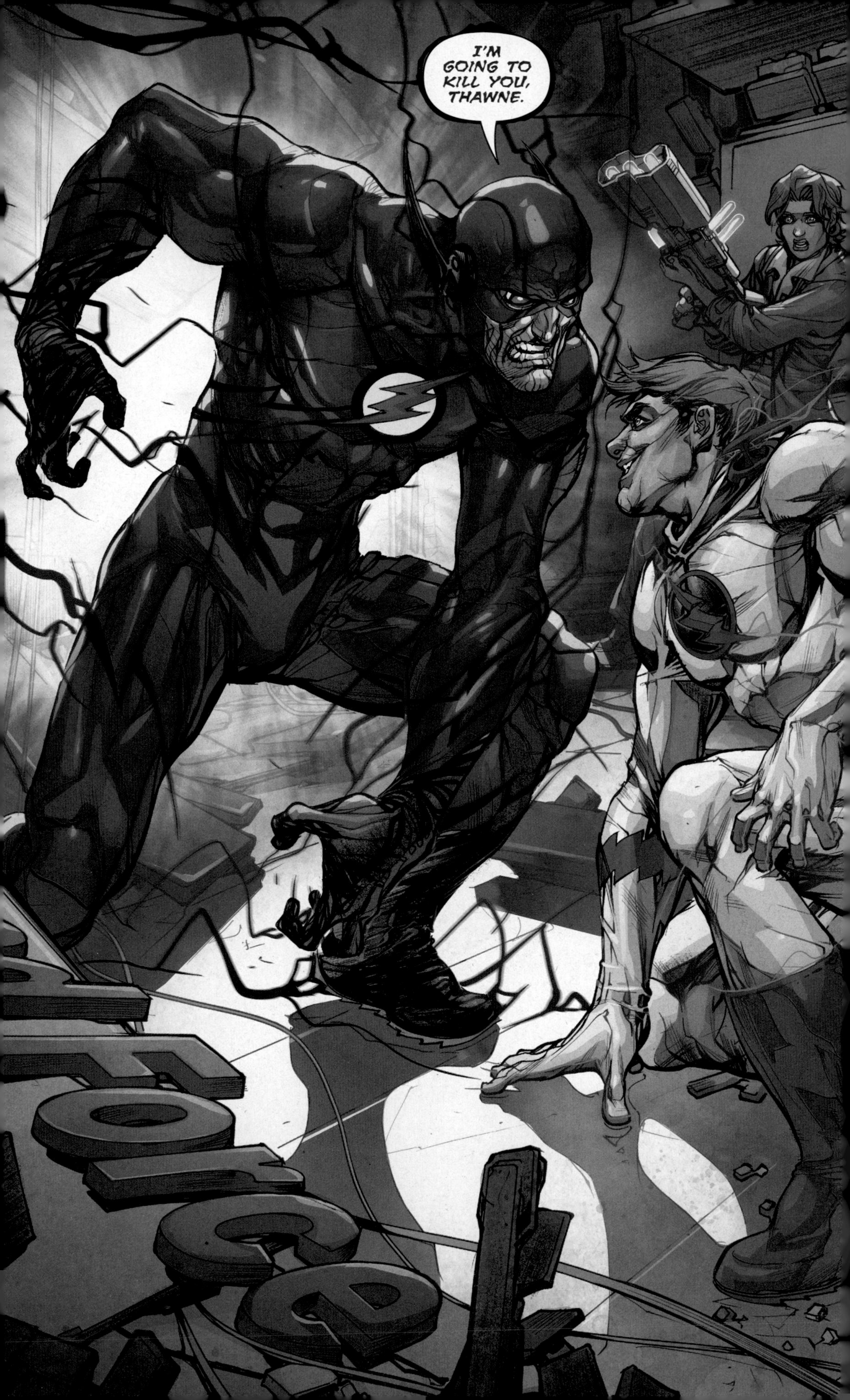
I'M GOING TO KILL YOU, THAWNE.

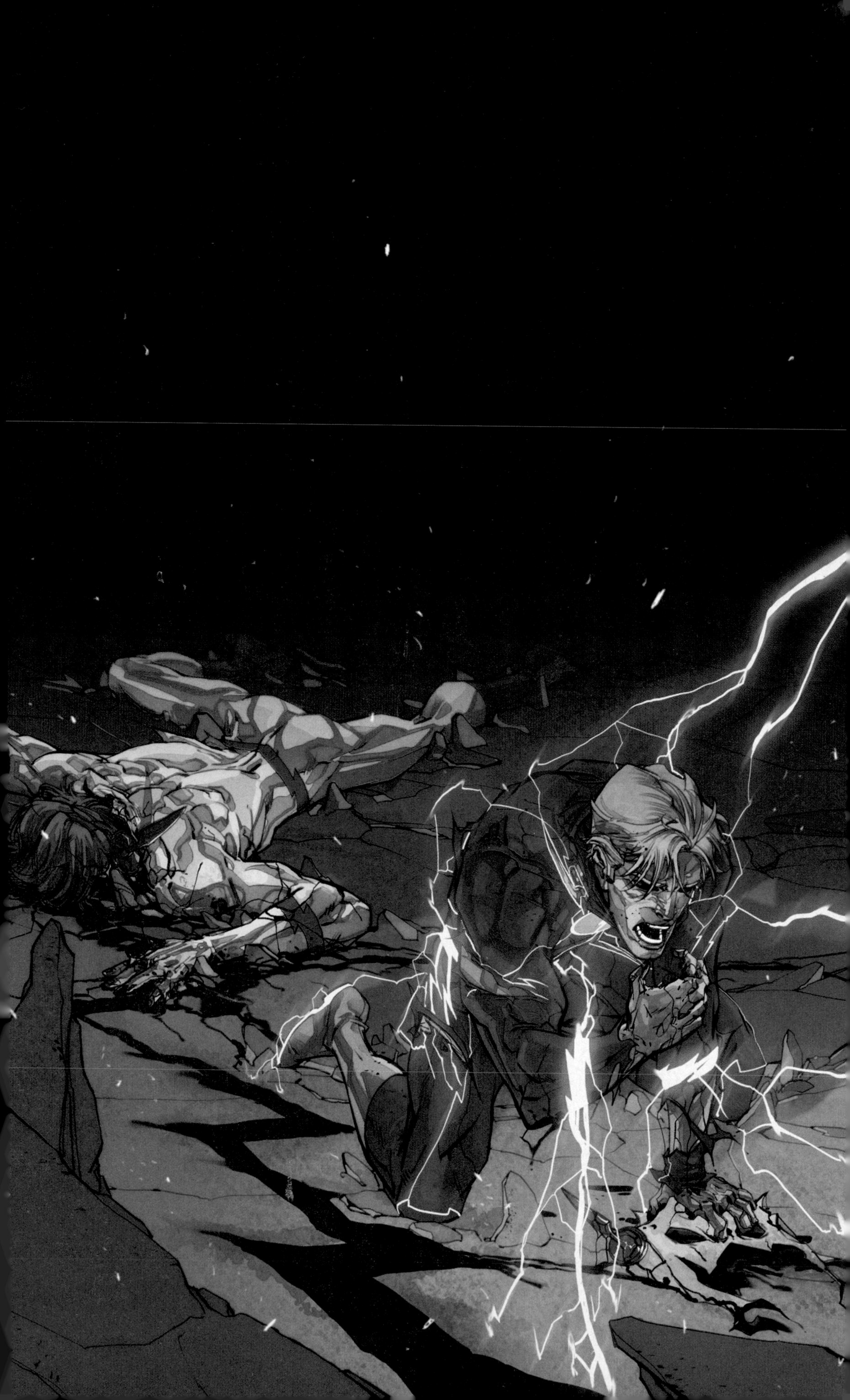

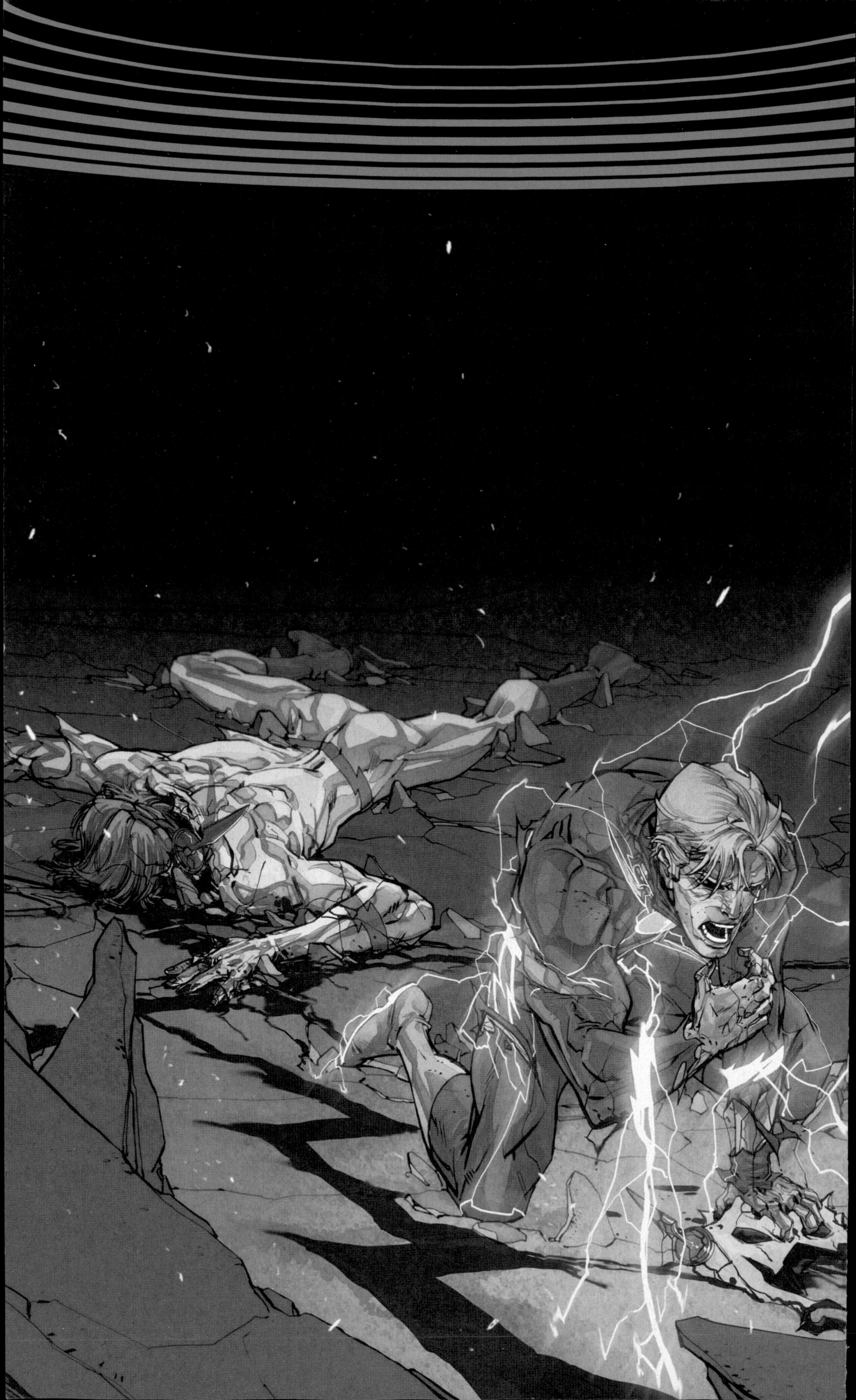

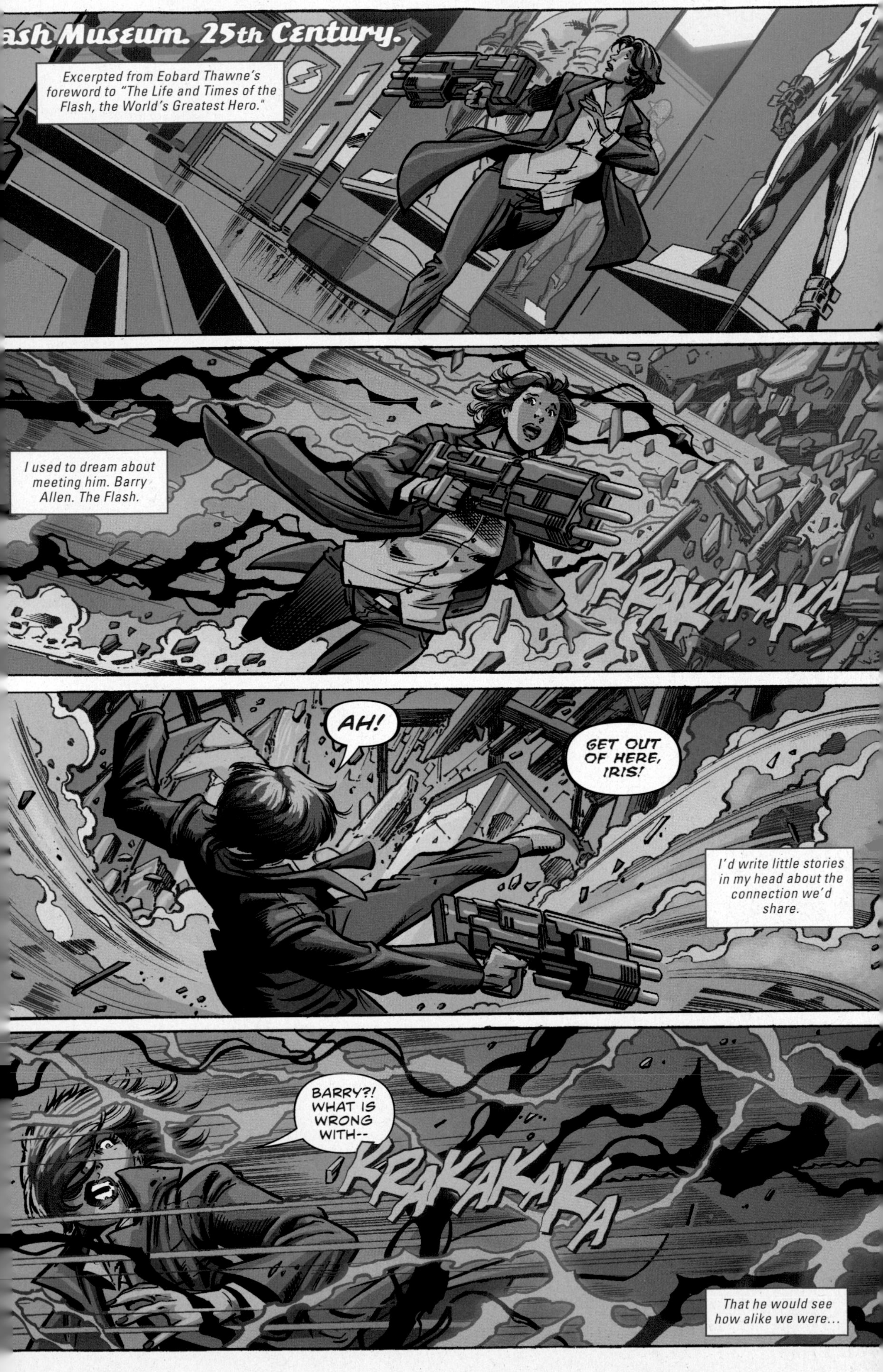
ash Museum. 25th Century.
Excerpted from Eobard Thawne's foreword to "The Life and Times of the Flash, the World's Greatest Hero."
I used to dream about meeting him. Barry Allen. The Flash.
KRAKAKAKA
AH!
GET OUT OF HERE, IRIS!
I'd write little stories in my head about the connection we'd share.
BARRY?! WHAT IS WRONG WITH--
KRAKAKAKAKA
That he would see how alike we were...

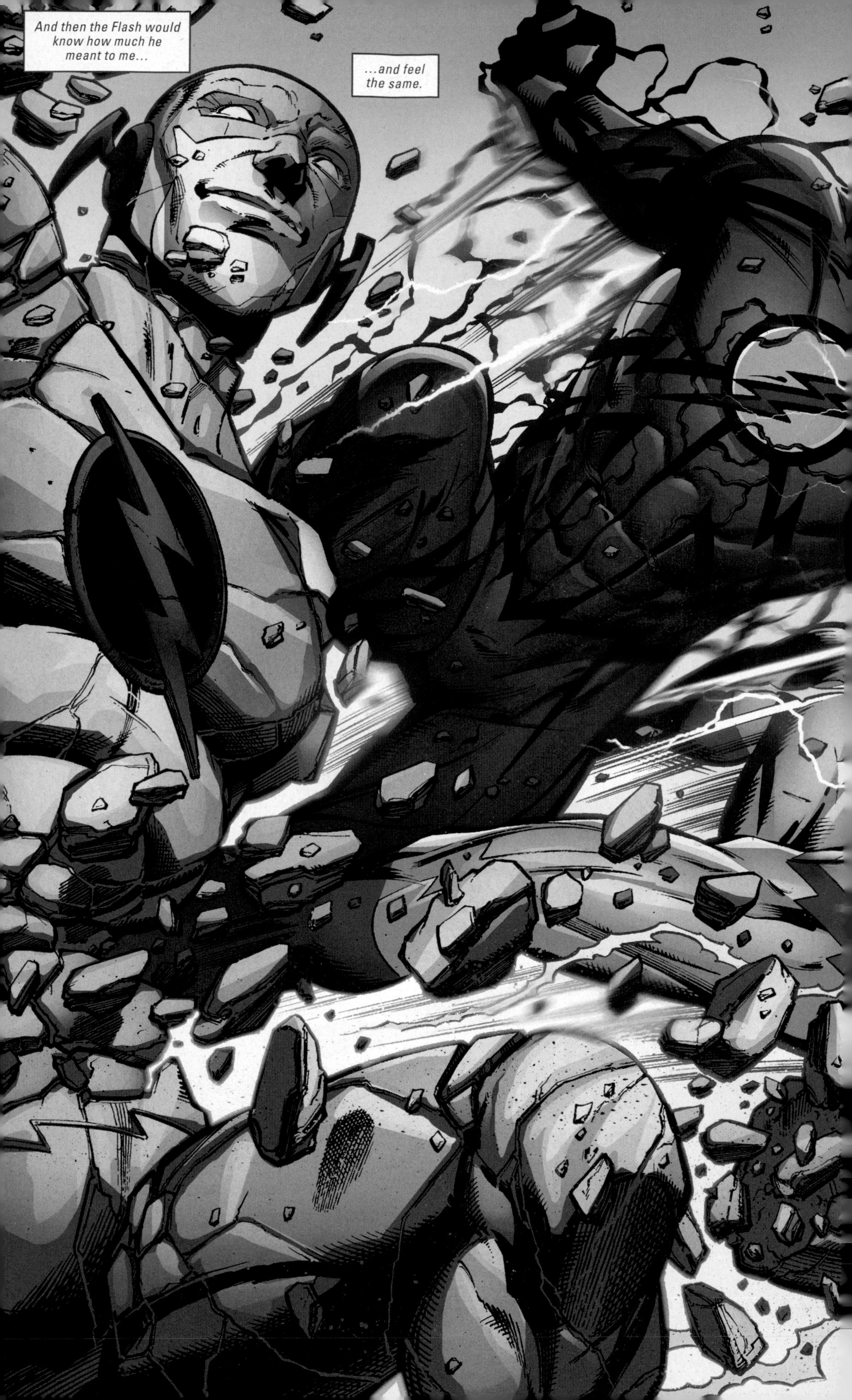
And then the Flash would know how much he meant to me...
...and feel the same.

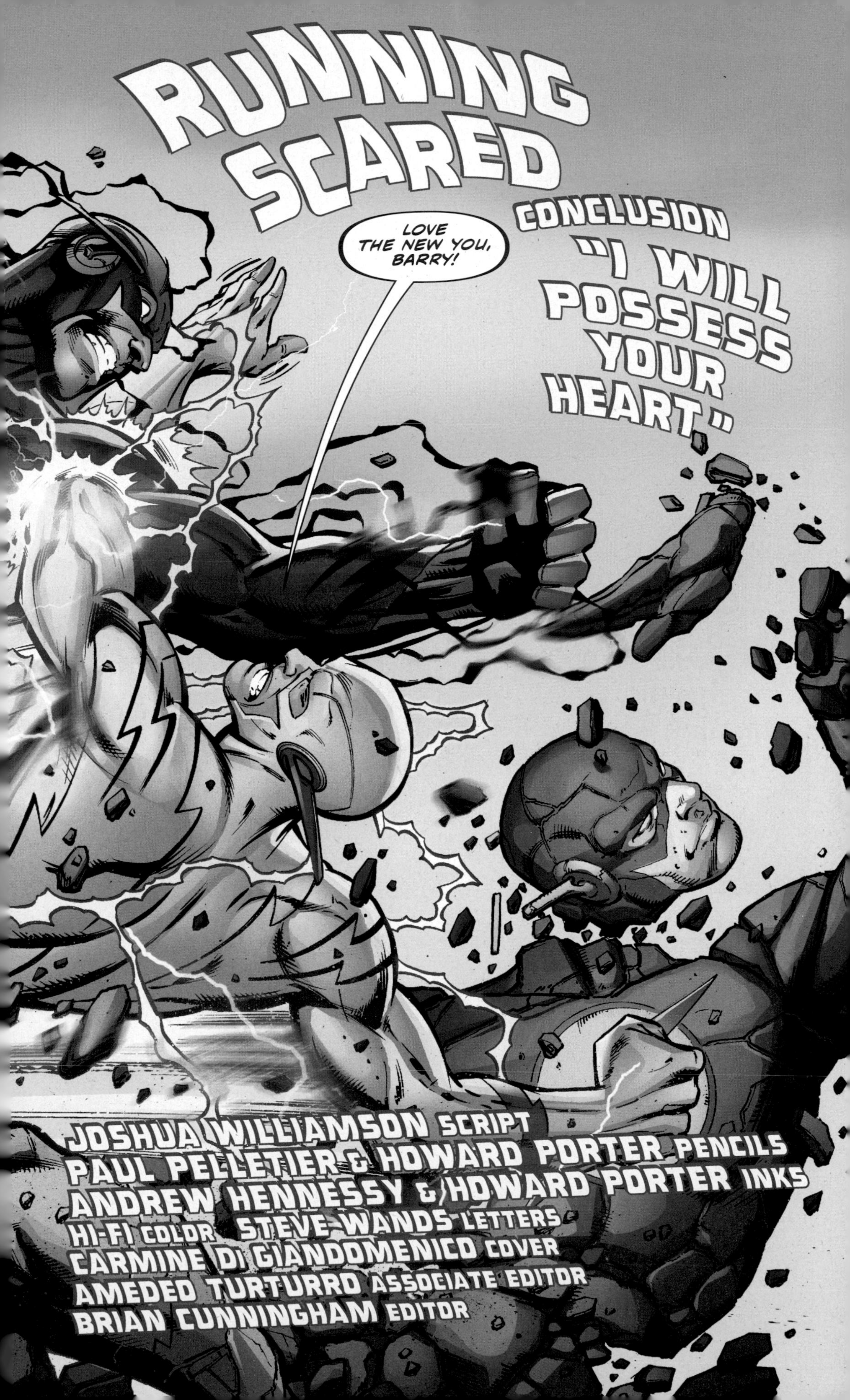
RUNNING SCARED
CONCLUSION
"I WILL POSSESS YOUR HEART."
LOVE THE NEW YOU, BARRY!
JOSHUA WILLIAMSON SCRIPT
PAUL PELLETIER & HOWARD PORTER PENCILS
ANDREW HENNESSY & HOWARD PORTER INKS
HI-FI COLOR STEVE WANDS LETTERS
CARMINE DI GIANDOMENICO COVER
AMEDED TURTURRO ASSOCIATE EDITOR
BRIAN CUNNINGHAM EDITOR

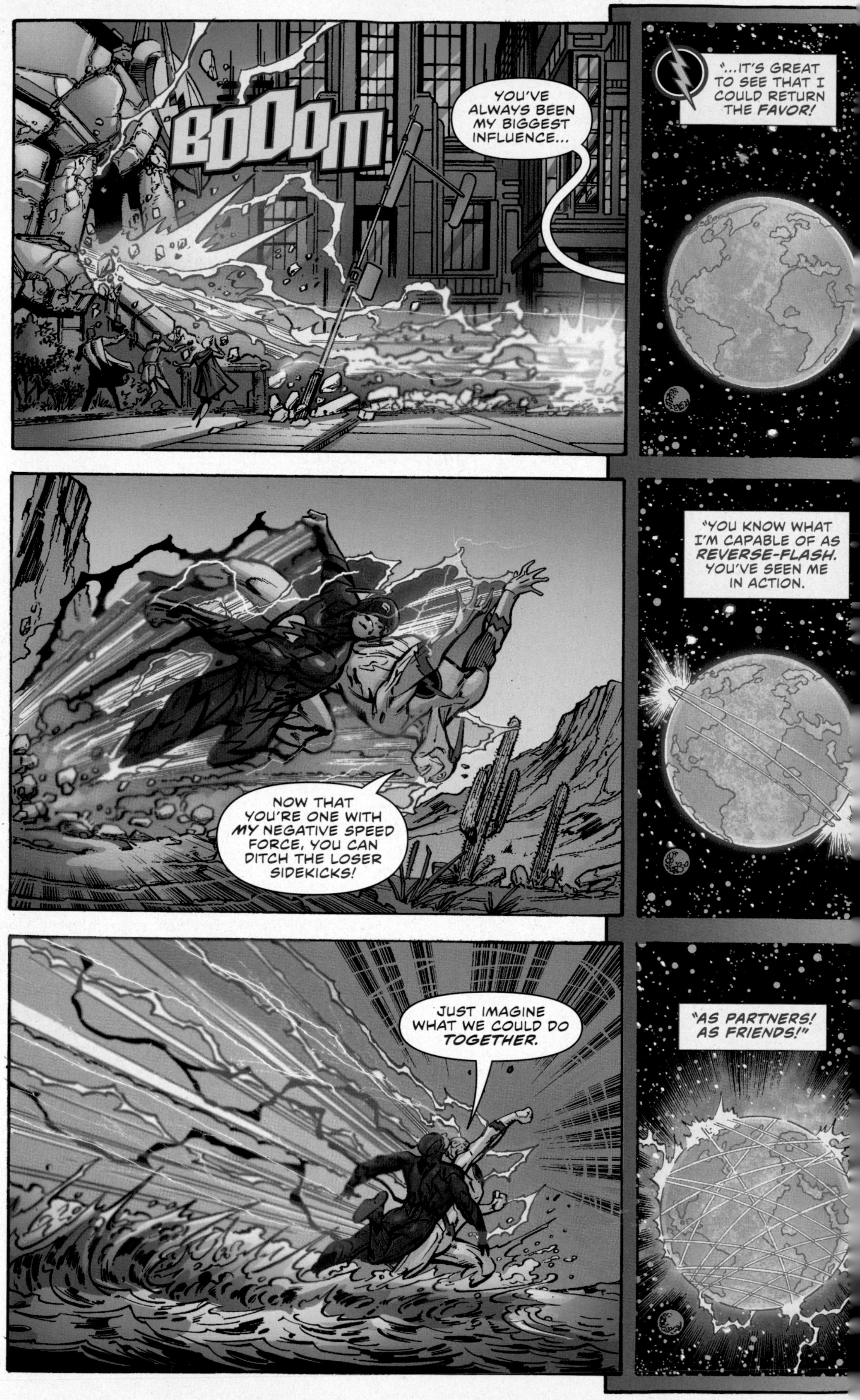
BOOOM
YOU'VE ALWAYS BEEN MY BIGGEST INFLUENCE...
"...IT'S GREAT TO SEE THAT I COULD RETURN THE FAVOR!
NOW THAT YOU'RE ONE WITH MY NEGATIVE SPEED FORCE, YOU CAN DITCH THE LOSER SIDEKICKS!
"YOU KNOW WHAT I'M CAPABLE OF AS REVERSE-FLASH. YOU'VE SEEN ME IN ACTION.
JUST IMAGINE WHAT WE COULD DO TOGETHER.
"AS PARTNERS! AS FRIENDS!"

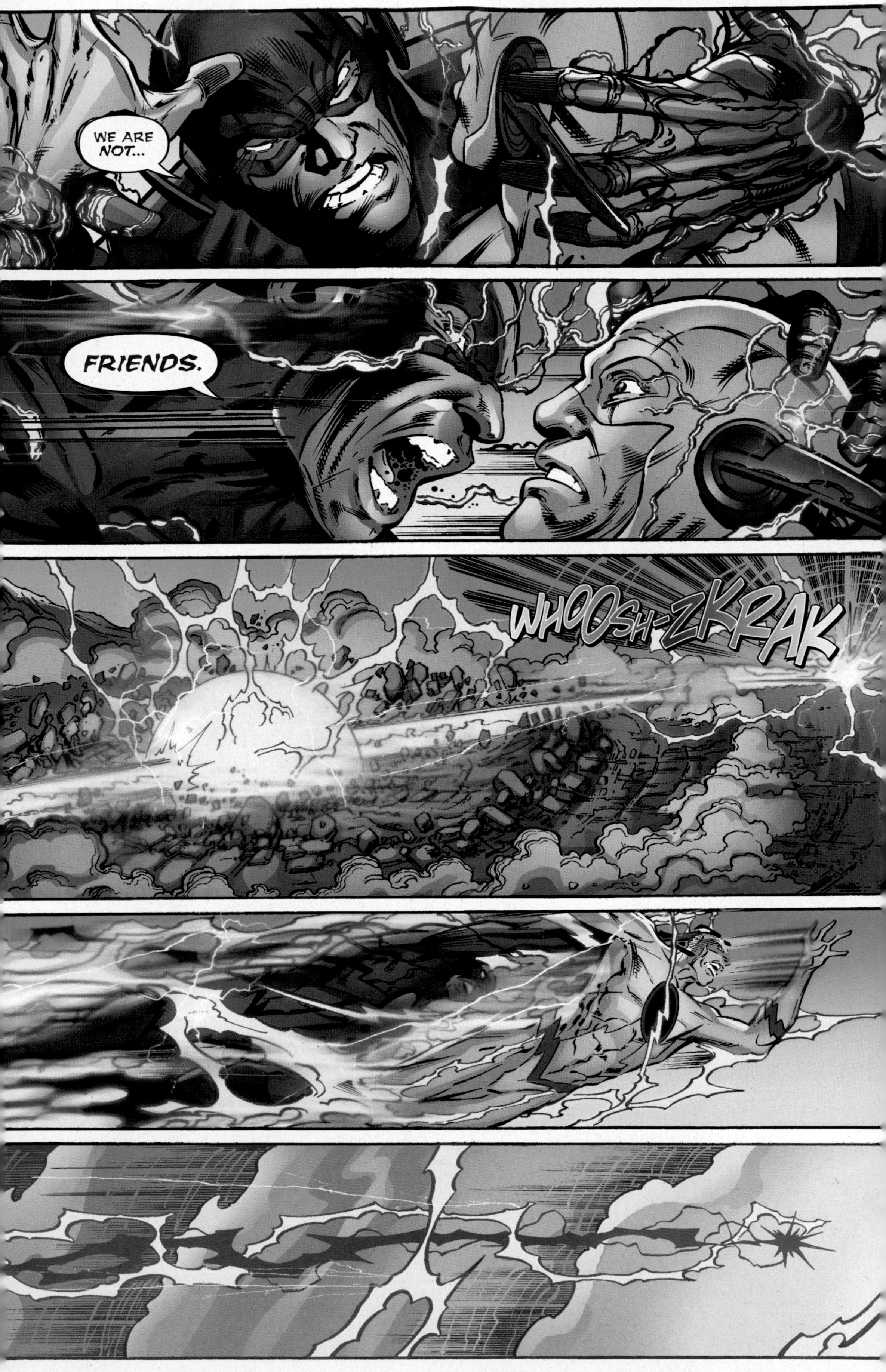
WE ARE NOT...
FRIENDS.
WHOOSH-ZKRAK

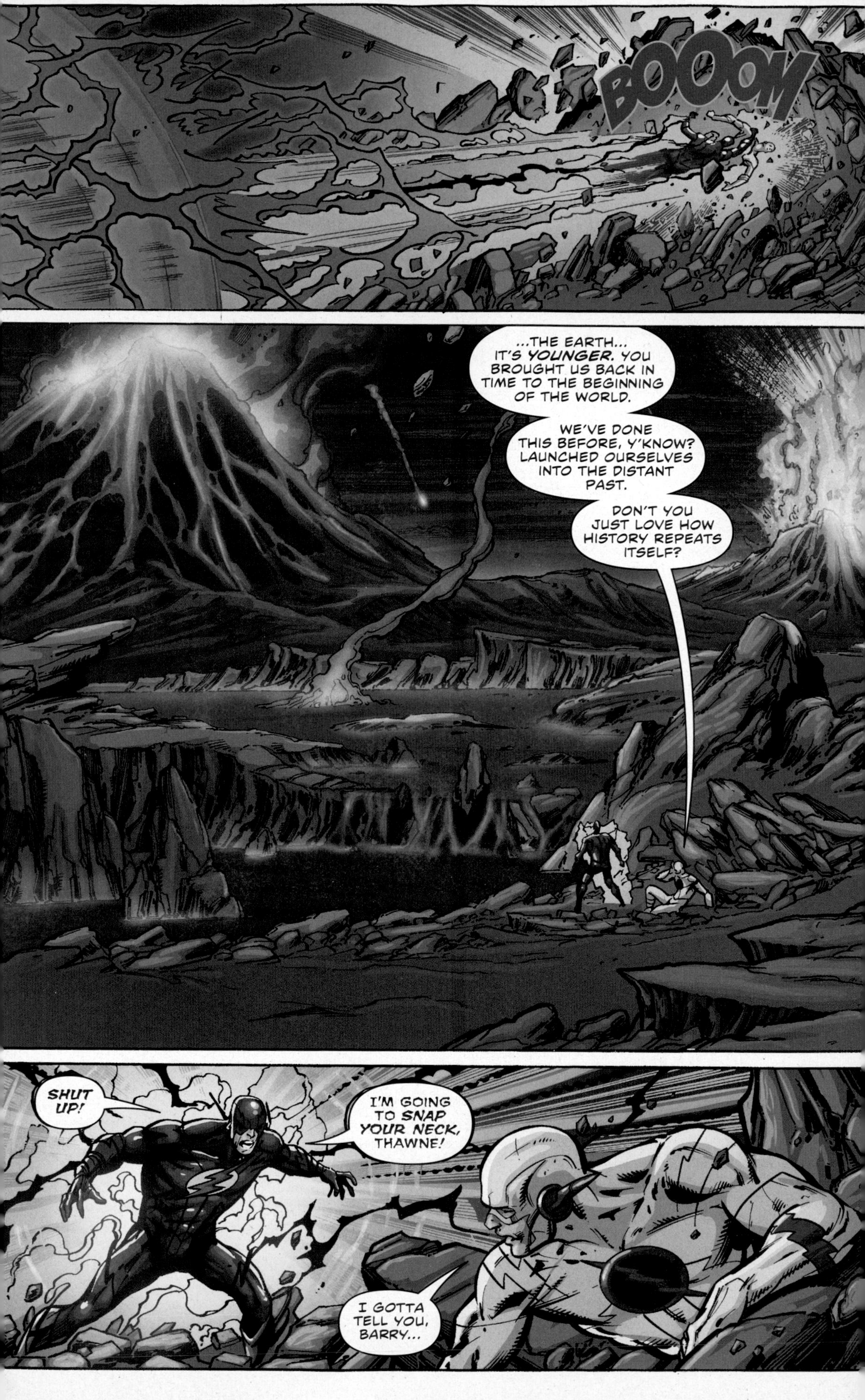
BOOOOM
...THE EARTH... IT'S YOUNGER. YOU BROUGHT US BACK IN TIME TO THE BEGINNING OF THE WORLD.
WE'VE DONE THIS BEFORE, Y'KNOW? LAUNCHED OURSELVES INTO THE DISTANT PAST.
DON'T YOU JUST LOVE HOW HISTORY REPEATS ITSELF?
SHUT UP!
I'M GOING TO SNAP YOUR NECK, THAWNE!
I GOTTA TELL YOU, BARRY...

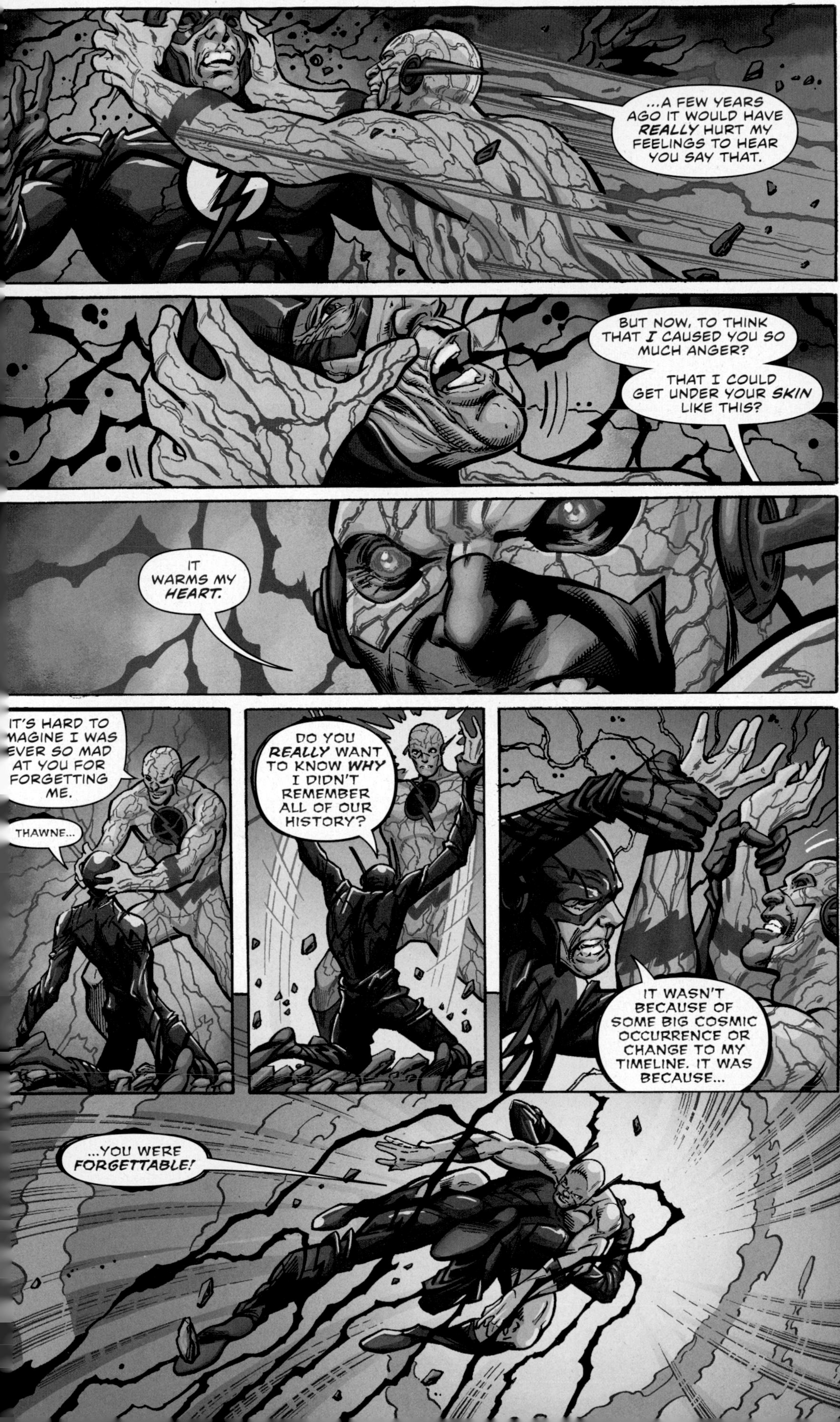
...A FEW YEARS AGO IT WOULD HAVE REALLY HURT MY FEELINGS TO HEAR YOU SAY THAT.
BUT NOW, TO THINK THAT I CAUSED YOU SO MUCH ANGER?
THAT I COULD GET UNDER YOUR SKIN LIKE THIS?
IT WARMS MY HEART.
IT'S HARD TO MAGINE I WAS EVER SO MAD AT YOU FOR FORGETTING ME.
THAWNE...
DO YOU REALLY WANT TO KNOW WHY I DIDN'T REMEMBER ALL OF OUR HISTORY?
IT WASN'T BECAUSE OF SOME BIG COSMIC OCCURRENCE OR CHANGE TO MY TIMELINE. IT WAS BECAUSE...
...YOU WERE FORGETTABLE!

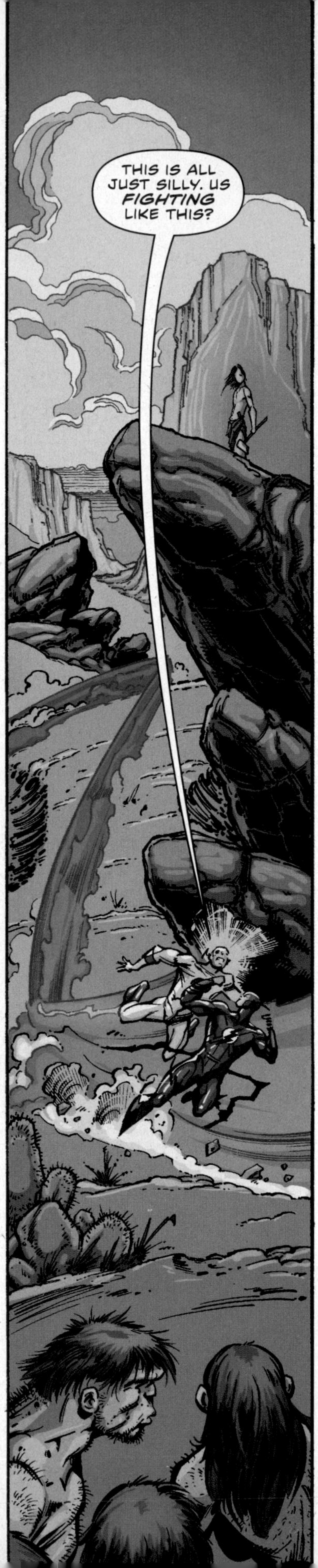
THIS IS ALL JUST SILLY. US *FIGHTING* LIKE THIS?

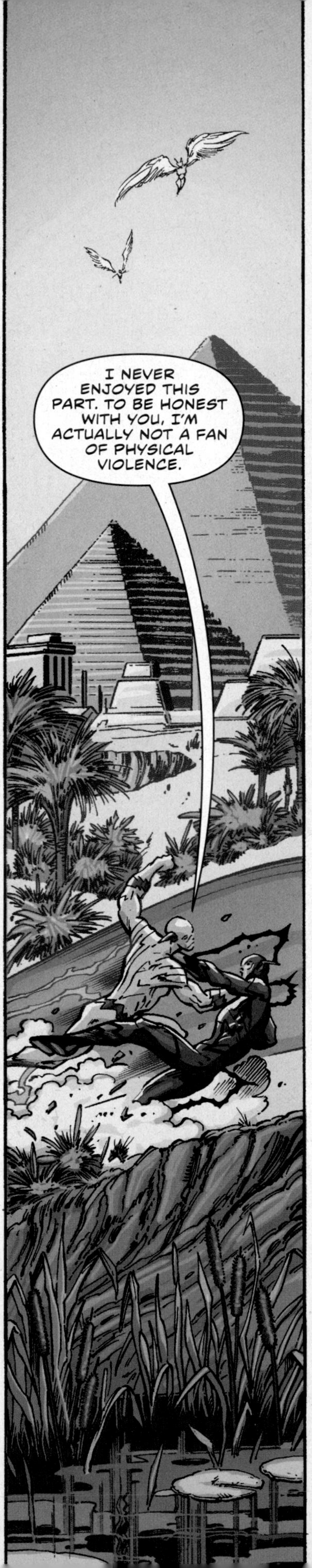
I NEVER ENJOYED THIS PART. TO BE HONEST WITH YOU, I'M ACTUALLY NOT A FAN OF PHYSICAL VIOLENCE.

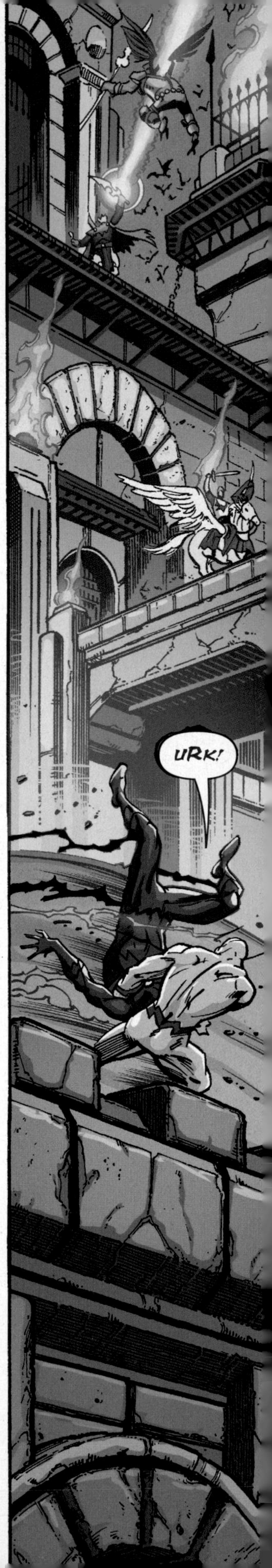
URK!

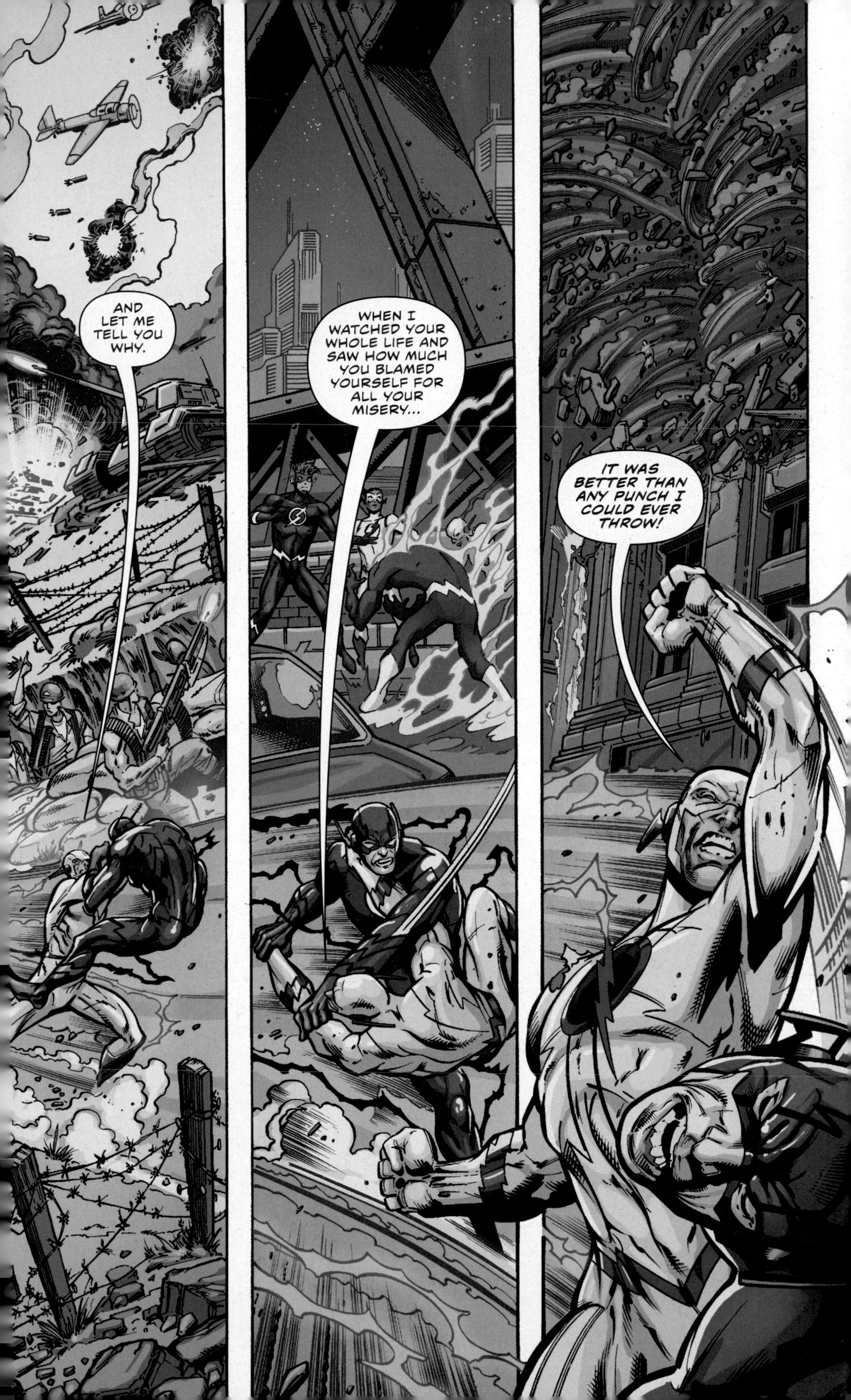
AND LET ME TELL YOU WHY.
WHEN I WATCHED YOUR WHOLE LIFE AND SAW HOW MUCH YOU BLAMED YOURSELF FOR ALL YOUR MISERY...
IT WAS BETTER THAN ANY PUNCH I COULD EVER THROW!

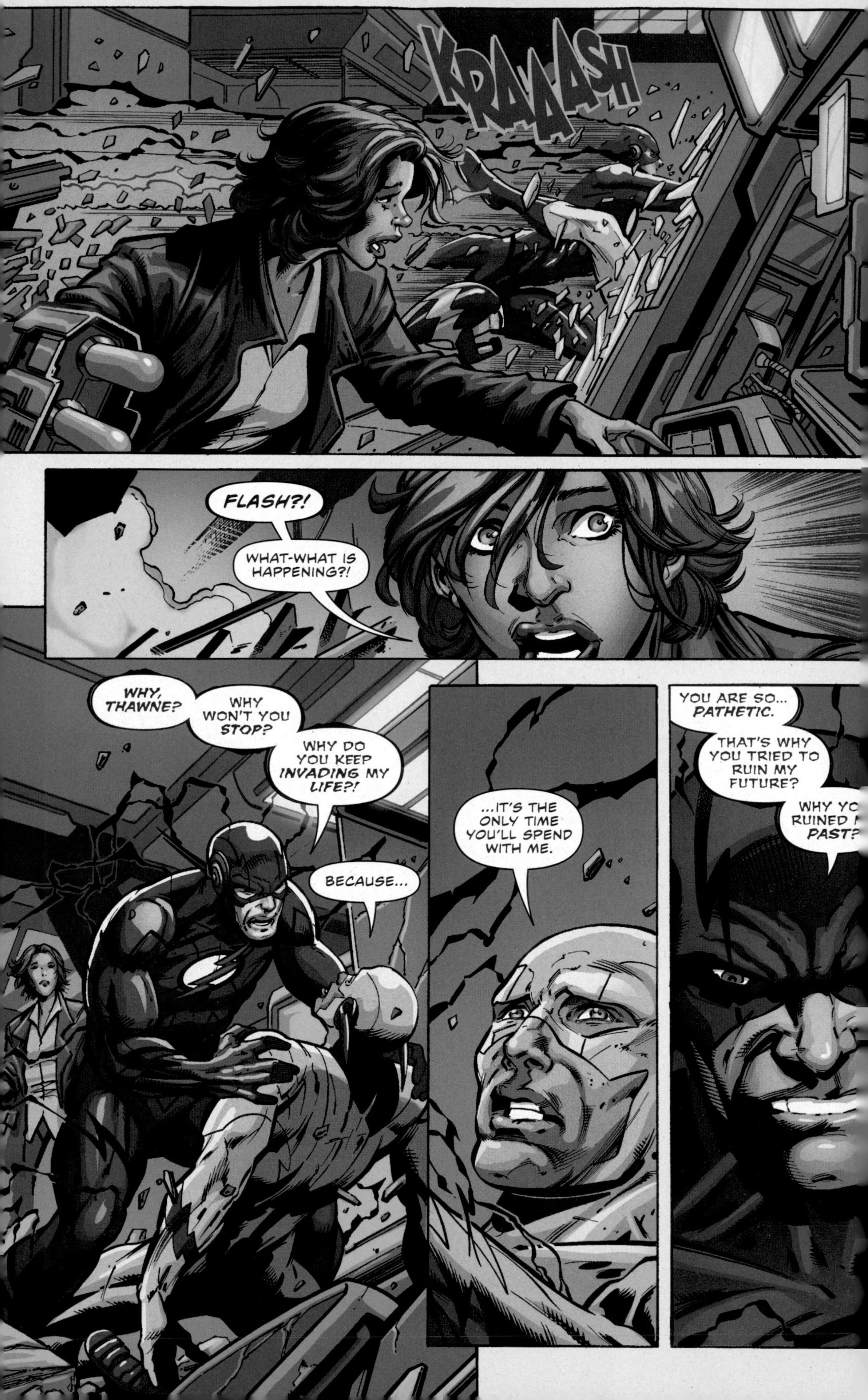
KRAAASH
FLASH?!
WHAT-WHAT IS HAPPENING?!
WHY, THAWNE?
WHY WON'T YOU STOP?
WHY DO YOU KEEP INVADING MY LIFE?!
BECAUSE...
...IT'S THE ONLY TIME YOU'LL SPEND WITH ME.
YOU ARE SO... PATHETIC.
THAT'S WHY YOU TRIED TO RUIN MY FUTURE?
WHY YO
RUINED
PAST?

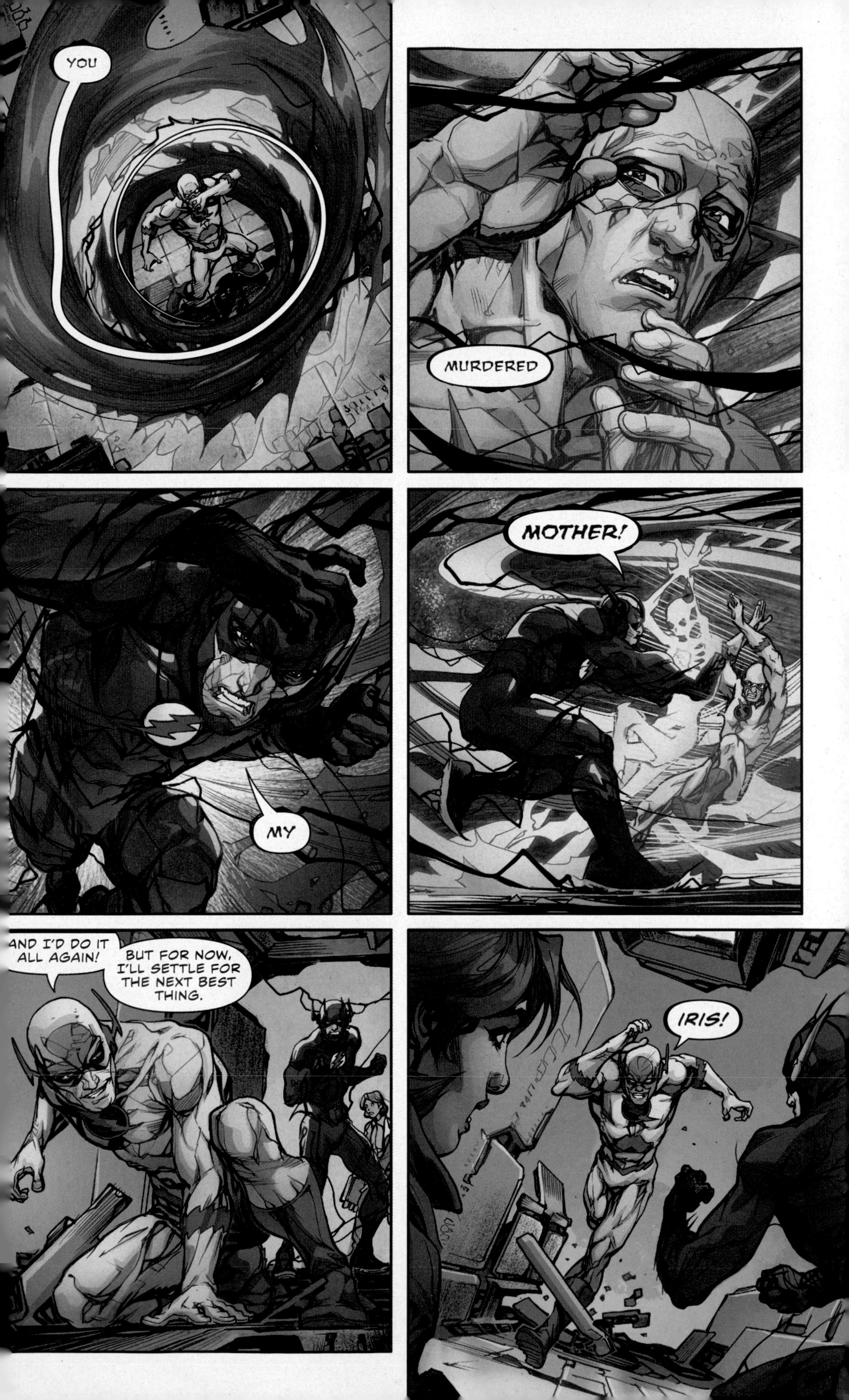
YOU
MURDERED
MY
MOTHER!
AND I'D DO IT ALL AGAIN!
BUT FOR NOW, I'LL SETTLE FOR THE NEXT BEST THING.
IRIS!

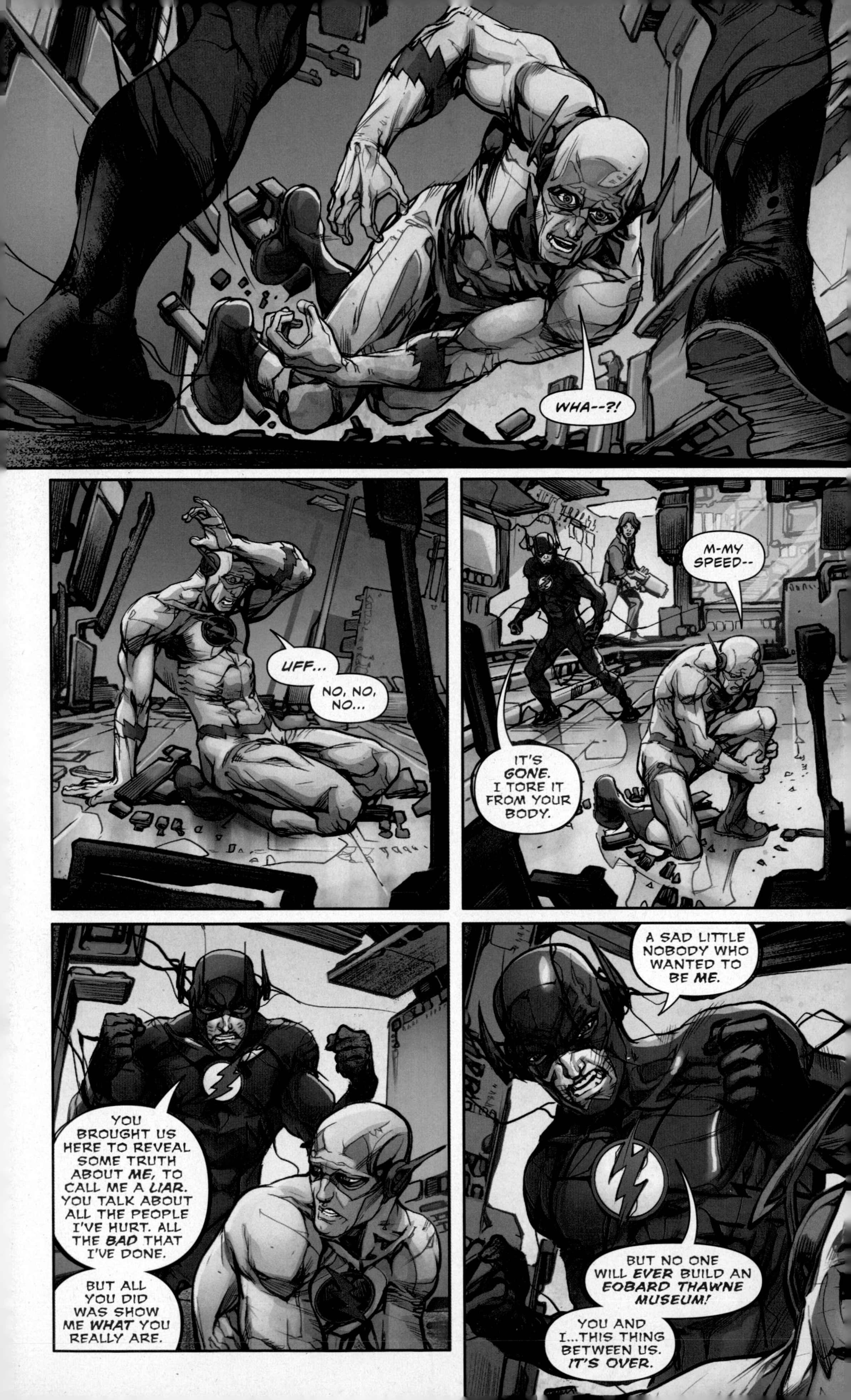
WHA--?!
UFF...
NO, NO, NO...
M-MY SPEED--
IT'S GONE. I TORE IT FROM YOUR BODY.
YOU BROUGHT US HERE TO REVEAL SOME TRUTH ABOUT ME, TO CALL ME A LIAR. YOU TALK ABOUT ALL THE PEOPLE I'VE HURT. ALL THE BAD THAT I'VE DONE.
BUT ALL YOU DID WAS SHOW ME WHAT YOU REALLY ARE.
A SAD LITTLE NOBODY WHO WANTED TO BE ME.
BUT NO ONE WILL EVER BUILD AN EOBARD THAWNE MUSEUM!
YOU AND I...THIS THING BETWEEN US. IT'S OVER.

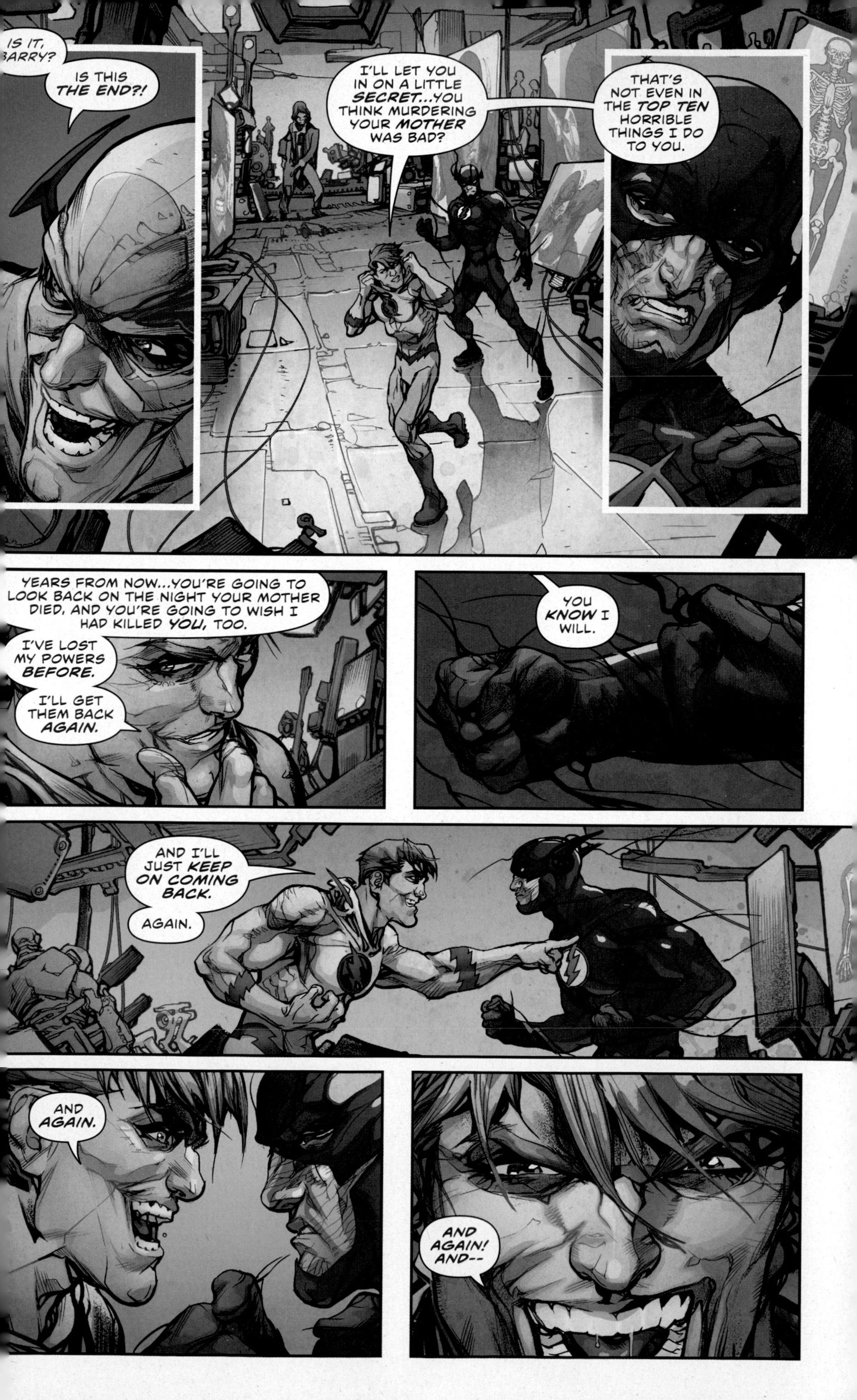
IS IT, BARRY?
IS THIS THE END?!
I'LL LET YOU IN ON A LITTLE SECRET...YOU THINK MURDERING YOUR MOTHER WAS BAD?
THAT'S NOT EVEN IN THE TOP TEN HORRIBLE THINGS I DO TO YOU.
YEARS FROM NOW...YOU'RE GOING TO LOOK BACK ON THE NIGHT YOUR MOTHER DIED, AND YOU'RE GOING TO WISH I HAD KILLED YOU, TOO.
I'VE LOST MY POWERS BEFORE.
I'LL GET THEM BACK AGAIN.
YOU KNOW I WILL.
AND I'LL JUST KEEP ON COMING BACK.
AGAIN.
AND AGAIN.
AND AGAIN! AND--

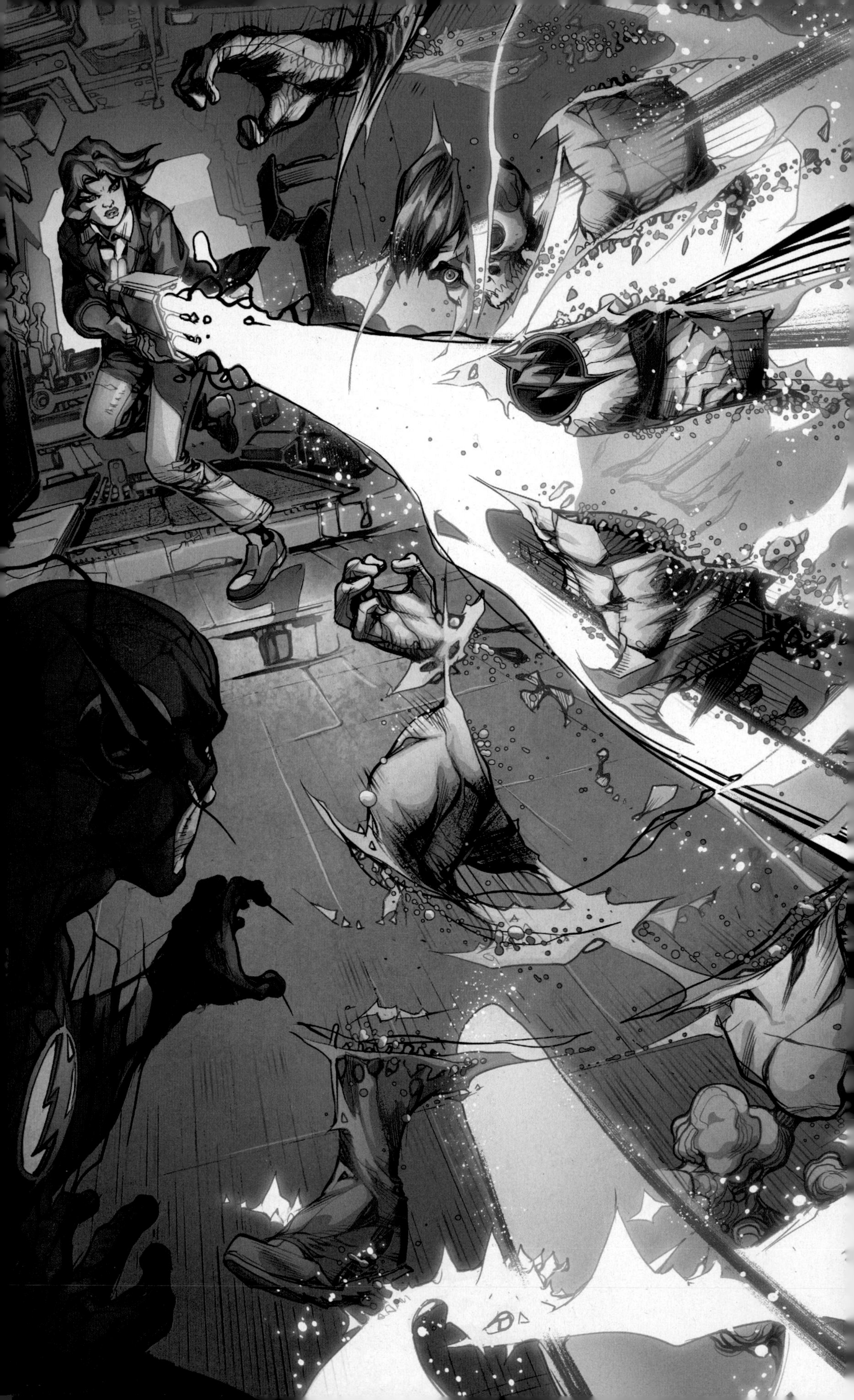

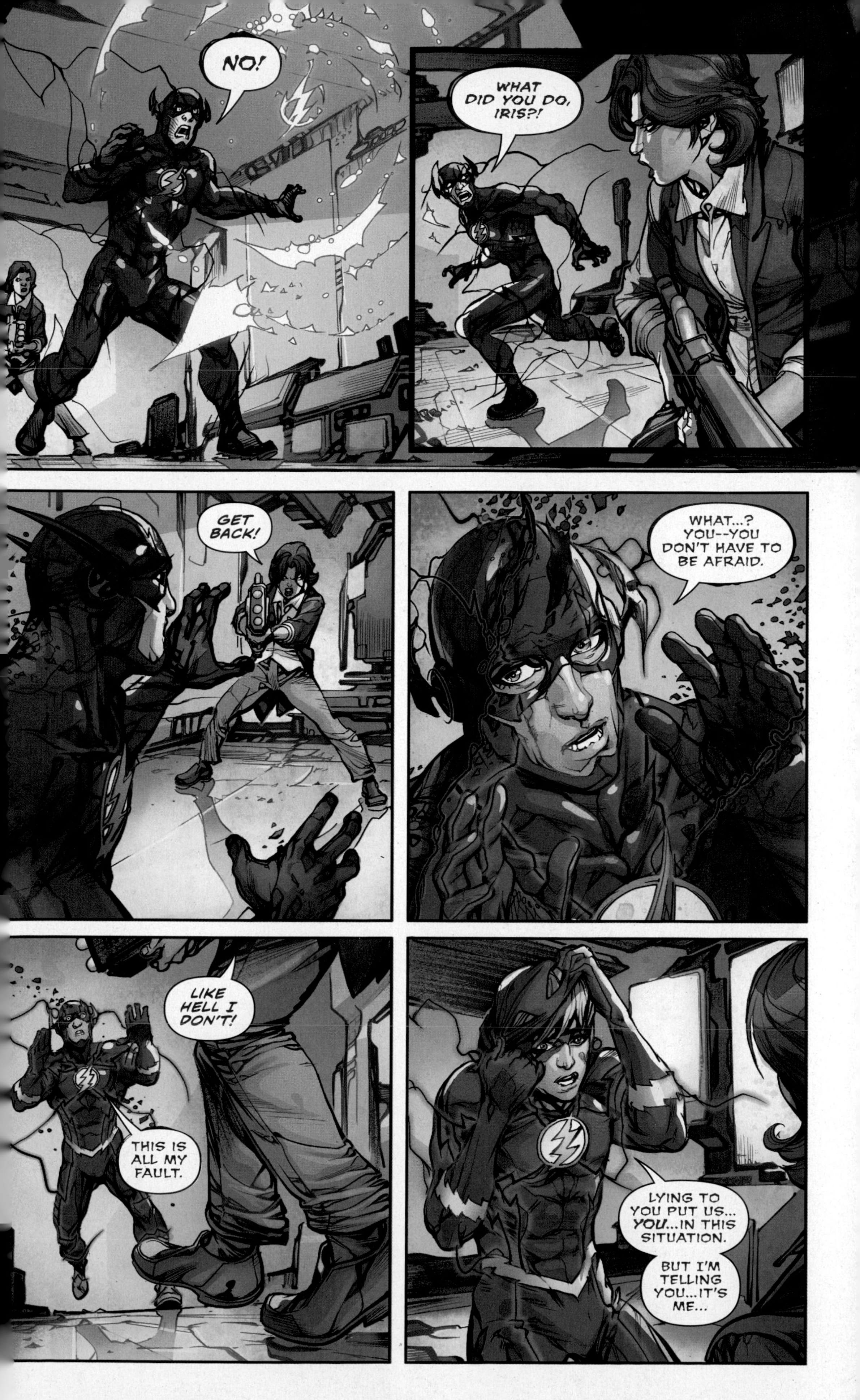
NO!
WHAT DID YOU DO, IRIS?!
GET BACK!
WHAT...? YOU--YOU DON'T HAVE TO BE AFRAID.
LIKE HELL I DON'T!
THIS IS ALL MY FAULT.
LYING TO YOU PUT US... YOU...IN THIS SITUATION.
BUT I'M TELLING YOU...IT'S ME...

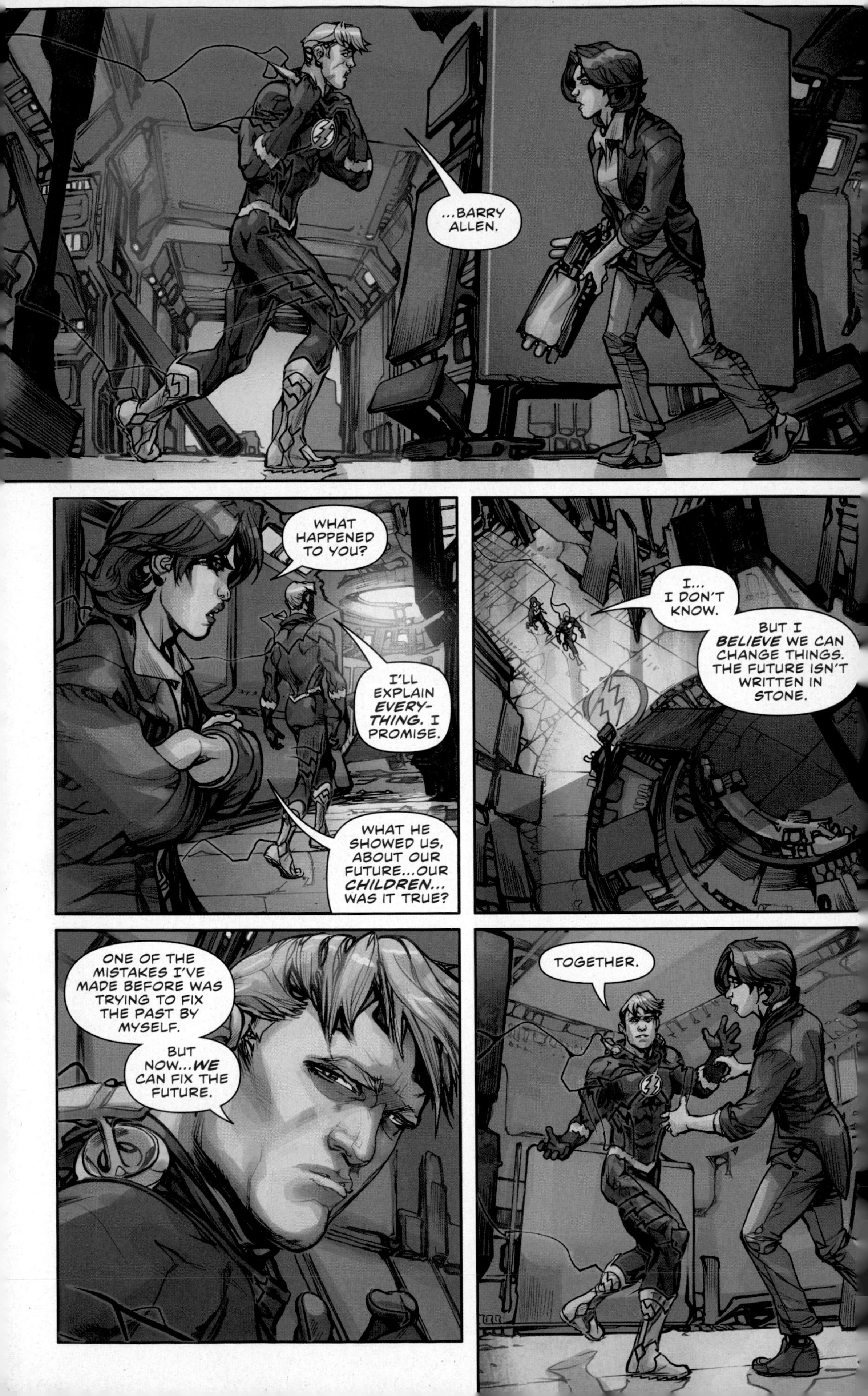
...BARRY ALLEN.
WHAT HAPPENED TO YOU?
I'LL EXPLAIN EVERYTHING. I PROMISE.
WHAT HE SHOWED US, ABOUT OUR FUTURE...OUR CHILDREN... WAS IT TRUE?
I... I DON'T KNOW.
BUT I BELIEVE WE CAN CHANGE THINGS. THE FUTURE ISN'T WRITTEN IN STONE.
ONE OF THE MISTAKES I'VE MADE BEFORE WAS TRYING TO FIX THE PAST BY MYSELF.
BUT NOW...WE CAN FIX THE FUTURE.
TOGETHER.

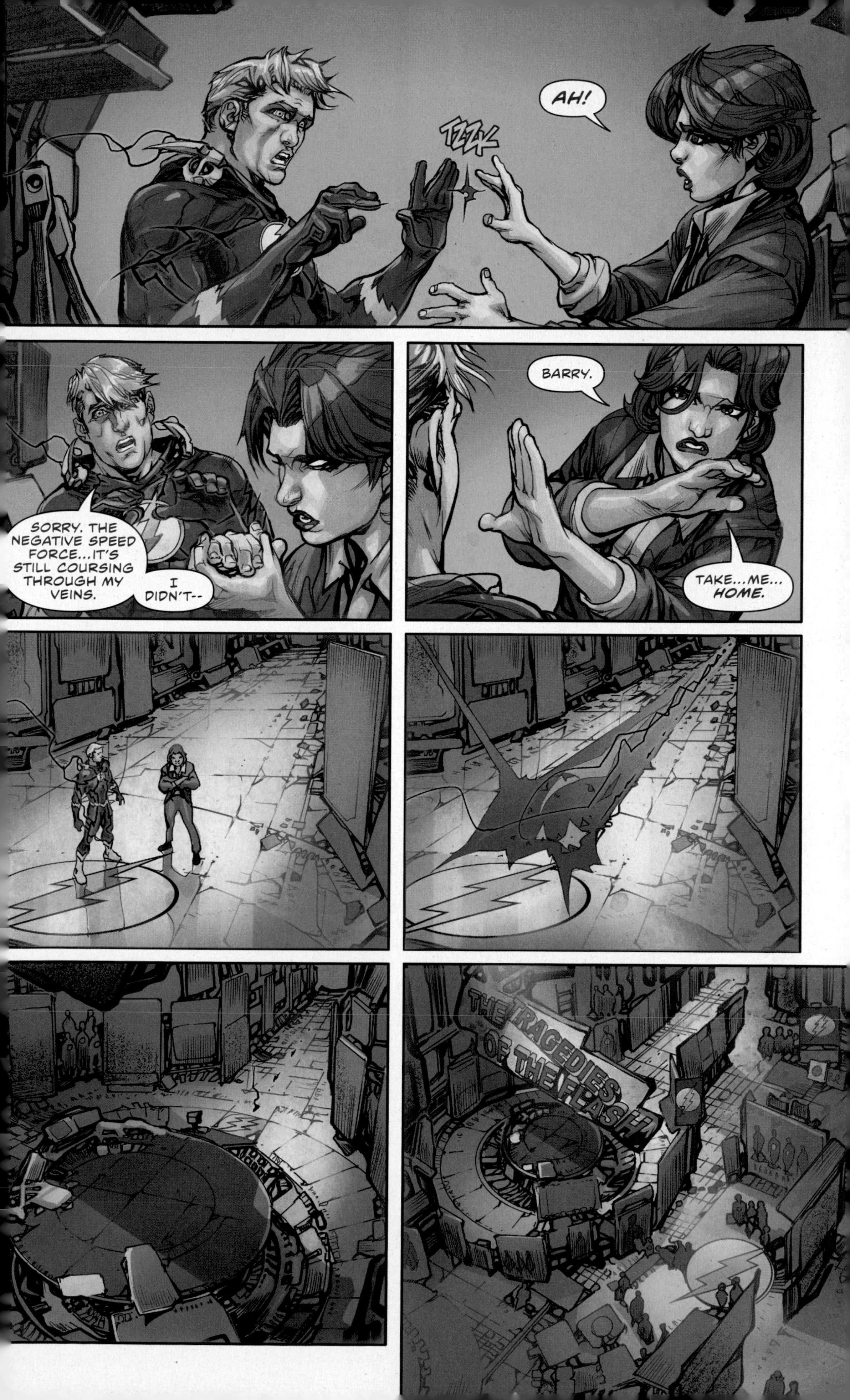
AH!
TZZAK
SORRY. THE NEGATIVE SPEED FORCE...IT'S STILL COURSING THROUGH MY VEINS.
I DIDN'T--
BARRY.
TAKE...ME... HOME.
THE TRAGEDIES OF THE FLASH

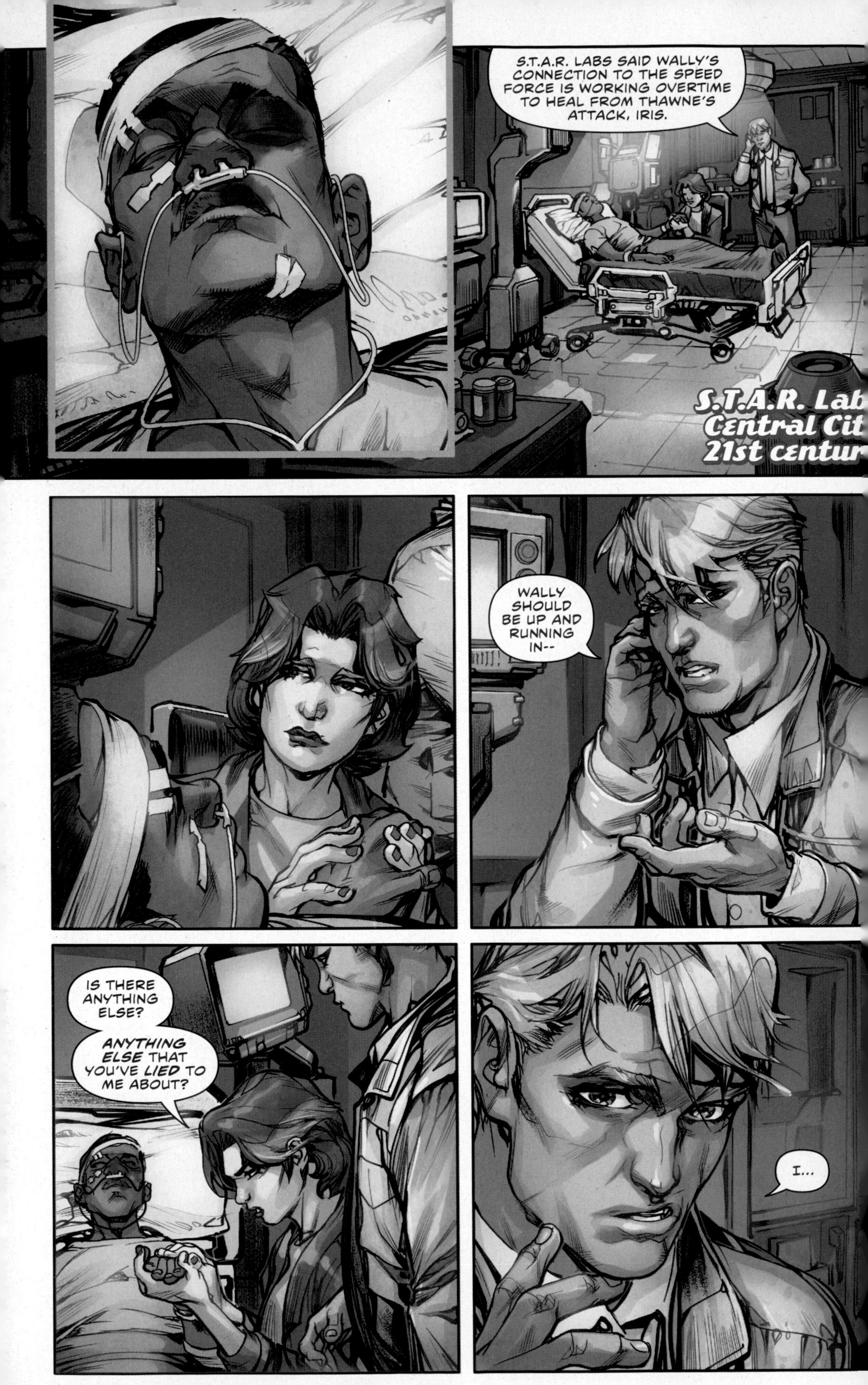
S.T.A.R. LABS SAID WALLY'S CONNECTION TO THE SPEED FORCE IS WORKING OVERTIME TO HEAL FROM THAWNE'S ATTACK, IRIS.
S.T.A.R. Lab
Central Cit
21st centur
WALLY SHOULD BE UP AND RUNNING IN--
IS THERE ANYTHING ELSE?
ANYTHING ELSE THAT YOU'VE LIED TO ME ABOUT?
I...

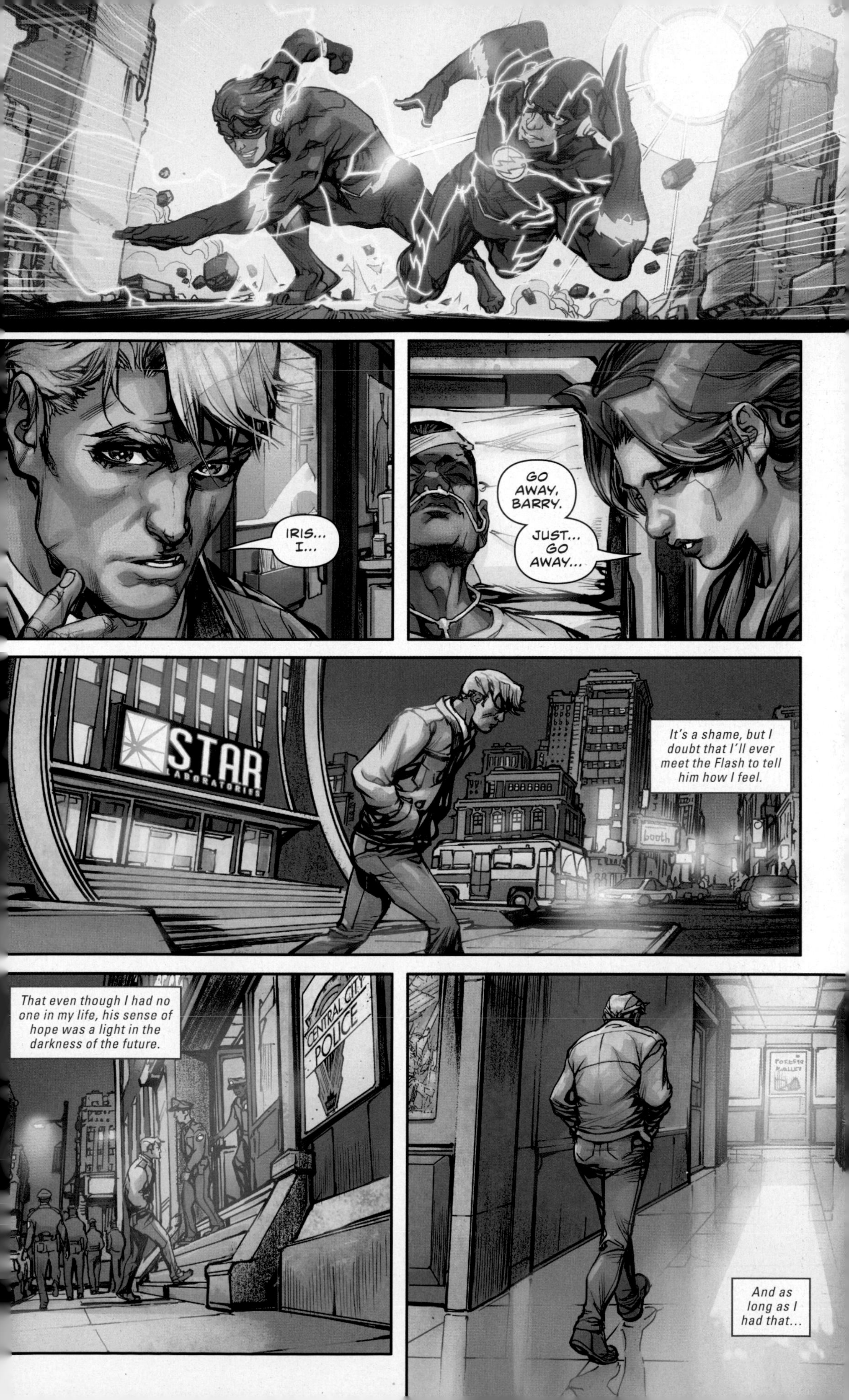
IRIS... I...
GO AWAY, BARRY.
JUST... GO AWAY...
S.T.A.R. LABORATORIES
booth
It's a shame, but I doubt that I'll ever meet the Flash to tell him how I feel.
That even though I had no one in my life, his sense of hope was a light in the darkness of the future.
CENTRAL CITY POLICE
And as long as I had that...

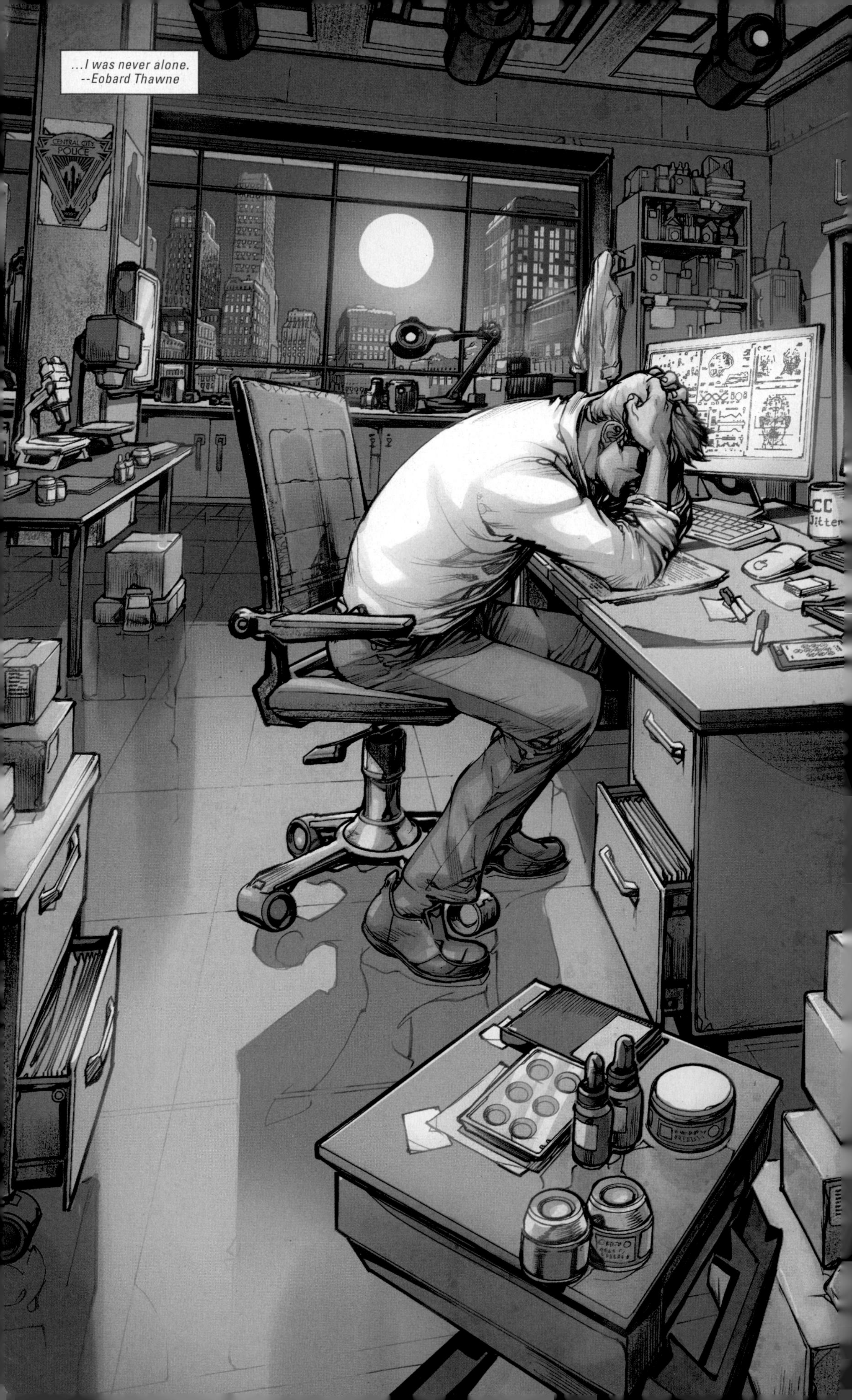
...I was never alone.
--Eobard Thawne
CENTRAL CITY POLICE
CC
Jitter

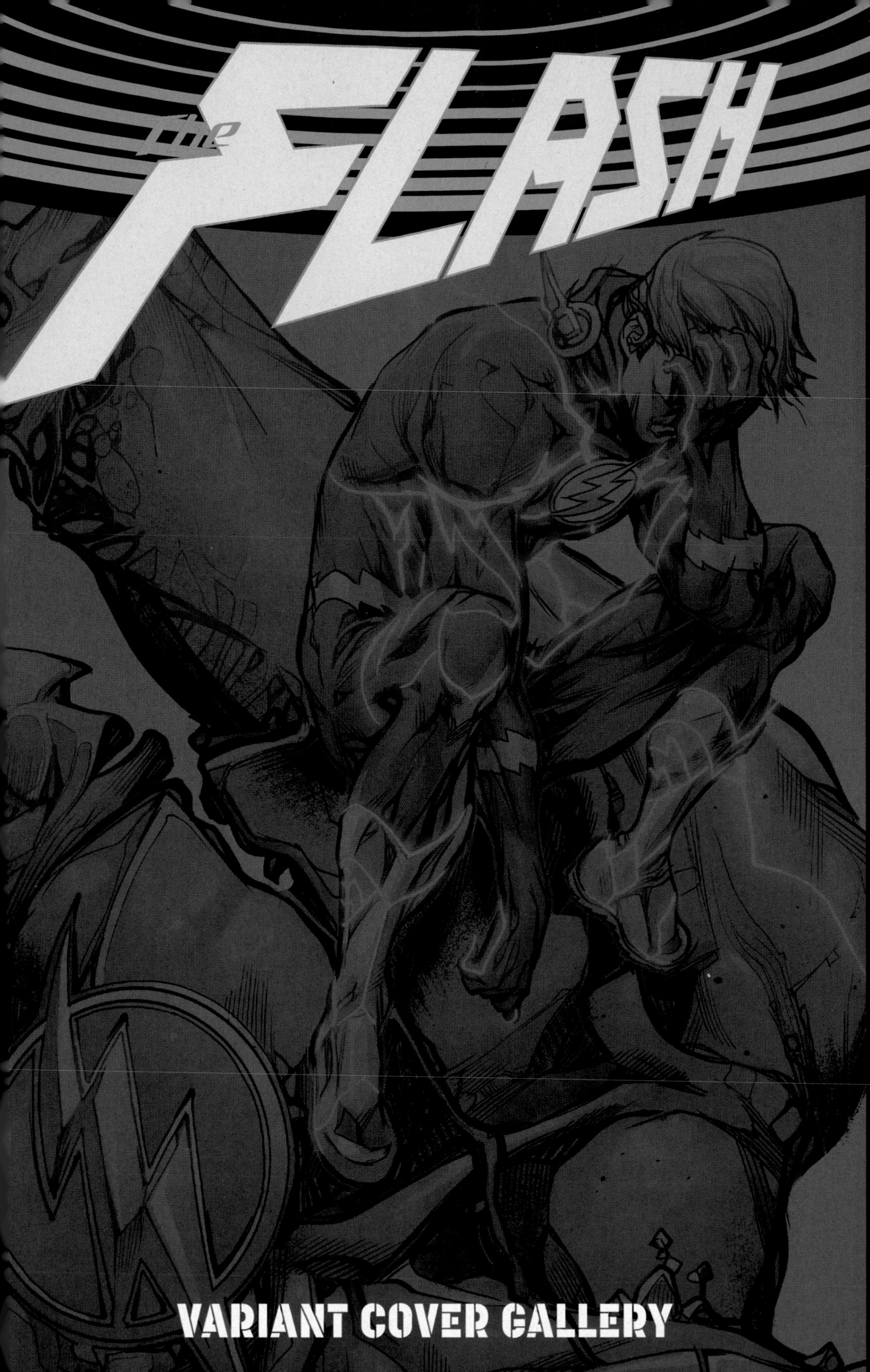

the FLASH
VARIANT COVER GALLERY

THE FLASH #23 variant cover by HOWARD PORTER and HI-FI

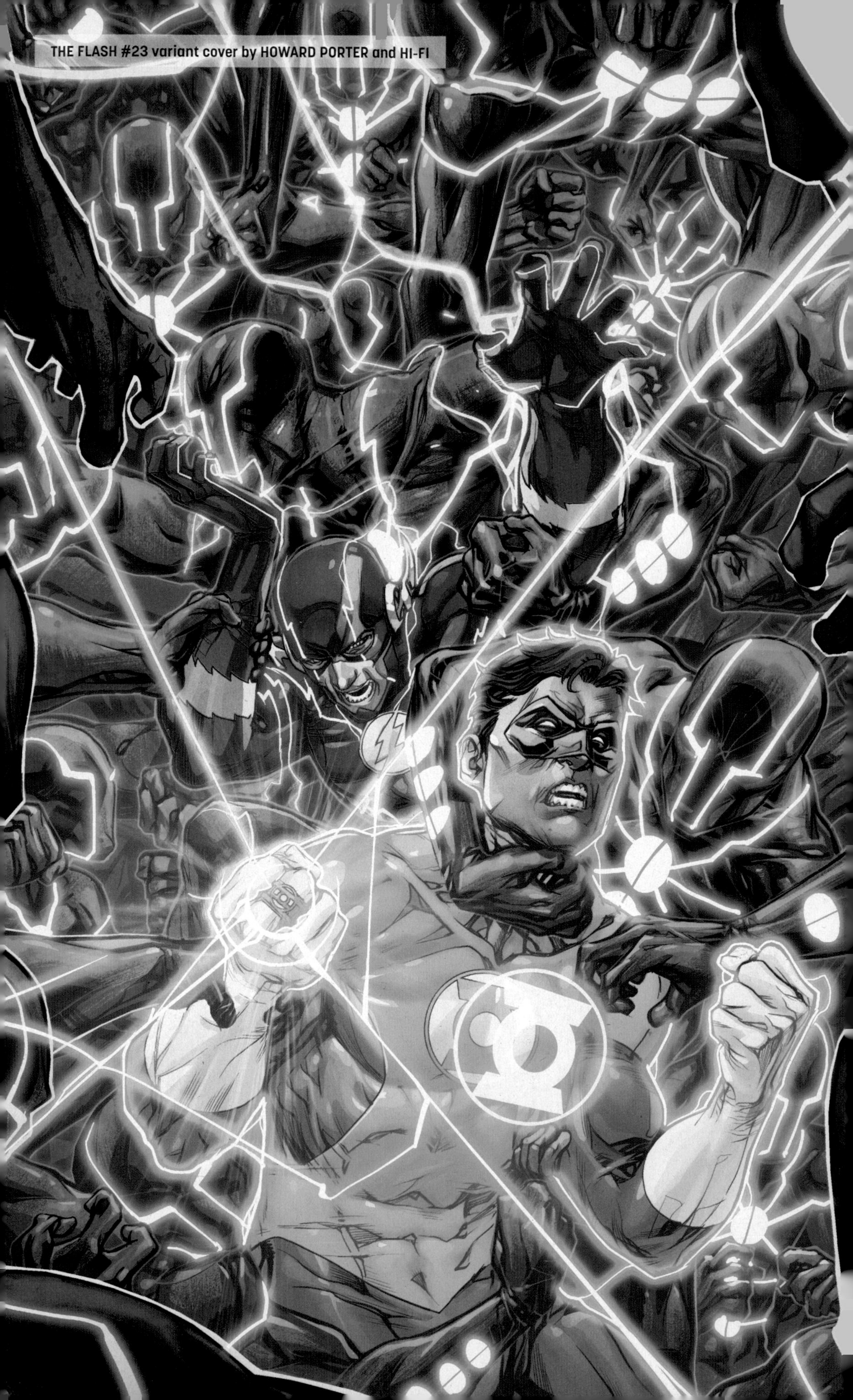

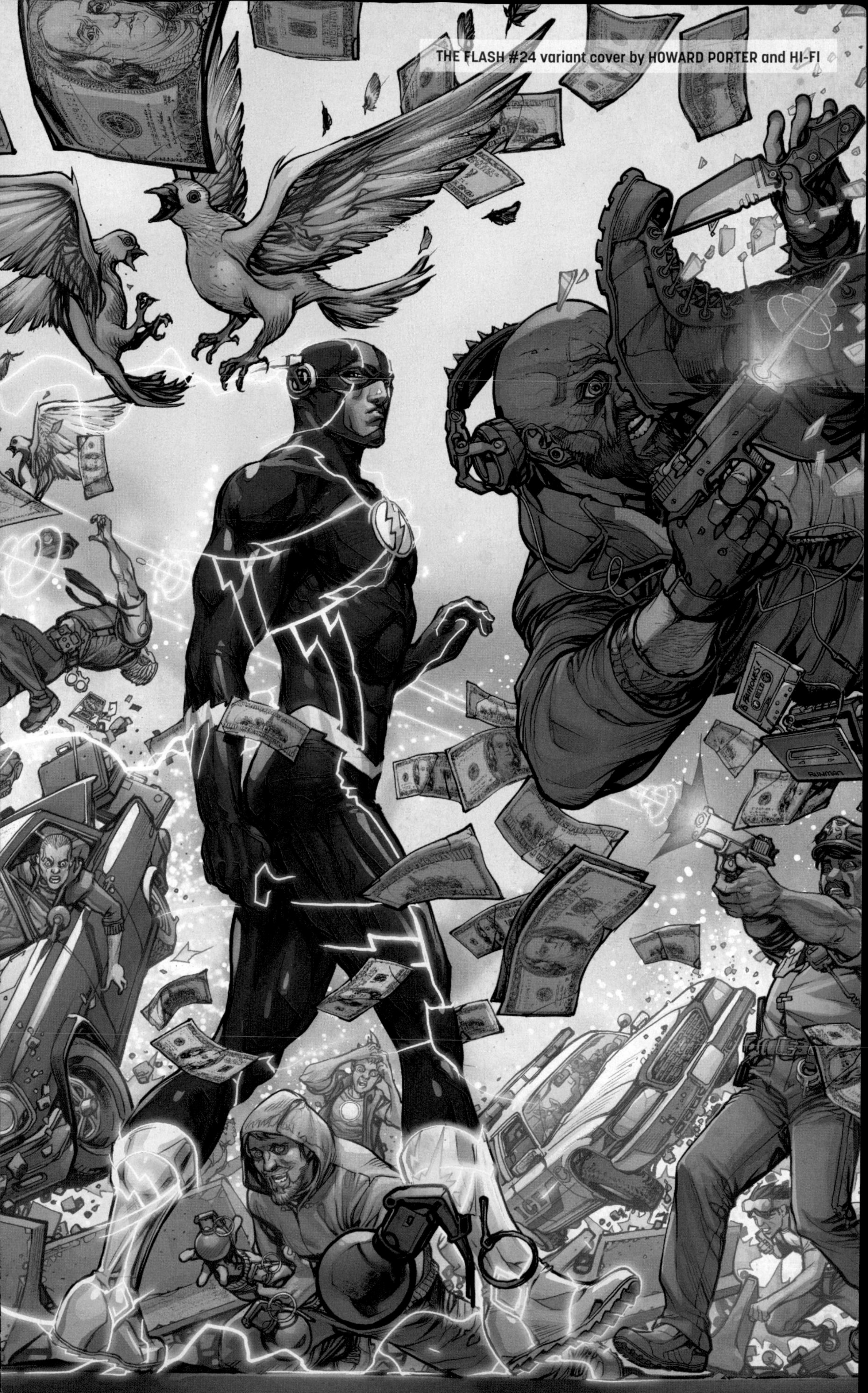

THE FLASH #24 variant cover by HOWARD PORTER and HI-FI

THE FLASH #25 variant cover by HOWARD PORTER and HI-FI

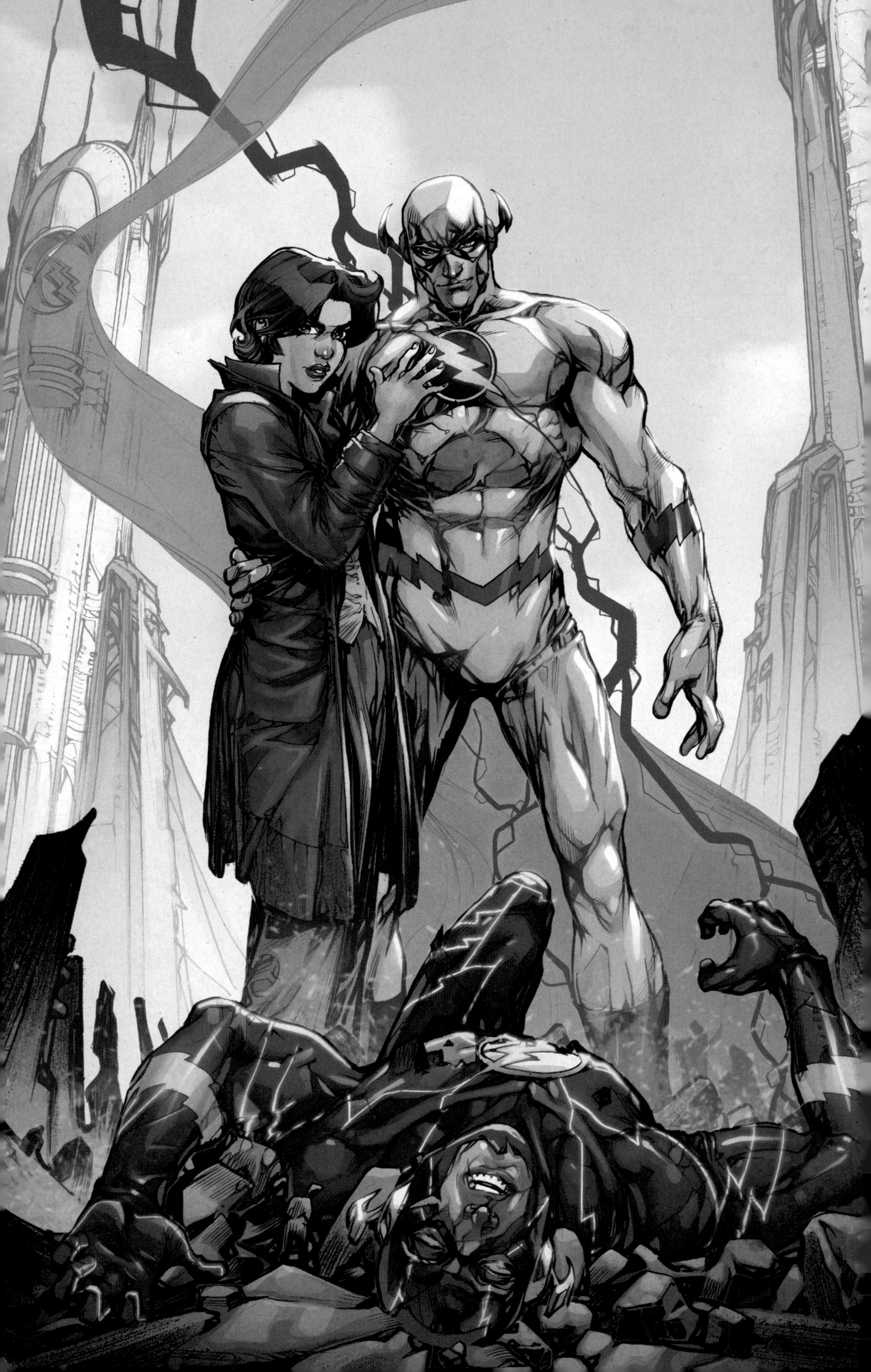

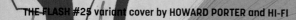

THE FLASH #26 variant cover by HOWARD PORTER and HI-FI

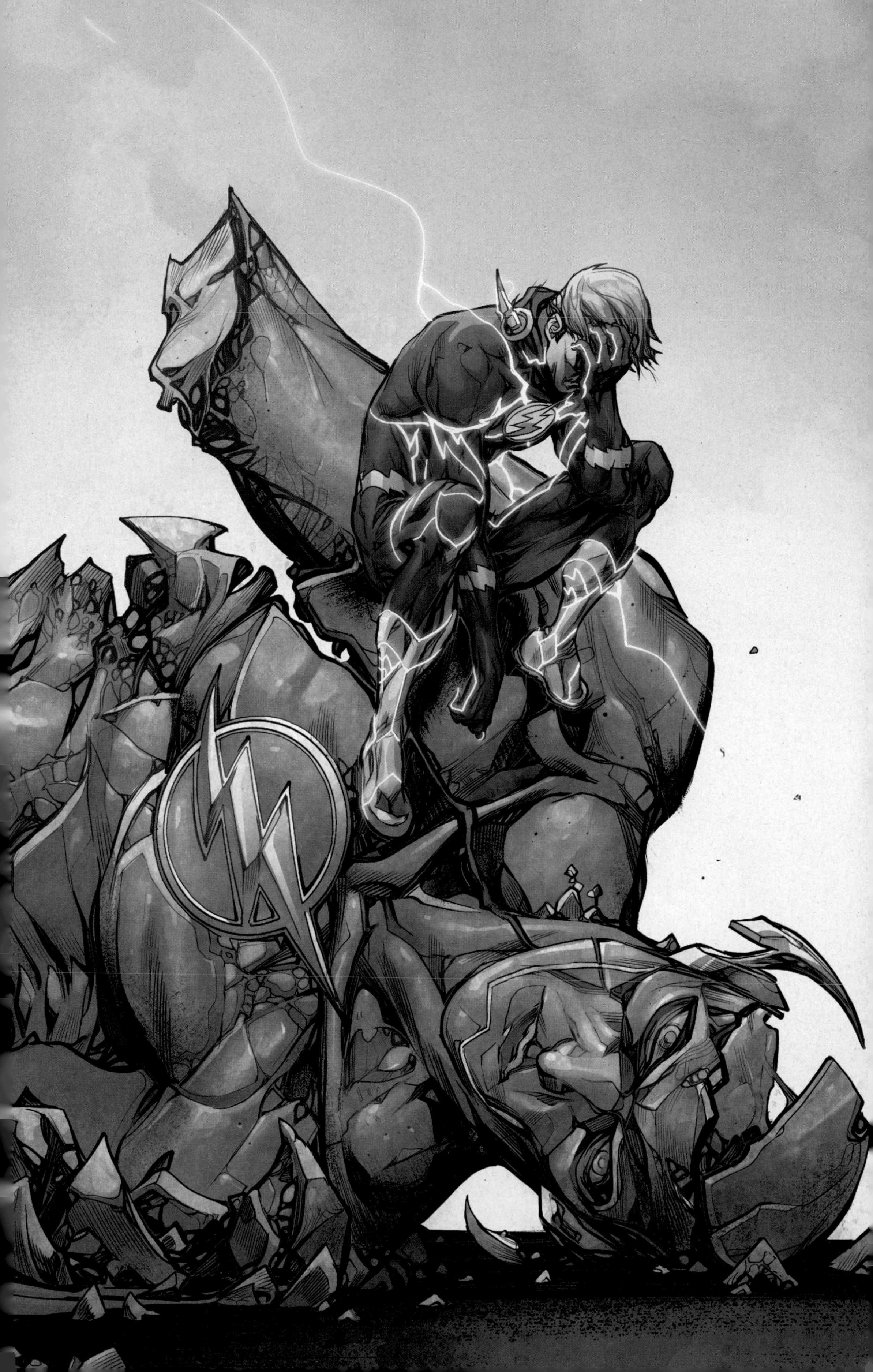

THE FLASH #27 variant cover by HOWARD PORTER and HI-FI

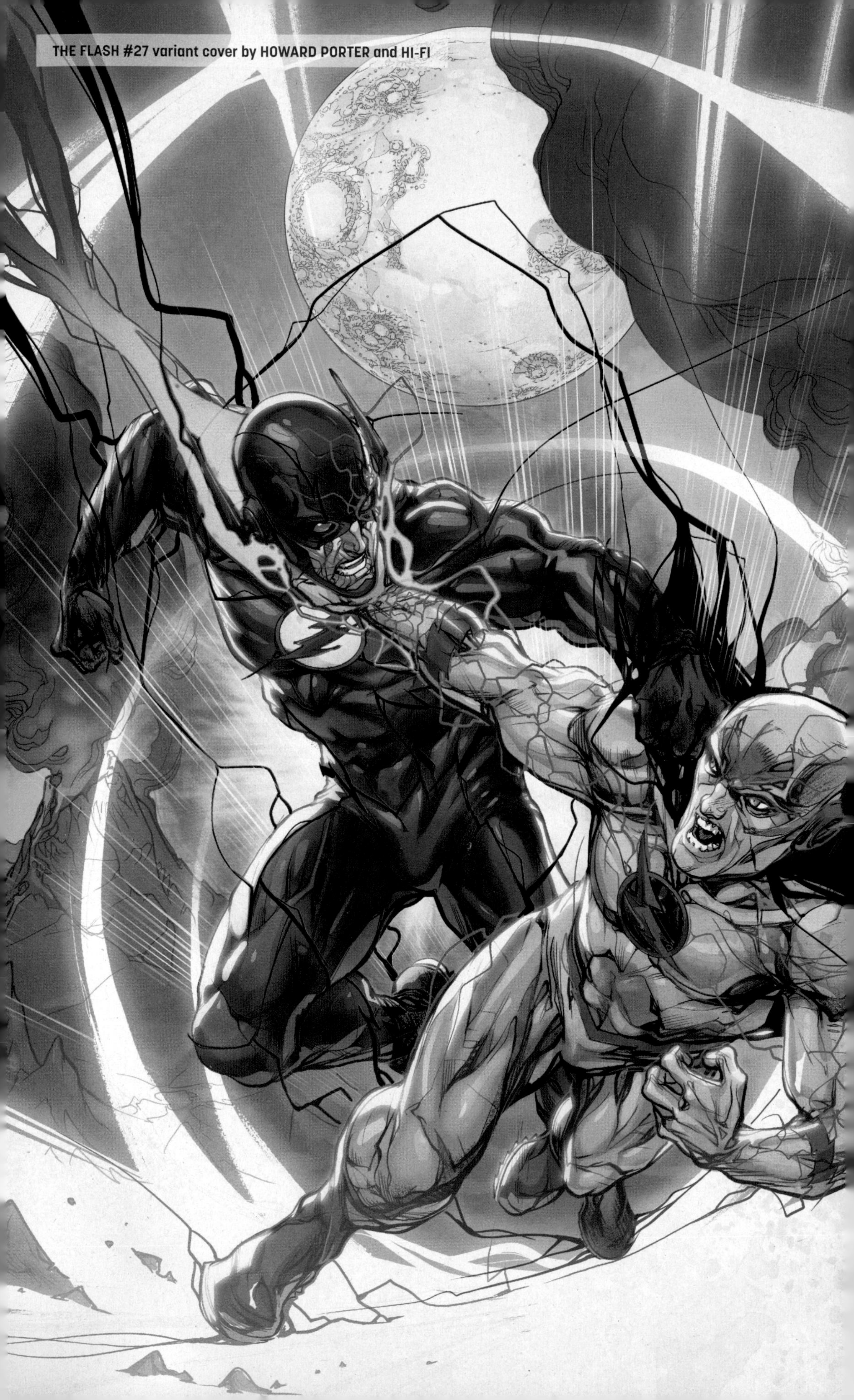

EOBARD THAWNE CHARACTER DESIGN
by HOWARD PORTER

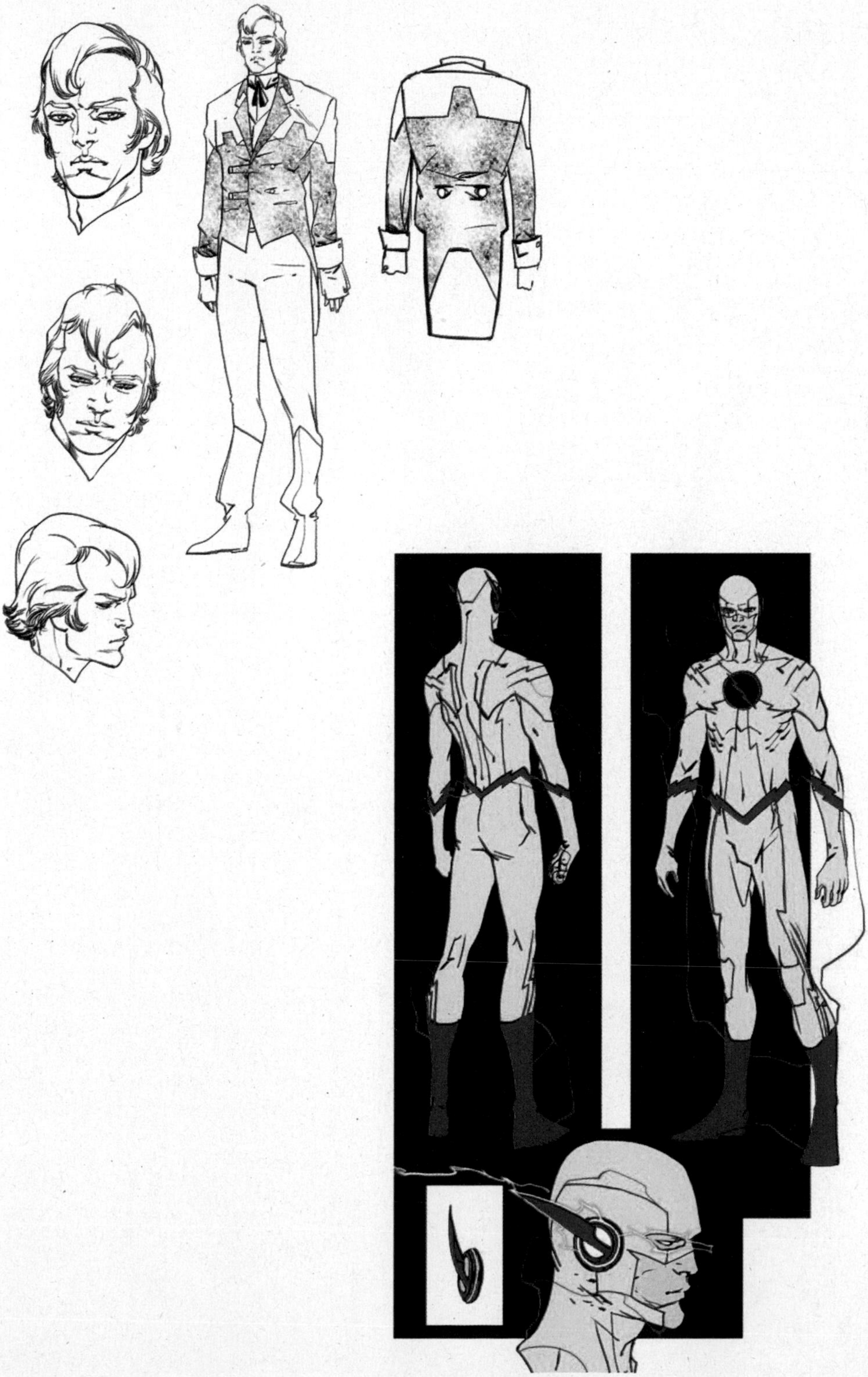

NEGATIVE FLASH CHARACTER DESIGNS
by HOWARD PORTER and CARMINE DI GIANDOMENICO

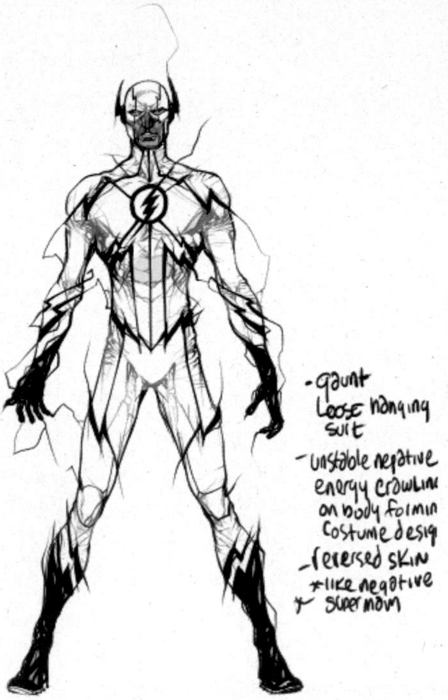

-gaunt
Loose hanging suit
-unstable negative energy crawlin on body formin costume desig
-reversed skin
*like negative superman

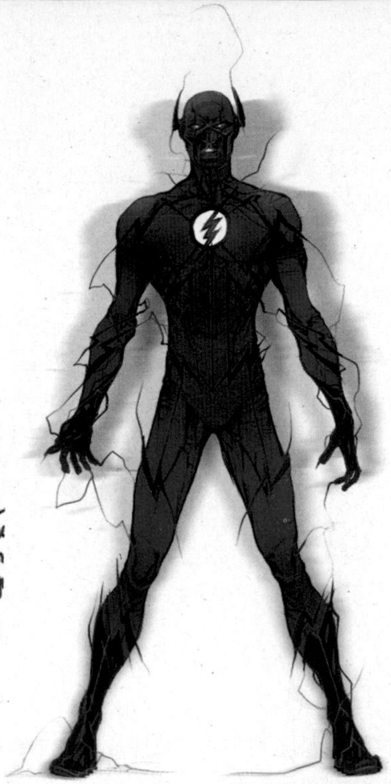

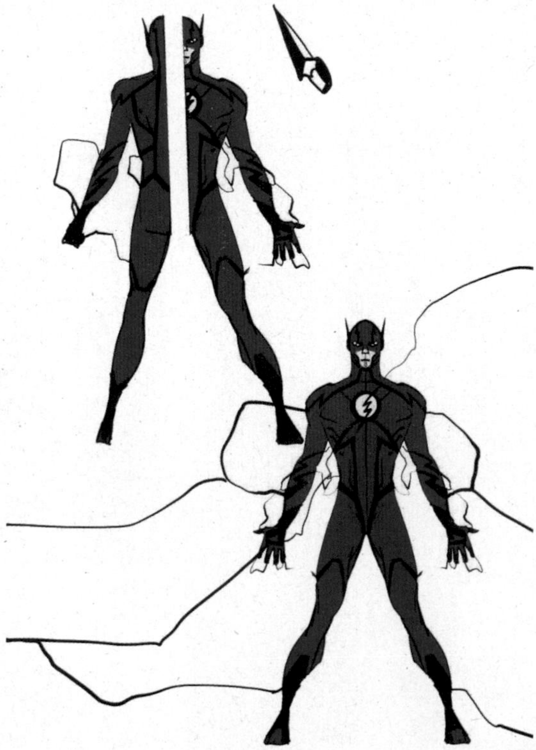

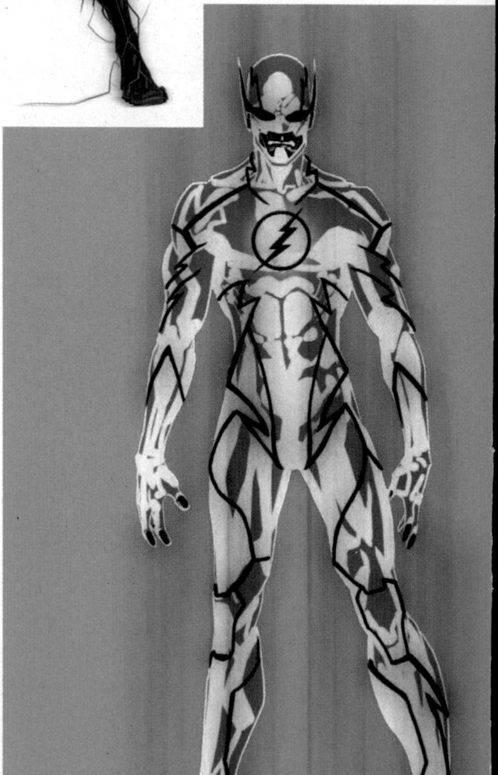

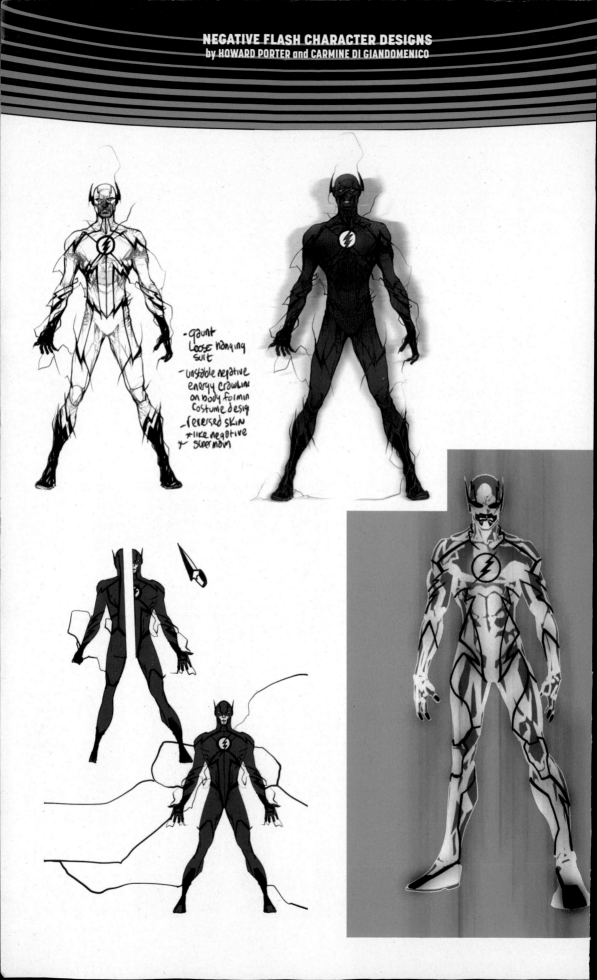

FUTURE IRIS WEST AND BARRY ALLEN AND TORNADO TWINS CHARACTER DESIGNS

by HOWARD PORTER

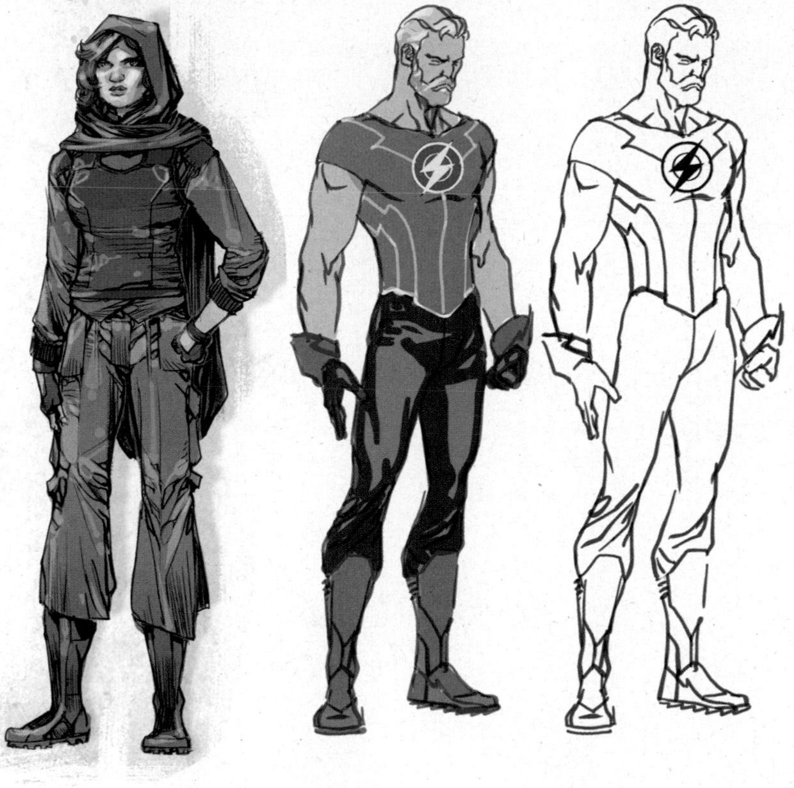

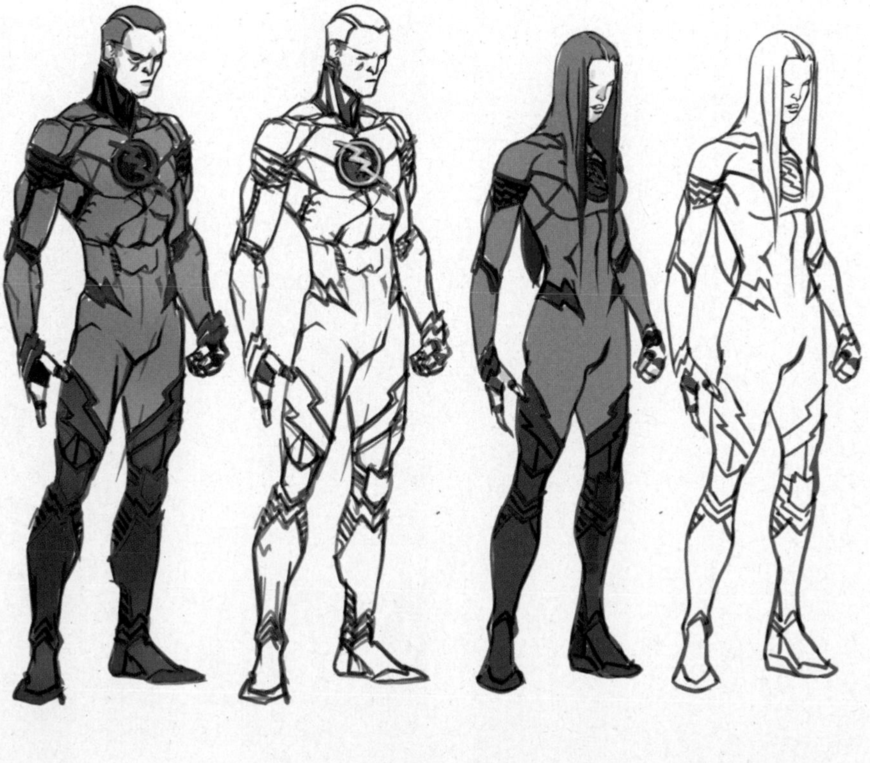

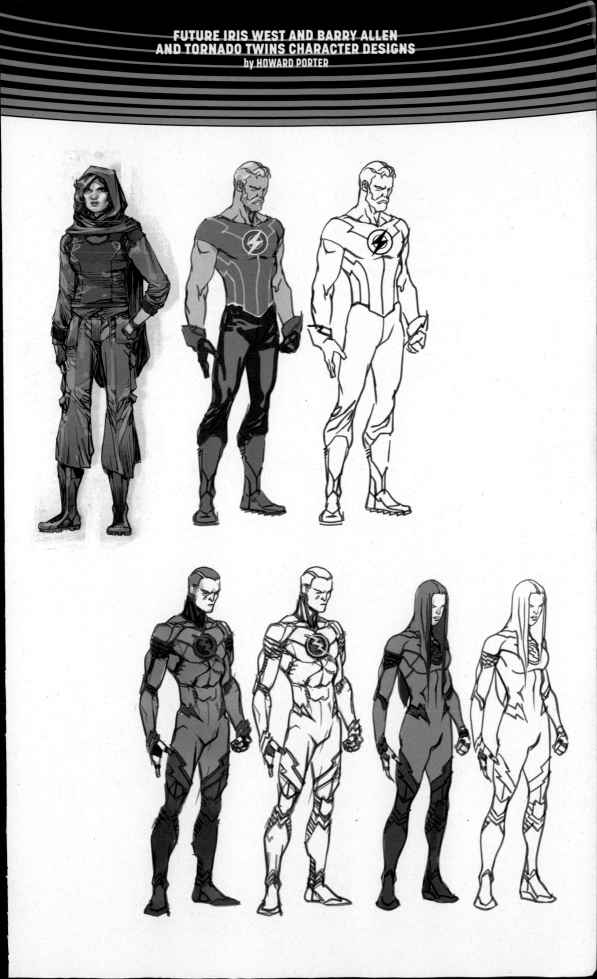

FLASH #25 PROCESS IMAGES
by RYAN SOOK

ALL COLOR SHOULD BE IN NEUTRALS. COOL BLUES AND BROWNS WITH THE ONLY REAL COLOR BEING THE RED AND YELLOW OF FLASH AND THAWNE'S SUITS ET "SEES RED". THE RED AND YELLOW TAKE ON AN ALMOST DIVINE NATURE IN ET'S DISTORTED VIEW OF REALITY

p.1: low angle. large empty room shadows evoke lightning bolt monitors loom over ET because Flash is" always above him". light from monitors washes out features. he has no identity until he becomes flash.

p.2 : from behind ET. again we dont see his face until he is in Flash's suit in mirror next page. One monitor shows Flash rescuing a woman from a burning building.

pp.3 : suit is pure, vibrant red and yellow. almost glowing, radiant. but mask evokes a skull without someone wearing it. haunting and creepy

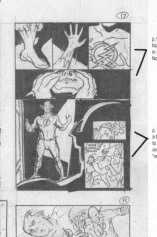

p.1-4 : ET's face stays largely hidden until he looks at himself in the mirror in full Flash garb. Now he sees his true self.

p. 5-6 : et rescues a woman from a burning building in similar fashion to monitor scene of real Flash on previous page. only in "reverse" angle.

p.1 : late afternoon. long shaodows cast on beautiful 25th century architecture. still in cool blues and neutral except for suits

p.2 : main image is Flash showing ET how to vibrate hand through solid object. but I see one large shot of ET's lab with multi images of both men flashing from one station to another sharing knowledge and info.

p. 3 : on blacony. late afternoon has become night

p. 4-5 : mirror images except angled so Barry is always looking down at ET

p. 2-5 : ET slowly moves from bottom of panel two, rising through the sequence to near the top of panel 5. He's overcoming but still "set apart" from those around him.

p. 6 : now he's happy in the museum but small. dwarfed by the Flash's history. And alone

p.1-2 : homage to Neil's page 4 but in "reverse"! Can this be a night scene? Works better for keeping the atmosphere. Barry and Eobard are night and day to each other.

ET is small in BG of scenes.

p.1-6 : all scenes are set at night to add shadow and atmoshere

p.1-4 : Night scenes continue. More nuetral cool tones except for ET's suit which is vibrant yellow and red.

p.1-4 : Museum at night empty. One large panoramic of museum over 4 panels with ET moving across from panel to panel

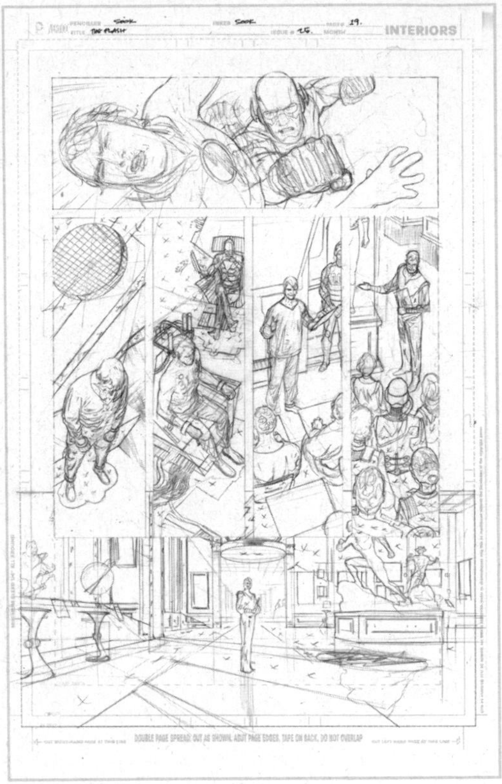
INTERIORS
DOUBLE PAGE SPREAD: CUT AS SHOWN, ABUT PAGE EDGES, TAPE ON BACK, DO NOT OVERLAP
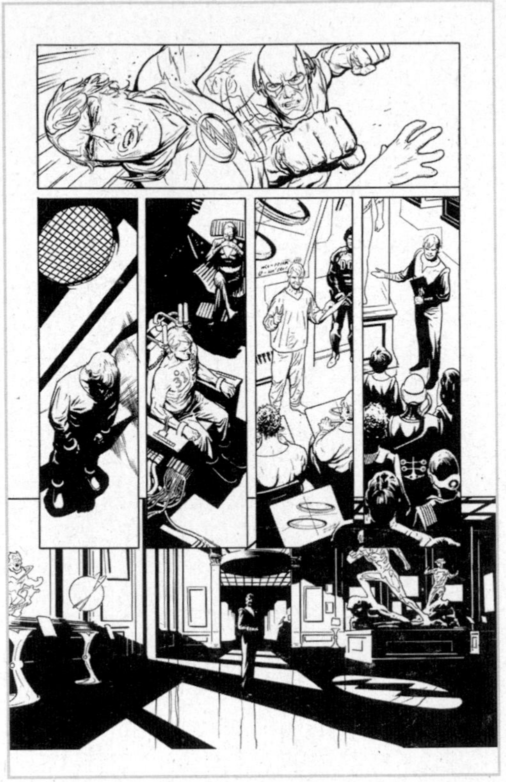
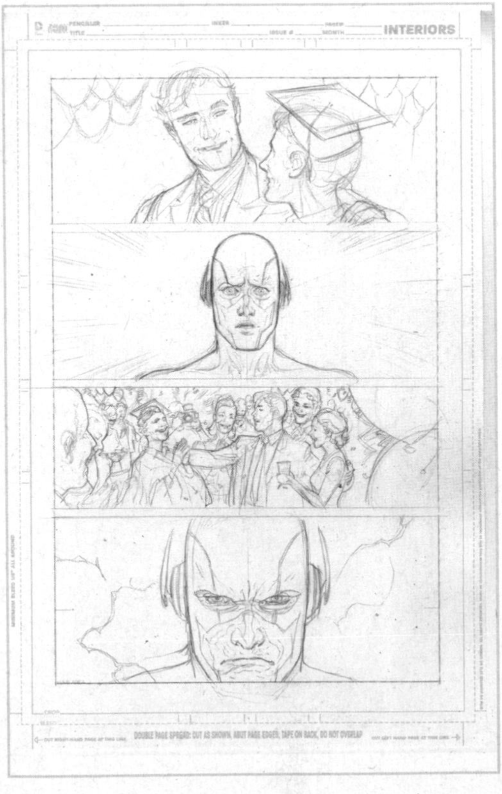
INTERIORS
DOUBLE PAGE SPREAD: CUT AS SHOWN, ABUT PAGE EDGES, TAPE ON BACK, DO NOT OVERLAP
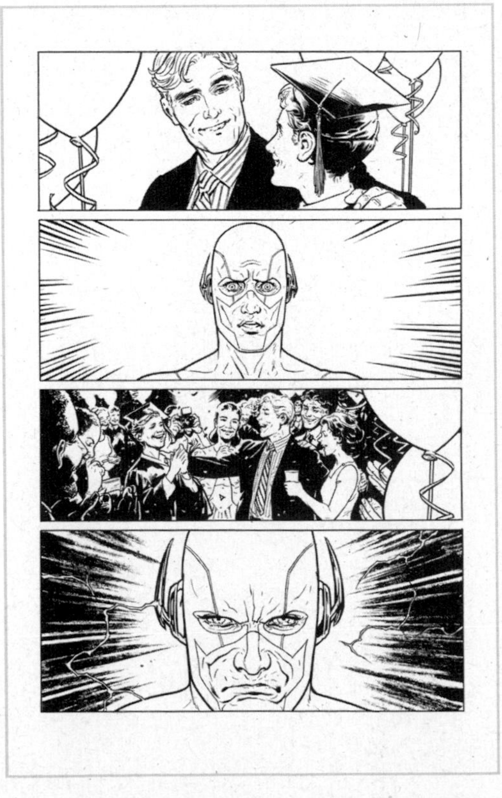